D1459806

Frank & Charli

Frank & Charli

WOODSTOCK, TRUE LOVE,
and the SIXTIES

Frank Yandolino

Skyhorse Publishing

Almost cut my hair,
It happened just the other day.
It's getting kinda long,
I coulda said it wasn't in my way.
But I didn't and I wonder why,
I feel like letting my freak flag fly,
Cause I feel like I owe it to someone.
—David Crosby, "Almost Cut My Hair"

Skyhorse Publishing books may be purchased in bulk at special discounts for sales promotion, corporate gifts, fund-raising, or educational purposes. Special editions can also be created to specifications. For details, contact the Special Sales Department, Skyhorse Publishing, 307 West 36th Street, 11th Floor, New York, NY 10018 or info@skyhorsepublishing.com.

Skyhorse® and Skyhorse Publishing® are registered trademarks of Skyhorse Publishing, Inc.®, a Delaware corporation.

Visit our website at www.skyhorsepublishing.com.

10 9 8 7 6 5 4 3 2 1

Library of Congress Cataloging-in-Publication Data is available on file.

Cover design by Laura Klynstra
Cover illustration by Frank Yandolino

ISBN: 978-1-5107-0640-8
Ebook ISBN: 978-1-5107-0641-5

33614057638123

Printed in the United States of America

Acknowledgments

I would like to take this opportunity to thank Jarred Weisfeld, Bobbi and Bert Padell, Sam Blake, Maureen McKeever, Maxim Brown, and my family for their support in publishing my husband Frank Yandolino's life story.

I could not have published this book with out your help and I will always remember your loving friendship which made a difficult time a little easier.

Thank you all very much.

Charli Yandolino

Contents

Foreword

I first met Frank Yandolino on October 5, 2012. It was right after my first production: staging the reenactment of the infamous Marilyn Monroe skirt blowing over the subway grates scene from *The Seven Year Itch* in honor of the fiftieth anniversary of her passing. Erika Smith, one of the top Marilyn Monroe tribute artists in the world, wanted me to meet Frank, who was her friend and a Marilyn Monroe expert, in the hopes we would develop a Marilyn Monroe project together.

During my initial encounter with Frank, he hands me a non-disclosure agreement and says, "Sign this!" It was akin to becoming a blood brother, and after signing I thought I'd better fasten my seat belt, because I was going to be taken on one hell of a ride. And I was! We went on this crazy journey together to develop the stage play, "Marilyn Naked." With his vast knowledge and passion for Marilyn, I remember he immediately drilled down on the list of possible actresses to portray Monroe. He was adamant about revealing her true story with "Marilyn being spiritually, emotionally, and physically naked!"

As a parting gift, four months before he passed away, Frank called me one day shortly before Thanksgiving (we spoke several times a week), and said, "Hey, I was thinking. How would you feel about developing Woodstock as a Broadway musical?" At this point I was a producer on four Broadway shows and had won a Tony Award for the revival of *Pippin*, so feeling that Broadway was in need of new productions, of course I was interested. Frank was a great "connector," and wanted to introduce me to Michael Lang, one of his closest friends and one of the four Woodstock founding partners. However, Frank's illness was advancing rapidly, and that introduction would sadly occur at his wake (even after his time with us Frank continues to work his special magic). I'm certain the day that the Woodstock Broadway musical opens in commemoration of the festival's fiftieth anniversary (August 2019), Frank will be smiling looking down upon the opening night with his Freak Flag Flying. Frank's Freak Flag still flies and now you are about to find out why in *Frank & Charli*.

I had the pleasure of knowing Frank the last year and a half of his sixty-nine years; a bittersweet period. I was introduced to his wife, Charli, only three weeks before his death on March 17. Charli and I have become fast and dear friends since then. Frank was a true renaissance man. He had this great philosophy to "grab the ball" and keep as many balls in the air as possible. When I'm embarking on a new project, I can still hear his voice in my head telling me to grab the ball!

The last time I spoke to Frank was a Friday conference call where we were discussing the Marilyn Monroe project. Frank was on speaker phone and sounded eerily far away. Frank told us not to worry, he could hear us, and participated in the call passionately and insightfully as he always did. He passed away the following Monday. I am not a religious person but I do keep Frank's Mass card on my night stand; the reverse side positioned in a card holder (a.k.a. roach clip). It has the following poignant David Crosby lyrics:

Almost cut my hair, it happened just the other day.

It's gettin' kinda long, I coulda said it wasn't in my way.

But I didn't and I wonder why, I feel like letting my freak flag fly,
Cause I felt like I owe it to someone.

Michael Rubenstein
Tony Award–winning producer

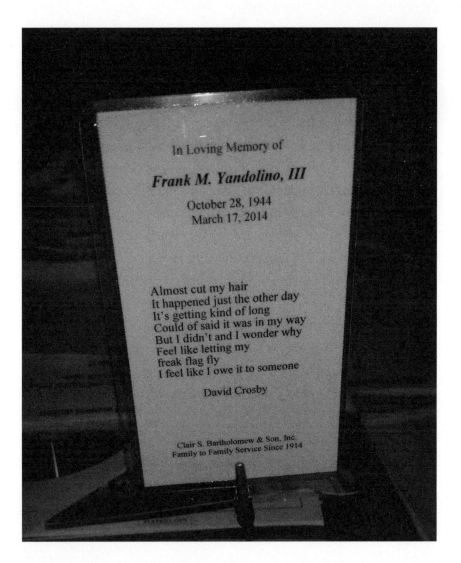

Frank & Charli

MEETINGS WITH EXTRAORDINARY PEOPLE

A True Love Story

CHAPTER 1

The Early Years

As I got off the elevator and opened the door to my apartment, I braced myself for the attack—the jumping and the kissing, the tail waving from side to side like a speeded-up metronome, sure to be followed by another ruthless onslaught of kisses, licking, and barking.

"OK, OK Bruno." Bruno was named after one of my self-appointed aliases, Bruno Fataché. Bruno was my best friend. My brother. A ninety-plus-pound Grand Champion Sieger bloodline German Shepherd with his shiny jet-black coat and perfectly symmetrical tan highlights around his head and legs and four-inch tan paws, Bruno was a magnificent regal specimen. He hated other dogs, people in uniform, and anyone sitting on his end of the couch. His relationship with people was love or hate, and he could switch sides at any moment. But he was always loyal to his adopted family.

I turned on the hall light and there she was, the girl of my dreams, Isalda, my beautiful Afghan woman. Adorning the wall just inside the front door, she was the first thing you saw after entering the apartment.

A free, nude, long-haired blonde creature resembling a mix of palomino horse and golden Afghan dog, with her own mane flowing in the wind. She glided through space on a field of flowers, following a white dove toward the end of the rainbow.

I searched everywhere looking for the real thing. But like a vision just out of reach, she eluded me, always a step ahead. Isalda was more than an image. She was my kindred spirit.

And everyone that saw her wanted her.

How the hell was I to know that my creation would one day come to life?

The huge ink and watercolor painting fit perfectly among the other treasures and tchotchkes in my haze-filled, six-room apartment on the sixth floor of the Chatsworth Building, just east of the Hudson River at the end of 72nd Street and Riverside Drive. A handmade, floor-to-ceiling, brown-stained wooden bookcase took up an entire wall. Nearly one hundred cubby holes of various sizes formed the shelves, each like a little altar for its occupant. The eyes of original ventriloquist Paul Winchell's Jerry Mahoney dummy followed visitors as they walked in. Pictures of Mao Tse-Tung and Al Capone quietly judged. Aboriginal masks, statues, written messages, and a plaster woman's hand with diamond rings were all eerily backlit with multicolored Christmas lights. Over the years, the bookcase grew. It now filled entire rooms of our current apartment, revealing the stories of my life and travels. Everything in there made a statement and had a story connected to it.

What brought me to this place and time? What event started my journey? Maybe it was that horny girl my freshman year of high school.

It was 1957. I was thirteen years old, living in Brentwood, Long Island. My family—Mom, Dad, my little brother, Jamie, and I—had just moved from Borough Park, Brooklyn. I was the new kid in school, sitting at my desk, minding my own business, when I saw this girl across the room finish writing a note. It traveled from one kid to another until the guy next to me handed it over.

I looked at it. "What the hell is this?"

He shrugged. I unfolded the paper and read:

Hi. My Name is Dottie. Do you like me?

I like you. Do you want to meet after school? Where?

Do you want to make out with me?

Was she kidding? Of course! So, I answered it.

Yes I liek you. Yes I wana

In the school yard

Yes Yes Yes

I didn't realize the teacher had witnessed the entire thing. He took the note from me without saying a word. Several classes later, I heard it for the first time, screeching over the loudspeaker:

"FRANK YANDOLINO, REPORT TO THE PRINCIPAL'S OFFICE."

Hearing my name scared the shit out of me. Walking to his office felt like heading down death row. When I got there, my mother was sitting on a wooden bench with a "Frank, I am pissed" look in her eyes. Dottie was sitting on the other side of the room with her parents. I knew what was up. This girl was throwing me under the bus to save her ass.

"He started the note. I just answered it," she said, not looking at me as she spoke. I wanted to give her the finger. "That's bull," I yelled.

"You're a liar."

It went back and forth until the principal couldn't take it anymore. Looking over the note, he had a great idea. "Let's have them write the note again."

That was the first time my dyslexia saved my life. There was no denying who wrote what. In my world, words move around like a shell game. When I was in high school, no one really knew what dyslexia was, who had it, or how to treat it. My mother and father didn't understand it or believe that I had it. They saw it as a poor reflection on them, and didn't want the guilt of having spawned what to them seemed to be a genetically damaged child. But I couldn't have been more loved; my parents showered all of their children with affection. They couldn't do enough for us. We came first and we knew it.

There were no books in my house, and growing up no one read to me except nursery rhymes like *Old MacDonald's Farm*, *Little Red Riding Hood*, and *The Three Little Pigs*, so it makes sense that my dyslexia went unnoticed. In school I was considered slow by teachers and quiet by classmates. My biggest fear was having my name called to read out loud or come up to the dreaded blackboard. That blackboard felt like being put on trial.

Looking back, I wonder how my frequent mispronunciations didn't tip anybody off. Sometimes I would read and write the wrong words entirely. Wouldn't became would, couldn't was could, wasn't looked like was, 683 became 368, and so on.

My world of words and numbers looked like a bowl of Campbell's Alphabet Soup. As you can imagine, I got many things wrong, and didn't do well on tests, especially with reading and math. My inferiority complex continued to grow and I developed zero social skills.

Never wanting to expose myself or be ridiculed, I did the best I could to camouflage my fear by becoming the class clown.

Not until my senior year in high school did I truly discover the root of my problem and realize that my struggles and poor grades were not because I was stupid. I began training my eyes and brain to slow down by scanning sentences and focusing on the words. Today I still struggle with dyslexia (just ask my editor!), but I have worked hard to overcome the problem. I can now read a book or two in one day; back then it would have taken at least a week. I have written screenplays, books, stories, countless contracts, and proposals. In a way, dyslexia saved my life. It ultimately forced me to develop a career based around art and creativity, to become an artist—or as I prefer to call myself, a "producer"—to be able to use the creative side of my brain. This ultimately freed me from my insecurities and shortcomings. I gained confidence and became more awake, more aware, and, most importantly, more willing to take chances and risks. Being creative felt better and was easier than trying to be an academic wiz. In fact, tapping into my creative side inspired me to work harder. I began to read things over and over. I became the king of underlining, and I still underline everything so that I remember the important parts of what I read.

I have come to learn of people who overcame dyslexia to achieve great things, like Albert Einstein, Thomas Jefferson, Alexander Graham Bell, Pierre Curie, Richard Branson, and scores of others. I'm sure there are those out there who don't even know they have it.

As my career developed, and I began to conquer my disability, I formed a company, Interconnections, Inc. Fittingly, the company's purpose was to introduce interactive voice technology to the masses. It was during this time that my dyslexia and social skills troubled me the most, especially at meetings, reading documents out loud, and giving PowerPoint presentations out loud. The emergence of social networking and the spread of live chats and meetings on the computer via text and email only made it worse. I remember sweating through plenty of those meetings. Luckily, I was able to purchase a laptop computer that allowed me to dictate to it. It transcribed the words I spoke to type, and it spelled way better than I ever could. I could even take my handwritten notes and scribbles and convert them to spell check–corrected type. I am using it now as I write this book and have used it to write other books, screenplays, and stories. So I've grown able to understand my problem and develop my own system of managing it.

On our way home after my trip to the principal's office and my three-day suspension, Mom threatened me with one of her standard lines.

"Wait till your father finds out, after two days in a new school you get suspended for writing dirty notes." But much to my surprise, Dad did not explode. He simply said, "He didn't start it . . . that's what boys do." *What? I thought. That's it? That's all he has to say? Okay . . . next!*

A couple of years later, when I was a senior, I got that same cold sweat feeling as the loudspeaker blasted out:

FRANK YANDOLINO, REPORT TO YOUR GUIDANCE COUNSELOR.

Shit, what now? When I arrived at her small, one-desk, two-chair office, she got right down to business. Motioning for me to have a seat next to her, she caught my downward gaze as she crossed her legs. Quickly adjusting her miniskirt, she barked out, "Frank, you're failing algebra."

I can still see the pity in her eyes, but her announcement was not a surprise. In my head, numbers and letters were still salsa dancing to my brain's unique beat. Nonetheless, I had applied to Northwestern University for a civil engineering degree. Never mind that I hardly even knew how to spell "civil engineer," let alone what a civil engineer did. Hell, the only thing I knew about Northwestern was that it was probably north and west of somewhere.

"Northwestern said they are interested in you. However, you have to pass all your courses." She looked through her folders. "You could drop algebra."

"I could? I'll do that."

"Well, yes. You could take wood shop instead, or . . . art?"

At the time I had never done much of anything artistic. But I did know I didn't want to get sawdust all over me (I was chosen best-dressed kid by my class), so I picked art. This decision not only would end up being the right one for my grades, but it would drastically influence the rest of my life. For that I have to credit Mr. Vega, my fabulous art teacher, who encouraged me to pursue what he saw came naturally to me, using my mind to create rather than to spell or add. Mr. Vega quickly became my mentor. Painting and drawing came fairly naturally to me. Seeing something in my brain, then putting it on paper was much easier than the reverse.

My first work of art was a black-and-white pen and ink-stippled drawing of a shirtless dark-skinned peasant farmer standing in a field of tall grass while grazing his two water buffalo, one white, one black. Viewing the drawing up close you could see what looked like a million pen strokes and dots of various sizes that formed the picture, while from afar the image looked like a black-and-white halftone with shades of gray. Mr. Vega submitted my piece to a Long Island Student Art Exhibition. I won first prize and a gold medal. I grabbed the opportunity, said yes, I can do this, and kept at it. My next painting was oil on canvas board, of two boxers, one black and one white, pounding the crap out of each other while the referee looks on. That painting also won me a first prize and an interview at the Pratt Institute's School of Art and at Parsons School of Design. Pratt didn't accept me; I didn't have a track record in fine art. Forget track record—I didn't even know what fine art was or who painted it. I really didn't know much at all about this art world. All I did was copy what I saw printed in magazines and add my style to it.

Parsons called. I listened. I was not a carpenter or an engineer. I was an artist. and Mr. Vega helped me put together my portfolio. I was accepted that fall and moved into the spare room of my grandparents' five-story walk-up on 167th Street and the Grand Concourse in the Bronx. My bedroom window opened to the black-tarred roof of the building. I can still smell it. That is where I started to paint my own, totally original work.

My first painting was a very detailed image of my left hand. I spent many days making it as realistic as I could, with skin tones, hair, blue veins, fingernails, and the small letter "F" tattoo that I had given myself with sewing needles and black India ink. People to this day ask what it means and I tell them it was a secret cult gang that I belonged to in high school, but that's not true.

Although I'd been accepted to Parsons, I of course had failed the written portion of the entrance exam. So I spent the first semester taking an English comprehension make-up course at the downtown New York University campus. Putting my own spin on it, I told everyone I was attending both Parsons and NYU. It sounded better. I worked my ass off, lassoing those dancing letters like a cowboy.

Being accepted by Parsons was a big step. I was a sheltered kid from Brooklyn with no direction or reinforcement, except for a lot of love from my family. Now I was a free bird with a new life of art, sex, drugs, and jazz. Shedding the shackles of academia for art allowed me to express myself. My work spoke for me. And the better I got at it the more self-confidence I gained. One of the first courses I took was a figure painting class.

I showed up to my first class brimming with my newfound confidence. The room was a large open area with thirty students sitting behind easels. Even if I had walked in with my eyes closed, I'd still have known it was a painter's studio by the pungent smell of turpentine, mixed with undried oil paint, freshly primed gesso, and stretched linen canvas. The smell and feel of the classroom were far from my mind, though; in front of me was a naked woman sitting on a stool in the middle of the classroom, posing as if no one else was there. Today, I would describe her as Rubinesque. Back then I would have said she was fat.

Even though I grew up on the fast streets of Brooklyn, my only exposure to women had been my cousins and the girls on the block my age or younger. I had definitely never seen a live nude woman with clumps of hair on her crotch and under her arms. It shocked the shit out of me.

I stared, totally in a daze. The silence made me more uncomfortable, so I decided I'd be funny and controversial—something I would often do to camouflage my dyslexia-related insecurities. Very deadpan, I shouted out at the professor, "CAN I TRACE?"

Everyone cracked up. The professor, however, did not even break a smile. He answered immediately: "You can trace . . . only if you make it better."

This was a lesson I would never forget. You have to make it better. I try to do this with everything I do, always making it better. Even if it's just making a sandwich for one of my kids' lunches, I am driven to try to do it better than it's ever been done. At the time, I didn't know how to do that. Colored oil paint in a tube was new to me. So was the big, white, blank canvas staring me in the face, not to mention this big, white, naked woman in the middle of the studio. Plus, I had never done any sketches as involved as this assignment was.

Seeing that I was frozen, the professor walked over to me. "What are you doing?" he asked.

"Nothing. I don't know what to do."

He handed me a brush and took my hand in his, guiding me to smear the bristles into a glob of burnt sienna. We painted that first stroke across the empty canvas together.

"Now you do."

It was as simple as that. Make the first mark. If it sucks, make another one over it. Add and take away, until you and your art are left. I became the artist.

One of my class projects started me on a road that followed me all over the world for many, many years. It required picking from a list of classic love stories, reading it, and interpreting it graphically. I chose "Tristan and Isalda." Little did I know I would come across several Isaldas in my life. Any time they would tell me their name I always won them over by replying that my name is Tristan. It has worked every time. And it may not be over.

Isalda the German Model at *Mode* nagazine. Isalda the Bolshoi Ballerina in Moscow.

Isalda the Russian hooker.

This is for sure: My years at Parsons exposed me to freedom, the arts, and their creators. It gave me a whole new perspective on life. Well, not new—it was the only perspective I had ever had.

CHAPTER 2

Drafted

Several months after graduating from Parsons I got the dreaded letter all young men in those days feared.

Selective Service Systems
ORDER TO REPORT FOR INDUCTION

The President of the United States
To: Frank M. Yandolino   Selective Service # 30 2 44 2318
17 6th Avenue. Brentwood, New York

Greetings:
You are hereby ordered into the Armed Forces of The United States. Report at the lobby of the U.S. Post Office Main Street Brentwood, New York on November 5, 1966 at 6:30 AM for forwarding to an Armed Forces Induction Station at 39 Whitehall Street New York, NY.

I can still see the day of my induction as clear as yesterday. It was dark, just before dawn, when I left my parents' home on eastern Long Island and boarded a westbound bus for a two-hour trip to the US Army's induction center.

Artists and war do not mix. I went from painting beautiful hairy women to standing in line after line with not-so-beautiful hairy men. White Hall, as the induction center was called, was built in 1886 and had become a dilapidated eight-story building of red granite, sandstone, and red brick with small slit windows on the ground floor. Above the arched front entranceway was a decorative granite panel carved with a cannon, a mortar, a knight in chain mail armor, cannon balls, and a spear. It looked like had been done by a kid in a sandbox. Inside, it smelled like a gym locker room. The entire place had walls painted shades of drab pea green with gray floors and sterile white ceilings with black trim. Hand-painted cardboard signs hung everywhere, telling me what to do like lifeless little fascists.

Gone were the Rubinesque big tits and furry bushes. Instead, I was surrounded by all sizes and colors of dicks, men and boys from every walk of life, with accents from every part of the country. All of us were now carrying the same thing: jars of piss. Standing in line, a doctor approached and requested I pull down my shorts. He grabbed my balls and said, "Turn your head and cough." All I knew while standing in my underwear with my own urine in my hand was that this was not the path for me.

"I gotta get out of here."

My father knew someone who knew someone who got me into the Army Reserve. I was sent to 42nd Street and 12th Avenue for training while awaiting my orders. Because of the enormity of the Vietnam draft, the Army had run out of uniforms, so I went to Reserve meetings in my dungarees and civilian clothes. After a few weeks, I was sent to summer camp, a two-week trip to Camp Drum, an Army training facility in Watertown, upstate New York—to learn how to survive in Vietnam by participating in simulated war games.

When we got to camp, wouldn't you know, they assigned me and five other recruits out of five hundred to become commandos. Two Special

Forces commando trainers arrived in helicopters and laid out the plan of attack for invading the other trainees. They gave the five of us gas masks, tear gas, and smoke bombs, along with the standard-issued M1 Garand rifle. The only gun I had ever had before was a carpet gun, made out of a two-foot piece of two-by-four wood with stretched-out rubber bands strung together and held down by half of a wooden clothespin. It shot out a one-inch-square piece of linoleum tile. You always aimed for the other guy's head, hoping to knock his eye out. I can still hear my mother: "Junior, stop that! You'll knock his eye out." Somehow, we never did.

During our briefing we were told that all we had to do was wear a soft cap to designate ourselves as Special Forces Commandos for the war games. I instinctively put mine on backwards and tied a white handkerchief around my neck, wondering if this was all just some bad trip.

As the games began, I took my defiant insubordination one step further. At times I took the cap off. I was starting to understand how the military mind worked. They expected me to not break the rules, presuming honor would prevail. They didn't know I grew up in Brooklyn and live by the credo: if you didn't grow up in Brooklyn, you didn't go through basic training.

In Brooklyn, you went to work immediately, always looking to get the edge, that little something different. You snooze you lose. No a'kees, olly olly oxen frees. Oops doesn't count. All that stuff stays with you forever, gets embedded in your character and influences what you must change in order to evolve. But first you must run as fast as you can, yelling the Brooklyn attack chant "ee awk ee, ee awk eeeeee." We're not like those who were brought up in Queens or Long Island. We are Brooklyn.

Not even the army can compare to growing up in Brooklyn, where I learned that rules are made to be broken, and that a little white lie applied at the right time is okay, or that bending the truth to your advantage is necessary to survive. The army didn't count on me hiding my cap so the other troops wouldn't know who I was. They were trained to look for guys in caps, and I didn't fit the bill. It was just like when my mother used to make me wear the ugliest, stupidest, most embarrassing ear-flapped, make-believe, leather fake fur-lined hat, complete with chin strap. I stuck it in my shirt every day and I still don't like hats.

Off we trekked into the woods, preparing our attack. Both sides took the game very seriously. Several from our side were captured during the war simulation and even lightly beaten. Once the 12:00 p.m. siren sounded a truce was struck. We all returned to the main base for lunch.

A lieutenant and I were walking back for our meal when we were jumped. I was hit with a rifle butt and we were detained. I didn't realize that the lieutenant and I were the only two Special Forces left. These overzealous soldiers were trying to end the war games early by cheating. I hate cheaters.

Strutting like peacocks, they marched us into a large command tent where all the brass sat eating. Our captors were there to claim victory to the soft-jowled men in ribbons and medals, but the lieutenant wasn't done.

"You still got those bombs?" he whispered. I nodded.

"On the count of three . . . one . . . two . . . three. *Gas!*" he yelled.

I rolled one of my tear gas bombs right down the center of the officer's lunch table. We quickly slipped on our gas masks and made an easy escape from the sounds of coughing and gagging. I disappeared into the woods.

For several hours, I haunted the base, randomly exploding and destroying things. Eventually, they sent out a helicopter. That's when I heard that nefarious loudspeaker again.

"PRIVATE YANDOLINO, YOU CAN COME OUT NOW. THE GAMES ARE OVER."

Bullshit! I didn't trust them, so I continued to set things on fire, hide, and attack. After several more passes by the helicopter, I got tired of it all. I came out of the bush. They snapped a picture of me walking out in a haze of smoke, my gun at my side, white handkerchief around my neck á la John Wayne, my soft hat on backward.

Ironically, it was that image that allowed me to grace my first magazine cover: the *Army Times*. I guess I took simulated war games pretty seriously. I really don't like to play games, especially if someone cheats.

Several months later my unit was called up for six months of basic training at Fort Jackson, South Carolina, before moving on to Fort Knox, Kentucky. For their part, and perhaps in response to my newfound fame, the army sent me to cook school to continue my basic training.

"Cook school," I proclaimed. "Why? I graduated college for art and photography; at least make me a sign painter."

The sergeant was dead serious. "Son, someone has to feed our boys over there in 'Nam." In basic training I met Joe Lombardo. He weighed about three hundred pounds and was unable to do any of the drills or exercises. The other soldiers constantly picked on him, and Joe was the target of all the drill sergeants. I believe they sensed something was very different about Joe. I overheard one of them use the word "queer."

I had no clue, just felt sorry for him. My brother James had faced the same ridicule growing up, from kids and adults alike, because he was very overweight. It made me crazy and still does. I deplore ignorance when people impose their ill-founded ideologies on others.

Joe and I became great friends. He was one of the most creative, innovative people I'd ever met, which is truly saying a lot. This super-special lost soldier taught me it was cool to have fun at what you do, to set yourself free. That's when I decided to let my freak flag fly.

Many years later when Joe and I were in Paris working on *Mode* magazine we had a conversation about his personal sexual preference, and what it meant for him to be gay, being from an Italian family, starting out straight, coming out of the closet, meeting Joe's girlfriend, Donna, going back in the closet. A key observation I have learned that people

14

need to realize that being gay isn't being a freak of nature or having some disease you can catch. It's not something you become because of your upbringing or your environment. It's not a choice. You are born gay, it is what you are, it is your genetics. From the beginning of time animals and humans have been bisexual. They are all on their own unique part on the spectrum of the four sexes, which I explain as something like this: straight men on one side and straight women on the other, with gay men and women in the middle sort of sharing a little from both sides. You may look masculine or feminine and inside be completely the opposite. Joe agreed with that theory. He was tormented by it all his life. Was he straight or gay? Feminine or masculine? Is it possible to be both? Well, he was. Unfortunately for the world, in the mid-eighties my good friend Joe died of AIDS.

I had already decided the army was not for me, even before the army decided to ignore my artistic experience and make me a cook. Fortunately, they made Joe a cook, too. Together, we were sent to Fort Knox, put in charge of the field mess truck, and assigned to prepare for a very important retirement parade for a general. We were told to clean the truck and paint it to match all the other equipment—missile launchers, troop movers, etc. The entire base would be on hand to witness the spectacle.

Joe and I went to work. We painted all night, finishing just in time to move the truck into position on the parade line. When the officers saw our work, all hell broke out; we had painted that food truck to the max. It was painted army drab green, with oversized white stars that covered most of the front doors. All the metal parts, bumpers, exhaust stacks, and tire rims that were once painted camouflage were newly painted gray and the black tires were now sporting whitewalls. Remember, Joe and I were artists first and foremost. Our mess truck was immediately pulled out of formation, yet the army still did not have the foresight to remove me from duty.

As a cook, I immediately understood that I had leverage and grabbed the ball of opportunity again. I had the goods to barter. I traded food for privileges. There was a rumor traveling at light speed around the world about how you could get high by smoking dried banana peels. Even in the military there was a market for Mellow Yellow. As cook, I had access to thousands of banana peels. I took the skins up to the barracks roof and I lined the entire barracks roof with aluminum foil, laying them all out to dry in the sunshine. I sold each dried banana peel for a dollar. One problem: it did not work. All you got was a headache.

My capitalist endeavor ended during a barracks inspection. The platoon leader saw the skins on the roof. I tried to blame it on the monkeys.

"What monkeys?"

Seems he knew that monkeys weren't indigenous to Kentucky, so that excuse unfortunately didn't fly. I ended up having to refund everyone's dollars.

My bartering did get me out of one of the worst military jobs, KP (Kitchen Police—the army's way of telling you to do the dishes). Avoiding the second worst job, guard duty, wasn't so simple.

In the military, every so-called Swinging Dick had to serve on guard duty. It was not only your duty, but supposedly an honor. Before their shift, every soldier reporting for guard duty stood in line for inspection. Your uniform had to be clean and pressed with razor-sharp creases, boots shined to reflect your face. Most importantly, the brass belt buckle had to be shiny and spotless. The sergeant stood in front of your face, barking out questions. Answers had to be perfect, without hesitation.

When my turn for guard duty came up, I shined my boots and my belt buckle. I even stood at attention. Yet I had no intention of standing out in the cold snow all night. So, when it came to the questions, I put my plan into action.

"Son, what is your third General Order?"

I stared straight ahead when I answered. "I don't know, Sergeant."

His iron gray eyes widened. "What is your first General Order, soldier?"

"I'm not sure, Sergeant."

Steam rose off his buzz cut. "Who is your Company Commander?"

"Uh, General Fataché?"

The sergeant stared at me for some time. I stared straight ahead as earnestly as I could.

"Son, do you realize that you just failed inspection? You will not serve guard duty. What will your mother say?"

"I'm sure she will not be happy, Sergeant."

"You're dismissed, soldier. Return to your barracks. You are confined for the weekend."

"Yes, sir."

I saluted and jogged back to my barracks. Sprawled on my bed, no one could tell me what to do for two whole days. That's about as close as it gets to paradise in the military.

From there, I got through the rest of my time in the army by following one simple rule: lie and always carry a clipboard. Looking busy, I quickly learned, was the fast way to avoid work. When asked to do something by my superiors I would point to my clipboard full of bullshit papers and say, "Sorry, sir, I am busy doing this." I perfected this art to the point that I was able to sport prayer beads and grew long sideburns like Elvis as my way of protesting. When told to shave off my sideburns or take off my beads I would say "Yes, sir" and later on, when questioned again by the same person, "Son, did I tell you to shave those things and get rid of the beads?" I would simply say, "No, sir."

They never caught on. Artists are great liars.

The reason I'm writing about the Army is not just to share some interesting experiences. It's about the lessons I learned. The most important thing the army taught me was that you must be in control and also must look like you are in control, especially when you've got the ball.

It could have been easy to give up or give in and conform to what the military wanted me to do and the way they wanted me to do it—always without question, without input from me. They taught you how to follow their ball. But I had my own goal and my own ideas on how to handle the ball and what to do with it. Ninety-nine percent of the people in the military are trained to follow. It's easier for them not to think, easier to follow someone else's ball. And it's not just in the military that this is prevalent; the same is true in most organizations, especially in the government. Sorry, but I'm not very good in that type of system, and I don't think many people belong in it, either.

One day I received a letter from Mom. She said my cousin, Frank Pedone (we share the same birthday, October 28), was also at Fort Jackson. He was the same cousin Frankie, the son of my mother's oldest brother, Tony, who was brought over from Italy when they moved in with us at Grandpa's house on 42nd Street. So Cousin Frankie and I grew up together.

Those little Italians who came over wearing short leather pants, knee-high socks, and little hats had to learn the Brooklyn way, so I had taken Frank and his siblings under my wing. Their hats got taken every day by other kids to play a game we called "salugi," where you take someone's hat or other item, and throw it back and forth to each other and don't let the kid get it. It took some fist-fights before my cousins completed their Brooklyn basic training, but they eventually learned to hide their hats, too. We became very close.

I remember looking outside my barracks window. It was pouring rain. Cousin Frankie was in a barracks on the other side of the base, where the troops were gathered for deployment to Vietnam. I put on my raincoat and headed to his barracks. Walking in, I immediately felt a deep sense of worry emanating from these very young men pondering their fates. I found my cousin sitting on a bunk. We hugged and kissed, a family custom even if you saw him just the other day. We were very happy to see each other. All the other soldiers were just sitting around wide-eyed, scared that tomorrow they would be in Vietnam. Frankie and I talked about his brother Ralph and, oddly enough, our other cousin Frank Sconzo, both of whom were already in 'Nam. I didn't think it was fair to have so many boys from the same family out at war at the same time. I asked him if he was looking forward to being deployed, but he didn't have to answer. I could tell he was scared by the look on his face. So I reminded him of something important.

"You grew up in Brooklyn. You already got basic training." He smiled. "I know that, Cuz'."

Cousin Frank's leg was stretched across his bunk. My eyes scanned the other soldiers in the room. I asked him again if he was looking forward to deployment, and before he could answer, without hesitation, I kicked him in the ankle, shattering the bone.

He yelled out. I walked out the door, back into the rain, smiling, knowing he would be going to a hospital, not 'Nam. We still smile about it every time we meet, even though he walks with a slight limp.

Although I was surviving the army, I knew my road led somewhere else. I had to get out. Art was calling. That's when the idea hit me. The army was clearly stripping me of my rights. Why not unionize?

I founded a union for soldiers against the officers. I called it the First Soldiers Union of the United States. The membership drive began in earnest. When the commanding officer learned of my endeavor, the captain decided it was time to send me back to New York, destination Fort Hamilton, for evaluation. I was back in Brooklyn where I belonged.

"What do you want, son?" I was asked during my first interview. This was the crossroads, one of the easiest questions of my life.

"I want to get the hell out of the army."

It was all they could take. I think the decision had already been made. Hippies do not belong in the Special Forces.

"You can go home, son."

I didn't know whether they ever wanted me to come back. I never did, but I always wondered if they would come find me. Two years later, I received an honorable discharge in the mail. I kept all my equipment—tents, shovels, uniforms, mess kits, all the stuff I was supposed to return. They must have waived that requirement to get rid of me.

CHAPTER 3

The Chatsworth

Most people called me Frank, but I went by other names, too. Back in Brooklyn, I was sometimes called Junior. And depending on who I was speaking with or the gravity of a situation, might I have called myself Cambo Shabuggabo or Bruno Fataché.

About a year later I moved into the Chatsworth Apartment at 344 West 72nd Street, the last building off of Riverside and the West Side Highway, facing the Hudson River. As everyone who ever visited me would say, it was the coldest and windiest spot in the city of New York.

The Chatsworth was like no other. Every day strangers and friends would bring something new to the party. At any given time, day or night, long-haired visitors and braless girls, some whom I did not even know, sat on my floor listening to music, smoking, drinking, crashing, and staring at the bookcased wall. We would talk for hours, sharing the kinds of thoughts that sustained the chi of the '60s. I liked to tell stories, as I still do.

One particular night, sitting in my white Indian robe and sandals, I told one of my classics, a visualization that I truly believe happened to me: I am not a Human Being Experiencing Spiritual things, but a Spiritual Being Experiencing Human things.

"Ever since I can remember, I have this vivid feeling that my first day started with me falling from the sky. People were looking up, talking about it."

I took a hit off the joint being passed around, and let the grass steep in my lungs. The smoke-filled room added to the image like the clouds in a René Magritte painting. I continued:

"There may have been some photos in the news. I remember the wind was holding me up, guiding me down to the Earth. My mind had no reference. Who am I? Where am I going? Where did I come from? As I was falling, I had to choose the right moment to enter life. I felt brand new, going with the flow, having no choice but to grab the ball floating in front of me."

I took another hit and passed the joint, continuing my oration:

"Like a snake shedding its skin. Like a caterpillar changing into a butterfly."

"What do you mean, 'grab the ball'?" someone asked.

The joint found its way back to me. I took another hit before replying very matter-of-factly to the question. "It comes from another philosophical visualization that guides my daily decisions. I'm sitting at a table with a group of people when the proverbial ball—an opportunity—is thrown in the air. Some people sitting at the table look at the ball but don't grab it, thinking maybe the ball will go higher. Others hesitate, thinking it is already on its way down. I, on the other hand, grab the ball right where it is, while it is in the air, before it goes up or down, and then figure out what to do with it, with no thoughts flashing through my mind other than to take advantage of the opportunity. There's nothing too complicated about grabbing the ball when the opportunity is there. And now it's my ball, while everyone else is left never having made a decision at all.

"But it's not just about having the ball; it's what you do with it once you grab it. That's what it's all about: I realize now everything happening to me is a direct result of me: how I think and how I react to situations, how I flow and when I grab. I accept that some outside force dictates how long I stay in any situation. I know it's only long enough to get the experience before it's on to the next. It seems like I was shot out by a force that controls my life. What a ride, but it's my choice whether to take control or crash to the ground. Some of us are free spirits with a burning desire to learn and evolve, knowing payment for man's evolution comes in the form of hard work, karma . . . and balls.

"Growing up in Brooklyn in the '50s was all about the ball—both proverbial and literal—and the many ways you can play with it. You got your baseball, basketball, punch ball, stickball, and handball, stoop ball, box ball, off-the-wall, on a bounce, and hit the stick. No matter what type of ball, no matter what type of game, simply grabbing it is never enough; it's figuring out what to do with the ball once you have it that counts."

As I was talking I had joined in with the background music, banging out the rhythms and beats on my wooden, hand-stretched conga drum my Uncle Bob gave me in high school. Someone else picked up the bongos and a tambourine joined in as we pounded along with Olatunji's *Drums of Passion* and Mongo Santamaria, nothing unusual for my apartment, of course.

The girl who had just moved across the hall came to the door.

"Hi," she said. "I heard the drums from my place. Come over. I want you to meet someone."

I followed into her apartment. Sitting on the floor was another guy with long hair sticking up and out all over the place. He looked at my own long ponytail.

"I like your hair, man," he said. "What's your name, man?"

"Frank."

"I'm Gerome, Gerome Ragni."

We got to talking and smoked a joint. He told me he had just finished working on a Broadway musical. "You want to hear something?" he asked.

Before I could answer "Yes," he started to play his guitar and sing.

Darlin', give me a head with hair, long beautiful hair
Shining, gleaming, steaming, flaxen, waxen
Give me down to there hair, shoulder length or longer Here,
baby, there, momma, everywhere, daddy, daddy Hair, hair,
hair, hair, hair, hair, hair, hair
Flow it, show it, long as God can grow it, my hair.

We finished the joint and talked some more about hair before I went back to my apartment, where I felt more comfortable among my bookcases and my "girls." In one corner sat an old ceramic toilet bowl with half a mannequin sticking out of it. Two perfectly formed female legs clad in black mesh nylons and garter belt, no panties, stuck upside down out of the bowl like scissors cutting through the bullshit. Black, patent-leather spike heels rested on her pointy, stiff feet. In the other corner of the room was a seven-foot female mannequin bust painted in day-glow colors and silver glitter with a large glass light fixture separating her waist from her legs. She wore a white motorcycle helmet with black plumed ostrich feathers and mirrored sunglasses, complete with whips and chains. Making a statement was important to me. Sticking that girl mannequin in the toilet was a message to all women and women's libbers. It was all done very tastefully, though, like a fine sculptor, something Warhol or Dali would do. The statement was simple enough: some girls should be stuck in the toilet.

The Chatsworth itself was legendary. This prewar apartment building was built in 1904 by George F. Johnson, Jr., and Aleck Kahn, and designed by architect John E. Scharsmith. William Randolph Hearst originally lived there. A cab driver told me Hearst had the railroad tracks come straight through the building so his mistress could come and go on the train without anyone knowing. He also told me that it had once been the most notorious whorehouse in New York City.

Little did I know in 1968 that my friends and upstairs neighbors Barbara and Peter Anders would eventually become my sister- and brother-in-law. Peter Anders was quite a character, a forerunner of the early rock culture. A singer, songwriter, and producer, he and his sidekick Vini Poncia were part of The Videls, The Tradewinds, and The Innocence. Peter wrote and recorded with Phil Spector, The Ronettes, Cher, Elvis Presley, Doc Pomus, Richard Perry, Artie Ripp, Joan Jett, Kenny Laguna, Bo Gentry, Ritchie Cordell ("Mony Mony," "I Think We're Alone Now"), Jay & The Americans, 10cc, Billy Joel, Steely Dan, Tommy James & The Shondells, Bobby Bloom, Kenny Vance, The Regents, and The Archies. Most of them passed through our apartments at the Chatsworth with their entourages and groupies, and I often joined them at their offices and studios at 1650 Broadway, known as "the music building." Half of the Chatsworth apartments were filled with musicians, artists, and writers. It was a notorious center of the music and art world.

The entire Chatsworth building smelled of pot and it was the kind of place where you never knew what would happen next. I sometimes did the laundry in the basement with would-be actress Susan Sarandon, who never wore a bra under her tight-fitting white T-shirt, and I'd occasionally see Clive Barnes, the all-powerful *New York Times* critic. Mary Travis from Peter, Paul, and Mary lived there, along with members of the band Chicago. Sissy Spacek slept on my couch. She showed up one night at my apartment, having come to New York to be a singer/songwriter with her band called Bull Moose and the Pelicans. They would practice vocals under the transverse tunnel in Riverside Park. I can't remember how they were introduced to our crew, but she was a cute little thing with a southern accent. As I watched her play guitar and sing, I couldn't help but think, "That's a big, flat nose you got there, honey!" It's been under the knife since. Now it looks like Michael Jackson's.

Walking into the building, you'd immediately notice the huge columns that rose from the marble floor. The elevator was to the left and

Terrie and Norman Marzano lived to the right in a ground-floor apartment with their little baby girl, Boo. Norman was a well-known musician, and their place was the hub of the Chatsworth for a time. Everyone coming or going would stop in and see what was up.

The Marzanos' apartment was open 24/7. I walked in one day, as I tended to do, and that's when I saw her sitting on the couch, about 5' 11" and skinny, with long, blonde hair. She looked Scandinavian. It would have been impossible not to notice such a beauty. Leggy Norse goddesses aren't sitting on every couch in the world. I realized immediately this stunning vision was from the painting hanging on my wall. My Afghan woman had come to life and was sitting in Norman's apartment.

I could not control my thoughts. "Who is that?!" I sputtered. Thank God nobody heard me.

Feeling uncomfortable in her presence, I nervously started talking to Norman, but all I could see was this girl deep in conversation with some guy sitting next to her. He had an ascot and a sports jacket and slicked-back hair. His name was Enzo, a shoe salesman who spoke with an Italian accent.

I could not take my eyes off her, but not a glance came my way. Why would she notice me? Just another hippie in a dungaree, embroidered shirt and worn, faded jeans, pony-tailed with a motorcycle helmet in hand. A far cry from Mr. Italy shoe salesman, she had me talking to myself.

"That must be what she's into." "What?" Norman asked. "Nothing."

I felt like the sore thumb in the room. The conversation kept on rolling like I had never walked in. So I walked out, leaving her with that Italian shoe guy, for some reason knowing we'd meet again.

In Charli's Words

I was born Georgette Sue Miller on January 10. When I was younger, everyone called me skinny Georgie. I hated that name. I was 5' 11" and weighed 110 pounds. At the age of seventeen, my mother signed me up for beauty school. I was forced to become a hairdresser, just like her. She meant well. Mother wanted me to be prepared in case I had to support myself in life. "You never know," she would say.

My first job found me cutting hair in Great Neck, Long Island. One day one of the other hairdressers said, "You're not a Georgie. You look more like a Charli."

The name stuck, and I became famously known as Miss Charli of Great Neck.

In 1968 I was twenty-one years old and had just returned from a vacation in Italy with a new boyfriend I had met there. I remember sitting at Terrie Marzano's apartment at the Chatsworth waiting for my sister Barbara, who lived in the building, when this guy walked in. I couldn't help but notice him. There was something about him. He was the complete opposite of anyone I would ever know, with his very long hair pulled back into a ponytail, scruffy long beard and embroidered jean jacket, and carrying a motorcycle helmet to boot. Definitely not my type. I wouldn't look directly at him even though I felt a strange essence in his presence. He had a definite vibe, and I couldn't help but wonder, "Who is this guy?" And somehow I knew, too, that we would meet again.

Often in life, we are tugged in two directions at a time. Do I go left? Do I go right? One thing I know is that you can't be in two places at once, even if that's exactly what you and everyone else might want. So initially, I go with the flow, which may take me to the right, but I always stay ready to take out my machete and go to the left.

After the army, it was time to make a new path in the jungle of my life, one that did not give up on being an artist. And now one that did not give up on Charli. That Italian shoe guy could just piss off.

Charli must not have given up on me either. One day she showed up at my door.

WOW! I almost blurted out. I couldn't help but give her the Brooklyn don't-get-caught once-over. It was her, the blonde beauty from Norman Marzano's couch, the Afghan woman in my painting, standing at my door.

"Hi. My name is Charli. The elevator's not working." I nodded, gawking. "There's an elevator strike."

"My sister said I should stop by on my way up to the twelfth floor for a rest, or maybe a drink. Is that okay?" She may have used the excuse that she was thirsty, but I believe that meeting was our destiny. This was a ball I would not only grab, but one I knew I would never let go. "Come in, Charli," I answered. "Who's your sister?" "Barbara Ann."

I knew Barbara. She was also a real beauty, and my first friend in the building. Everyone knew her. Once a go-go dancer with Joey Dee and the Star Lighters at the Peppermint Lounge, she was now married to Peter Anders. His friend wrote the song Barbara Ann sung by The Regents and later covered by The Beach Boys about her.

Ba ba ba ba Barbara Ann
Ba ba ba ba Barbara Ann
Oh Barbara Ann, take my hand
Barbara Ann
You got me rockin' and a-rollin' Rockin' and a-reelin'
Barbara Ann ba ba
Ba Barbara Ann

I didn't know, however, that Barbara had a sister, or that I had drawn Barbara's sister walking through a field of flowers years before ever seeing her in person. Once Charli was inside, I knew I had her; entering my apartment was like entering Svengali World. I Svengalied her. I don't think Charli knew that at the time, though. If you asked her then, this moment of destiny had more to do with being thirsty and needing a rest.

Either way, the figure standing before me was more beautiful than any work of art. I could feel the heat of her spirit warming the air between us. She had on this miniskirt—a mini-miniskirt. I was in a fog the whole time. What could she be thinking? Probably something like, "Who the hell is this guy in white robes and sandals, smelling like patchouli oil?"

Way too soon, the moment passed. I walked her to the back steps. As this stunning blonde walked up the stairs, I watched her go. I am almost sure she wasn't wearing underwear. I stared at those thin, long legs. Six-foot legs! She was really special.

After finding my Afghan woman I wasn't going to lose her. I knew from the start, and I found out later so did Charli, that deep down we were meant for each other.

In Charli's Words

That summer during the citywide elevator strike I would stop by the Chatsworth after work and climb the twelve flights of stairs up to my sister Barbara's apartment, always complaining how exhausting it was. Barbara suggested I stop at her friend Frank's apartment on the sixth floor to rest. I think her real motive was that I meet Frank, not knowing it was the same guy I'd purposely ignored at Terrie's apartment a few days prior. Although I would never let him know, I did think he was cute. So the next time I visited Barbara I stopped at Frank's apartment and ended up doing that several times.

We got to know each other as friends, or so it seemed to me. I would tell myself he was not my type.

I never thought of being lovers, although I must admit deep down I did feel a warm feeling when I was with him. Now looking back I'm not sure about Frank's motives. He is and always was very cunning. I felt a bit like a spider in his web.

Coming from Great Neck, I had never been exposed to anyone like him or anywhere like his apartment, which I somehow thought was painted dark brown and very cool, just like the amazing music he would play on his tape recorder. I began to learn about his life, and slowly but surely his world felt less like a foreign land.

My sister had always been the wild one, leaving home immediately after high school and becoming a twist dancer at Joey Dee's Peppermint Lounge, a really crazy, famous place. She was considered extreme in my very straight, middle-class family. I decided to spend that summer with Barbara until I could find my own apartment. Time went by and I finally found a place on Horatio Street in Greenwich Village. I did not see Frank again for a while. Barbara moved to California with her husband, Peter, and her little daughter Petra.

Months later Barbara came back to New York to see the Mohammed Ali–Joe Frazier fight even though she was eight months pregnant. As I said, she was not a typical sister. But I was happy to have her stay at my apartment. She was always Frank's friend first so she invited him over. He had never been at my place. I came home from work and both he and my boyfriend were there with Barbara. I didn't know what to do. Frank had brought me a gift. I was used to real gifts, but Frank brought me a brown paper lunch bag with a piece of Bazooka bubble gum and one black-and-white little photo of him from one of the machines that gives you four pictures for a dollar. It cracked me up. Was he trying to impress me?

Well, it worked. I took a look at him, his long hair, jeans, motorcycle, crazy life. I'd always liked blue blazers, Gucci shoes, and limousines. Then I looked at my boyfriend, and back at Frank. I went over to my boyfriend and said to him, "We're breaking up. You have to go now." He was shocked.

I looked again at Frank and I knew he was perfect, not because of the outside but in that moment I saw him totally for the first time and I fell in love with the inside. I just knew he was a good man. After that Frank and I became inseparable and our lives together have been an adventure in every way.

The other day, my Frank asked me about our first date. I laughed.

"What first date? You never asked me on a single date that I can remember."

I have no memory of how Charli and I met again after the elevator strike. I just assumed she would go out with me. Barbara must have put in a good word. Whatever it was, we had a mutual attraction to each other. We both could feel it. Her character was my dream; prior to meeting me, she would always say that guys like me had been her nightmare. Still, somehow she accepted me. We disagree not only on how our first date came about but on how, a few months later, we decided to get married, too.

Anyway, on what I believe to be our first date, we took off on my motorcycle to a French restaurant in the Village, with Charli's miniskirted long legs dangling to either side. After dinner I took her back to her apartment. When she opened the door, I saw all the walls had been freshly painted.

"Why's everything brown?" I asked.

She smiled and looked at her walls. "I liked your apartment so much I wanted to get the same feel."

"Huh." That was strange to me. My walls weren't brown. Now that I think about it, it seems my Afghan woman's memory is open to question. Maybe I'm the one who's right about our first date after all.

CHAPTER 4

Woodstock

Just before I met my Charli, a nation within a nation rose from the earth—drenched in mud, springing forth on waves of pot, psychedelics, and long hair—against the war, tied forever together as one living breathing mass of hippiness. Never one to miss an opportunity, I thrust myself into the middle of it, a hippie in hippie land. Out of the soaking rain emerged a parade of people casted to be a part of my life forever. It all started when I met Artie and Linda Kornfeld. I was introduced to them by Charles and Harvey Estrin, better known as Harvey and Charlie Tuna. The Tunas lived on the other side of the Chatsworth. Charlie Tuna was a very savvy, honest, and spiritual man. Back then, while everyone else grew long hair, mustaches, and beards, Tuna shaved everything off his shiny head except a thick, black, Gurdjieff-type mustache.

Still in my early twenties, I was interested in learning more about who we are and where we are going as a human race. Tuna gave me several books to read on that subject and I instantly became a follower and student of the philosophers Gurdjieff and Ouspensky.

At this point I had a full-time job as an assistant art director at the MPA Agency, a full-service advertising and promotion agency in Manhattan. I got along great with one of the chief executives, Marshal May. He, like Mr. Vega at Brentwood High School, took me under his wing. As I have come to learn, independent things happen in my life that later become connected. Marshal belonged to an organization—a school of higher learning—that was an extension of the master, teacher, writer, and philosopher George Gurdjieff and his student and master philosopher Peter Ouspensky. Ouspensky wrote the most fascinating book I've read to this day, *The Psychology of Man's Possible Evolution.*

The school held classes and workshops dedicated to studying questions like: What does the evolution of man mean? What are the necessary conditions for this to happen? Marshal saw I was interested in such exploration and suggested I join the school. He set up a meeting with a woman named Mrs. Benson, so she could evaluate whether I was worthy of being accepted. Marshal already said he would sponsor me. I walked over to the Upper West Side to meet her at the institute.

As I entered the room, I could feel the intensity she projected. Without saying a word she directed me to sit across from her at the small table. Our bodies were three feet apart. I was shaking as she began her inquisition, her face no more than six inches from mine. "The first thing you must do," she began. But before she continued I nervously took out a cigarette and lit it. Looking directly in my eyes with total disdain she barked out, "How dare you! Without asking me?"

Thinking she meant she wanted one as well, I sheepishly answered, "Oh, I'm sorry. Would you like a cigarette?" She went off. "No. That is not what I meant. How dare you break our concentration? I am trying to see who you are, and you decided to stop that process; look what you did! Instead of looking at me with undivided attention, you look away, grab a cigarette, look for a match, light your cigarette, take a puff, and blow it in my face. All while I am trying to communicate with you. You must always remain awake and aware. Do you understand?"

In total shock I put out the cigarette.

"Please forgive me. I will never forget that lesson." And I never did.

33

I was on my way to becoming awake and aware. Mrs. Benson went on with her thought. "What I was about to say is you must cut your hair and shave off your beard in order to evolve. In the early stages of growth you cannot stick out like a sore thumb by bringing attention to yourself. That will get in your way and may cause wrong impressions as to who and what you are." I am still working on this. Studying and reading Gurdjieff and Ouspensky revealed to me the root of my goal in life: to constantly be awake and aware and to continue to evolve as a human being. But I have come to realize man's evolution comes with a price. To evolve, man must work hard, be tenacious, and be dedicated. It doesn't happen overnight.

Ouspensky spoke of three stages to man's evolution. Stage one is sex, stage two is money, and stage three is power—power to be in control. Most people get stuck in one stage or the other. Many never get out of the sex stage, believing everything evolves around it. Although I like sex and money, I'm striving for power, the power to control each stage and live a more awakened life. And I especially believe that power can be yours when you have the ball.

One day, Tuna stopped by my place.

"Hey man, you want to help me with this?" "What is it?"

He showed me a 45-rpm vinyl record entitled *Stickball*. I put it on my record player. As the disc spun, a haunting voice filled the air: "Mrs. Bruno, can Tony come out and play?" I was taken back to my childhood, to the innocent times of stickball and playing in the street, and . . . was that a church hymn in the background? Gregorian chants?

"Far out."

I was about to tell Tuna it sounded a little boring, but I didn't have time to get the words out before Tony Bruno's lyrics took a hard left.

Love was love.

Love between two people is out of sight. But let me say this

Love between five people, now that's heavy. That could be a groove.

That's when it changed. A spiritual orgasm. Stickball was an X-rated, irreverent recording amid hymnal background singers. Tony screams it out:

The world is built on sucking.

Now suck me, now suck me, now suck me. Whip some skull on me, bitch.

"That's wild!" I'd never heard anything like it.

"Right on. It's going to be the first street-distributed record. You want to help?" The ball was in the air. "Sure. I'll do it."

Tuna and I went around to mom-and-pop record stores handing out *Stickball* on consignment, picking up the cash later. After a few days of hanging out, we got to talking. Tuna opened another door and threw up the next ball.

"I'm working on a music festival with two groovy guys. You'll like them. They're originally from Brooklyn, fellow Brooklynites, as we say. Artie Kornfeld and Michael Lang. Maybe you can help. You want to meet them?"

I didn't need to answer; Tuna knew me well enough by then. We drove over on my black street scrambler motorcycle to a new, very modern high-rise apartment building on East 56th Street and went up to the 62nd floor.

Artie met us at the door. His intense yet friendly dark brown eyes stood out, framed by his long curly hair and almost pubic hair–like beard. He was smiling before he knew who I was. He was barefoot and wearing a sleeveless shirt.

"Hey, man." He sounded genuinely happy.

Tuna answered. "Artie, this is Frank Yandolino, the guy I told you about." "Far out. Come in."

By the look in those eyes, I knew he was special. We embraced in a hippie power hug. I didn't know that it represented the beginning of our long working and very personal relationship. How could I? I was staring at the beauty behind him with her own sparkling eyes.

I have no recollection of how long Artie and I hugged, but I remember I kept trying to look at this girl wearing cut-off shorts and a shirt tied up under her breasts, until he finally let go and motioned to her.

"This is my wife, Linda."

"Hi Frank, nice to meet you."

"Hi Linda." She looked directly into my eyes, and I'm sure my mind. She smiled. "Far out."

The hug that followed that introduction was much more enjoyable. Contrary to rumors that exist to this day, I did not have sex with her, then or ever, at least not physically.

A child's voice came from down the hall. A second later, a cherub of a little girl appeared. She had her father's curly hair and just like her mom had a twinkle in her big green eyes that I haven't seen since.

Linda, as if proudly introducing her to the world, said, "This is our daughter, Jamie." "Hi, Jamie Jell-O. I'm Frank."

I put my hand out. Her tiny little fingers gripped mine. "Frank the Bank," she answered.

Linda and I became instant friends, but not as instantly as their little two-year-old Jamie and I did. Linda was the other half, or maybe three-quarters, of the Kornfelds, who I took to affectionately calling the Kornstalks. She sometimes called Artie "Arthur" whenever she wanted to make a point or get his attention. Otherwise they called each other "Kid" and sometimes "Babe." They were kindred spirits that at times transformed into oil and water.

Something big was in the air at the Kornstalks. Artie, along with Michael Lang, was building on an idea—a three-day music festival. I came in and out, adding some input here and there, but I spent much of that time with Linda. We listened to the group Traffic and rode my motorcycle around NYC, tripping through Harlem, as Artie busied himself creating Woodstock.

Artie and Michael claim to be the fathers who thought up the idea of Woodstock and found the perfect site for the festival. In my opinion, however, Linda Kornfeld is the mother of Woodstock; she started it all. She once told me her version of the story.

"Artie was vice president of rock music working for Capital Records. I thought it would be far out to have all the artists he signed at Capital come to a picnic in the woods. He and Michael worked on the idea, yin and yang, and the rest just kept growing."

Linda may have opened the door, but the Woodstock festival broke it down and the idea went viral. In those days, that was about as fast as the Pony Express, but because of that it developed as a real grassroots movement, a tremendous wave rolling toward the shore, deeper than today's flash-in-the-pan Internet sensations.

Those first meetings were primarily about what the 1969 festival should be, could be, and would be. It was never clearly defined, and the first original poster simply said:

WOODSTOCK MUSIC & ART FAIR PRESENTS:
AN AQUARIAN EXPOSITION
Wallkill, New York—August 15, 16, 17

Weeks before that announced date, the site was moved due to permit and legal problems. Everything was trucked to the famous Yasgur Farm. It then was re-billed as:

WOODSTOCK MUSIC & ART FAIR PRESENTS:
AN AQUARIAN EXPOSITION White Lake, NY
3 DAYS OF PEACE AND MUSIC August 15, 16, 17

The fact is the Woodstock '69 music festival was never held in the town of Woodstock, New York. The name stuck just because the press thought referring to the festival by the nearby town would simplify any confusion. I can't say I blame them. What's an aquarian exposition supposed to be, anyway?

Kornfeld was in charge of promotions and getting people to come to the festival. Lang was in charge of producing and putting on the event. But after Linda's suggestion the concept grew wings, and from there it started happening without them. It certainly didn't happen as claimed by one of the two organizers who, to this day, claims it was his spectacular promotional and marketing genius that brought the Woodstock Nation together. In truth, no one person can take sole credit for the spectacle that changed the world.

The Woodstock Nation, fueled by its own energy, spread daily until it divided the country. The hard hats spoke out in favor of the Vietnam War, claiming to be anti-drug and anti-sex, yet were secretly perverted. The Hippies joined the fight on the anti-war side as supporters of peace, free love, any way and anywhere, and as revelers in drugs and rock 'n' roll. The rift had started in the '50s when those same hard hats tried to take away our rock 'n' roll by banning it on the radio and in record shops. That didn't work, though; it just energized the cause, making way for the four Horsemen of Rock—two long-haired hippies, Artie and Michael, and two straight businessmen, John Roberts and Joel Rosenman. Yet right from the beginning there was no unity among them. They did not even share the same motives, and it's still an active disagreement to this day. One says Woodstock was about peace and love; another says it was a political protest against our involvement in the Vietnam War. In truth, the media helped convolute the message by adding spin and shock value with headlines like "Nude Bathers, Pot Smoking Rebels."

A man died, a baby was born, and Woodstock became a city larger than some of the biggest in the United States, a true microcosm of a new society. Abbie Hoffman was the first to call it the "Woodstock Nation." Young and old came from all over America to demonstrate our right to be free in mind, spirit, and body, and to believe in what you believe, not what is forced on you. It was really all about freedom, whether it was for peace and music or to protest the war. A million people showed up to unite, along with millions more worldwide who took part spiritually. Richie Havens's opening song, "Freedom," set the tone and brought it all together:

Freedom Freedom Freedom Freedom Freedom Freedom Freedom Freedom

It was as simple as that.

Working with Tuna during those early days, I became very close to Artie. I visited his apartment almost daily, and he often came to my place. Our friendship led to one of the greatest tales of my life, and it's time to fess up.

Some people will know what I'm talking about. For decades, I have told the same story over and over again. People liked to hear it so I kept telling it. It's hard to keep a good story down, whether it's real or not. Even Artie confirmed it. It goes like this: two weeks before the festival, he and I were flying to Yasgur's farm in a helicopter. In the story, I turn to him just before the farm comes into sight over the ridge.

"How many people do you think will come?" "Hundreds of thousands," he says without hesitation.

Then we see it. Thousands of people already there at the site, clearing land and pitching tents. It was a heart-stopping moment, a life-changing experience. The problem is it never happened. I never did fly in that helicopter, and as a matter of fact neither did Kornfeld. I have no idea who found the Woodstock site. I was drawn into the controversy by Artie. He and Michael both claim to have made the deal to secure Yasgur's farm.

If you want to press me for my honest opinion as to who found the site, I'm not sure. Elliot Tiber, who lived in Woodstock and knew a bit about Michael's site predicament, had ties to Yasgur's farm in Bethel,

New York. He knew Max Yasgur through the Hotel El Manaco his parents owned across the lake, and when he heard Wallkill, New York, refused to allow the festival, he may have reached out to Michael Lang and introduced him to Max Yasgur and the hallowed ground farm site. Who knows? All I know for sure is I wasn't on any helicopter ride and neither was Artie. *There. It's out in the open. Now I never have to repeat it again.*

Here's what I do know. According to Artie, before the festival, I was at his apartment, sitting on the floor playing with Jamie when the phone rang. Not knowing who was on the other end, I remember Artie leaving the room to answer it. He came back excited. I can't swear to the exact words, but he said something like this to Linda: "Babe, I think we can get a site. My cousin knows a guy who has a farm in Bethel." That's all I remember, all I know. Thirty-five years later, I received a call from Artie. He was writing a book and wanted proof to his version, which went something like this:

"Cheech." (Artie likes to call me that. It's an Italian nickname for Frank.) "You were in my apartment, right, when I got the call offering me the land? And I accepted." Now he was looking for assurance. "Will you verify that you were in my apartment?"

I should have been more aware of his usage of the word verify. But Artie's my friend, so I said, "Sure." A few months later, I received a letter. It started out:

I, Frank Yandolino, swear that . . .

So I ran with it.

To this day, in 2012, every time I talk to Artie, he reveals a new tidbit. As I was writing this he called me, and I asked him when he first saw Yasgur's farm. He surprised me with his answer.

"I didn't see it until the first day of the festival when Linda and I hitchhiked to the site. Michael had to come to the security gate to let us in."

"What? You never saw the site?!"

I was surprised by his admission and his transformation. I asked if he saw the original site in Wallkill. He again surprised me.

"I never saw that site, either. Michael wouldn't let me."

"Holy shit! What about the helicopter ride? Didn't you take a ride that I was supposedly on?" I asked. "No. The only helicopter I ever took was after the festival when everything had fallen apart and we were being sued. Michael told me to take the helicopter and go into town to fix it. Dysfunctional, the whole thing." My first day at the festival I walked from the hotel that was set aside for special guests near the site, and as I got closer to the stage, I saw Linda Kornfeld leaning against a fence while Bert Sommer was performing on stage. It was very surreal and bizarre to me, the revelation that this was finally actually happening. On the other hand, somehow it all felt very natural and that I was meant to be there, which was different than those who say I wish I had gone or say they did but didn't. So far I have met over two million and counting who say they were there, when in reality it was more like half a million people.

I still have on my fireplace mantle a small glass bottle from the festival stage. Inside it I have twelve hits of psychedelics—Timothy Leary's blotter acid, orange sunshine barrels, mescaline, and the famous Brown Acid. Oddly enough, I didn't take any psychedelics during the festival. It was the ultimate natural trip. And I was an insider, one of the invited guests. Little did I know how famous some of the people standing around me would become, or how much of my life would revolve around many of them: Michael, Artie, Abbie Hoffman, The Hells Angels, Joe Cocker, Bert Sommer, Paul Butterfield, Rick Danko, Levon Helm, and The Band. I was twenty-four years old when, as I like to say, I was reborn at Woodstock.

Everyone knows what happened at the festival. It has been documented on film and written about as many times as there are people who say they were there. The characters behind it, particularly Lang and

Kornfeld, are a story unto themselves. If you ever knew or crossed paths with Michael Lang, you may not recall where or when, but you always remember that you did.

Artie was a true representation of the hippie movement; he saw and experienced Woodstock as a kid tripping along with a million other kids who were sending out a collective vibe. He got the spirit in him through the elevator of the hallucinogen psilocybin, gliding through it all, going with the flow. I myself left the Woodstock festival in 1969 a new man. I designed a poster reflecting that time. It read:

To have a head is hard enough.

Getting it together with the rest of our body even harder.

Then to get all our heads together, WOW.

Unfortunately, when they got back to reality, Artie's and Michael's heads were nowhere near each other. The Woodstock aftermath took its toll both emotionally and financially. Owing millions of dollars to creditors and investors, the partners split into three camps. First, it was the original investors John Roberts and Joel Rosenman's camp versus the producers Artie Kornfeld and Michael Lang's camp. Then Michael and Artie turned against each other, especially regarding their debt and future income, including the ownership of the house and land in Woodstock, and most of all the rights to the title and name "The Woodstock Music Festival." You see, both of them wanted to be king. It really was a great house, just outside of town. Michael still owns it. Just after the festival we would go up to the house, known as "Tapooz," just Michael and his inside crew—not Artie—like Robin Hood and his band of merry men and dogs, big dogs. It was a special place.

Not wanting to give in to the other but still totally joined at the hip because of the media's interest in Woodstock, Michael and Artie came up with a plan to form two separate production management companies that they would each control. Michael's was called Lang Kornfeld and

Artie's was Kornfeld Lang. In 1970 I became art and advertising director for Kornfeld Lang Productions, responsible for Eluthera Records, ads, album covers, and taking photos of Artie's acts Buzzy Linhart/Music, Swamp Gas, and Bert Sommer.

Even though I was working primarily with Artie I occasionally visited Michael at his small, one-room office at Columbus Circle in the Gulf & Western building. He shared the space with his new partner, Marv Grafton—but that didn't last long. Marvin flipped out and disappeared. Unfortunately for me, years later he surfaced again. I'll get into that later. At this time, though, in 1971, Ray Paret entered the picture. Ray co-owned a recording studio, was the manager for the group Quill, and worked with Aerosmith. He and Michael formed Just Sunshine Records and moved into larger offices.

Billy Joel was a new artist who hung around the Sunshine office, sometimes sleeping on the floor. At the time, Michael and Artie Ripp were his managers. Thinking that "it's covered," Billy's first master recording was cut at the wrong speed, and he sounded like Alvin and the Chipmunks. When the record came out Billy freaked and ran away to LA to hide, changed his identity, and started singing solo in piano bars. That's when he wrote and became "The Piano Man." In yet another example of things of my past merging together, Elizabeth Joel, Billy's first wife and at the time his manager, would years later become my assistant in New York during the pre-production of the Rivera 76 festival.

Debbie "Blondie" Harry was another singer who came around Sunshine with her band The Wind in the Willows. I loved her from the night we went to see her perform in the village. Artie Kornfeld asked me to design the cover for Bert Sommer's new album Inside Bert Sommer. In order to get the project going I invited Bert to stop by the apartment so we could work on the concept. When he arrived he headed straight to the refrigerator. He took out all the sweets he could find, sat down on the floor, and ate everything. I had no idea that he was a junkie at the time.

The album cover depicts Bert walking from the front to the back cover. When opened, he continues to walk as an artist. I have always been interested in the subliminal use of images, the behind-the-scenes meaning. In most things I created, I tried to make a point, a political statement. Not many people got my early messages. Take, for example, a poster I made for Bert. I meant to show his true inside as a troubled and helpless junkie. The poster had a negative image of Bert's face, his eyes as dollar signs, and a brain filled with drugs. There were hypodermic needles stuck into his ears, and he was swallowing pills and LSD, smoking a joint, and had electrified, blown-out hair. When I showed the image to Artie and Bert, they laughed, thinking it was funny. But it wasn't. The last time I saw Bert was a few years later, I was hailing a cab in the village when I felt someone tug at my pant leg. Looking down, there was Bert on the sidewalk selling belts. "Hey Frankie, want to buy a belt?"

"No thanks, Bert." I pulled out my wallet and handed him some cash. "Thanks, Frankie. I'll call you."

He never did. Bert died a short time later, the ultimate victim to a life filled with enablers. His life, like so many others, reflected the struggle of the artist living in a colorless, capitalistic world, not willing or able to do anything else but write and sing.

But I knew it didn't have to be that way.

Working with Artie, I spent many nights that morphed into days at various recording sessions. Not only was I designing album covers, ads, and promotion pieces, but I was now becoming familiar with the music production side of the business. I first met Buzzy Linhart and his group Music in 1970 and created one of the first artistically designed psychedelic album covers. It was a work of art, not just a photo like most covers. We were recording Buzzy's album *Music* at the Record Plant studio, with Shelly Yakus engineering. Artie put some sort of psychedelics in a drink that he passed around to everyone in the studio. He was already tripping his brains out and began taking off the just-recorded tracks from the tape machines, throwing them in the air, unwinding the tape, and placing them on everyone's head and body until we were covered in tape laughing our asses off. I don't remember how it ended.

On another fun-filled occasion Kornfeld and I went to Electric Lady Recording Studio, owned by Jimi Hendrix, at 52 West 8th Street in Greenwich Village. The building had round windows, like some sort of spaceship. Areas of the space were still under construction, but it was equipped with a light machine that generated multi-colored ambient light designed to relax Jimi and enhance his creativity. The main studio had a sweeping, wall-to-ceiling, psychedelic space-themed mural painted by artist Lance Jost. The whole place was spectacular. Kornfeld went there to meet with engineer Eddie Kramer, who worked with Jimi Hendrix, The Rolling Stones, The Beatles, Led Zeppelin, Bowie, and many others. When I arrived, I heard strange sounds coming from an adjoining studio. I slowly crept into the room. There he was Jimi all by himself, making guitar-like sounds with his voice and his fingers replicating those very sounds on his guitar. I could not tell one from the other. Different than songs you expect from him, this one had a slow jazz feel. He must have felt my presence. He looked at me, nodded his approval of my existence, and kept right on playing. Not knowing what to do next, I nervously said, "You were great at Woodstock."

"I try," he politely answered.

Imagine. Jimi Hendrix said he tries. He went on playing the guitar, sounds I'd never heard before or again. I politely sneaked out backward the same way I entered. My time with Jimi Hendrix was up.

Hanging out at Kornfeld-Lang Productions, Eluthera, and Just Sunshine Records kept me in the middle of the music scene in New York. I was showing up for work at MPA later and later and many times not at all. That's when I realized the art agency let me get away with it because I was very good at what I did and their clients would request that I direct the art campaigns. It then developed into more of a freelance arrangement. I would show up when I felt like it or when the project was interesting to me, and I was able to be creative and use my artistic talent.

One night while recording at the Record Plant, Shelly Yakus told Artie that John Lennon was recording in the next studio. Artie jumped up and went to see John. He came back so excited; as a matter of fact, just today he told me that story again for the hundredth time, how he and John went to the bathroom and as they were talking, Artie, being the klutz that he is, turned to talk to Lennon standing at the urinal next to him, and proceeded to piss on Lennon's shoes. This, of course, is according to Artie.

As part of my hoarding nature I still have original notes, documents, photos, art, objects, and trinkets—you name, it I got it—dating back fifty years in one of our spare rooms in our apartment that Charli calls our garage. Much of the garage is filled with artifacts from these years working with Artie. Every one of the people I have met along my way pokes fun at that room and my ability to present proof of those experiences and people. One of those prized possessions came from the bass player from the group Swamp Gas. He borrowed some money from me, saying if he didn't pay me back the next week, I could keep his bass. As collateral he gave me a pre-CBS Fender precision electric bass guitar, which he said he got from Noel Redding of the Jimi Hendrix Experience, complete with a Power to the Black Panther Party sticker on the back.

I never was paid back and I still have the bass. Many musicians since have used it to record and perform live shows. It hangs on my wall, among many other artifacts and my personal memorabilia. When I look at any of our collections from all over the world I am often taken back to that time and place, and I see the image as if it were yesterday.

Artie asked me to come up with some ideas for his first and only personal record album cover for *The Artie Kornfeld Tree—A Time to Remember!*

The concept was to show an example of his beliefs and a reflection of our time. He and Linda would form the tree trunk of life, both beautifully nude, with their outstretched arms forming the branches, colorful, long-haired hippies singing and playing music, peace, and love. The back cover illustrated what was going on in our troubled world. A foreboding mushroom cloud of madness resented the result of the war in Vietnam. It was the black-and-white negative of the tree of life on the front.

On a side note, when I first presented the idea to Artie, it was only a rough magic marker draft illustration, just to show the concept. I didn't know that he'd turn it in to Dunhill Records as finished art. I was never really proud of that cover, but in retrospect, there are subliminal points there. Little did I know Artie's album cover would actually happen to him. Life blew up in his face.

In 1978, Linda Kornfeld died on Mother's Day, according to the press, of an apparent drug-related aneurysm. Five years later, little Jamie Kornfeld died of a drug overdose. She was only fifteen years old.

I would rather be wrong than right.

CHAPTER 5

Dominica

*B*efore Artie was able to settle down into his music business, he needed a change. The pressure with Michael and their finances was getting to him. He called me one day, after Woodstock was over, sounding frazzled.

"Cheech. I gotta get out of here. Linda and I decided to get away from it all by taking a vacation to the island of Dominica."

I lit a joint. "Are you okay, Kornstalk? Where the hell is Dominica?"

"I'm not sure. I think it's an island in the British West Indies."

"Wow." That's far out.

"Yeah, I rented a house for a few months from the president of the United Steamship Lines. Why don't you come with us?"

"To Dominica? Okay, when?"

"Come as fast as you can. We'll see you there. One other thing . . ."

"What?"

"You can't bring Marsha. Linda and I are adamant about it."

Marsha was my girlfriend at the time, a wild beauty, a model-actress who posed nude on the cover of *Evergreen* magazine. She wore suede short-shorts and a knife strapped to her hip, her blonde hair hanging halfway to her ass. As you know, I have a thing for blondes.

"We've decided you should bring Charli instead." I was surprised. "Why Charli?"

"Because Linda says you should. Just bring Charli. Okay? We'll have a great time." We made plans to meet there in about a week.

I did actually like Charli more than Marsha, but I've always been reluctant to ask women on a date, or even to dance. Maybe it's because of an encounter I had at an all-you-can-eat resort in the Catskill Mountains.

I was about ten or eleven years old that summer of 1954 when we drove for what seemed liked days from Brooklyn to the Catskill Mountains. My father loved those places where he could go see Italian music headliners like Al Martino and the comedy acts of Pat Cooper, Buddy Hackett, and Jackie Mason. Dad checked us in to the Nemerson Hotel, a sprawling complex covering several acres of land. The main building housed the cabaret theaters, the bars, and the gigantic restaurant that fed a thousand people. There was golf, tennis, volleyball, and badminton, but to most everyone who visited it was all about the shows, eating, and drinking.

On the first night there, I sat in the audience listening to Mel Torme, Steve Lawrence, and Eydie Gorme sing "I Got You Under My Skin." I hated that music; I was into '50s rock 'n' roll, constantly walking around with my RCA portable radio on my shoulder listening to any DJ, especially Allan Freed, who would spin the best new rock music in the country. Bored to death, I slunk down in my chair, and, staring at the embarrassingly corny stage show, I let the tip of my open-toed, crisscrossed, shiny brown leather sandals my mother made me wear get closer and closer to the woman's hair hanging over the seat in front of me. The words of that song pecked at my brain like a giant black crow.

I've got you under my skin.
I've got you deep in the heart of me.

49

So deep in my heart that you're really a part of me.
I've got you under my skin.

"Gross." I hated the thought and image of that song. As much as when the Stones sang "Under My Thumb." I think it has something to do with being under someone's control, a situation I've never liked. Those songs conjured up a visual in my mind of being stuck under someone's skin, which not only sounded disgusting but also as unpalatable as being controlled by somebody.

The next day, I felt restless. I stalked the resort looking for kids my own age. I found a crew of boys a little older than me and we spent the rest of the family vacation traveling in a pack, mostly hanging out at the pool. Surrounded by grass and concrete walks, it was larger than Olympic size, with roped-off areas separating the kids and adults. One day, while standing by the water, one of the boys got excited.

"Hey!" He pointed to the other side of the pool. "Look at that girl. She's cute." I checked her out. My first instincts warned me something was wrong.

"You mean the one sitting on that blanket?"

Her blanket was on the concrete walkway—not on the grass, despite the one hundred degrees blazing from the sun. "Yeah, that one. I'd kiss her."

We all laughed. Someone told him he had about as much chance of doing that as he did of landing on the moon.

"Oh, yeah? Let's see one of you go talk to her."

"Not me," I answered, knowing I'd never done anything like that before. I never asked for anything. In fact, I never even liked trick-or-treating because I felt like it was a form of begging. Right from the beginning, as a kid I knew I couldn't beg for anything, especially candy, or, more importantly, women. And I still don't. So I didn't volunteer myself. How could I? Instead it was decided we would draw straws.

They squabbled about the size and the order. All the while, I kept staring at that girl.

"I don't care if she is cute," I told myself. I still had reservations something was wrong. I hadn't fully learned my grab-the-ball philosophy yet.

Some might think the opportunity to talk to that girl was winning, but when I picked the short straw, it felt like I lost. The guys slapped my back and cheered me on, so I took my first steps toward the little girl lying on what must have been a scorching hot blanket.

With each step, I got a better look at her. I stared at her little bathing suit, at her hair tied up so neatly in a nice ribbon, and the cat-eye sunglasses she was wearing. I imagined seeing myself in those lenses as I went over my opening line.

When I reached her I paused. She looked up, her head tilted just a little bit. I fidgeted. I cleared my throat. "Anyone sitting there?"

I pointed at the corner of her blanket. When the words came out, I wanted to smack myself in the head. "Anyone sitting there?" On her blanket?

When she didn't respond, that song came back to mind—"I've Got You Under My Skin." Maybe she didn't hear me.

"Hi!" I shouted it this time. "Can I listen to your radio?"

That's when she took her sunglasses off, revealing her beautiful, large dark eyes. I stared into them as she extended her hand, her fist clenched. She answered calmly, uttering the bizarre words that would ring out like a siren whenever I tried to pick up a girl from then on:

"Squashed banana." It made my brain ache.

"Squashed banana? What the hell?"

Her fist slowly opened, and there it was in her delicate palm, a very squashed banana, oozing between her fingers. I froze, unable to move.

The girl arched an eyebrow, repeating: "Squashed banana."

Those words floated out of her mouth as if she was clarifying her earlier declaration. I backed away, unable to take my eyes off that squashed hot banana that haunts me to this day. What did she mean? Does anyone know? Whatever it was, I've never looked at a woman, or a banana, the same way since.

After Artie told me about his Dominica plans, I thought about that story. When it comes to women, despite my reluctance to initiate conversation, in my mind I feel like I'm a vampire looking for a giraffe.

So this time I decided to trust my friends over my own questionable experience. Linda was right. Charli was special and I think I was already in love with her. Mind made up, I called my father to tell him I was going to Dominica. His matter-of-fact response was surprising.

"Dominica." He never questioned why or where it was, as though it didn't matter. "That's probably a good idea. Maybe you should get out of town for a while."

"What do you mean, that's probably a good idea?"

"Nothing to worry about. I have a little business problem. It'd be best if you weren't around for a while, that's all."

He didn't tell me what the problem was at that time, and since I'd already decided on going, I headed to the bank to withdraw a few thousand dollars. Charli was at her place when I drove over on my motorcycle to see her. The door opened and there she was, looking incredible.

"Hi, what's up?"

"I'm taking a little trip. I'd like you to come with me."

"Where?"

"To Dominica with Artie and Linda."

"Where's Dominica?"

"I don't know." I laid out the cash I'd withdrawn. "Here, this is for you. Get a ticket and meet me in Dominica."

We made plans to meet there in a few days. Charli never questioned me, and she still doesn't. Early the next morning, I started to pack. Tuna came by to help hide my stash. Joe Lombardo and Donna had made me the Frank Hat just for this occasion. It was a stash hat, full of nooks that Tuna had filled with drugs. Fully prepared, I headed out for a 7:30 a.m. flight to wherever I was going.

The ticket had a connecter in San Juan. I checked in when I got to the airport. The woman working the counter frowned.

"Sorry, sir, there are no connecting flights today."

"I have to meet the Kornstalks."

"Sorry, sir, I can only send you to Antigua today. From there, tomorrow you can catch a 7:00 a.m. flight to Dominica. We'll even cover your room and a car. There is a young woman that will be accompanying you, is that all right?"

"Young woman?"

Obviously, I agreed. I had visions of a tropical plush hotel room, air conditioning, a pool, and a hot young woman in need of saving. Then I met her. She spoke with an island accent.

"My name's Suzie, but I'm better known as Antoine."

She was a great big fun-loving woman, hair tied back, neatly dressed in a huge multi-colored, flowered sundress. I never did find out why she liked to be called Antoine.

Not wanting to get too familiar I formally announced, "Hi, I'm Cambo, Cambo Shabuggabo."

We arrived in Antigua and drove just out of town to the hotel, which sat on the side of a dirt road, surrounded by small shanty shacks, chickens, roosters, and lots of dogs. So much for a plush hotel. I was in the Antigua ghetto. I could not believe this was the hotel they were putting us up in, until I saw the chipped, faded sign hanging outside:

MAIN ROAD GUEST HOUSE

The person in charge introduced himself as Mr. Mills. He was an older man with a tremendous goiter protruding from his neck and missing teeth that caused him to whistle when he spoke, just like President Obama. I'm surprised *SNL* comedians have not picked up on this.

"Good evening (whistle), Madam, Sir. I'm here to (whistle) give you a room."

The room had a bed and a chair, a light, sheets, and one pillow. No food, no drink. "For both of us?" I asked. He whistled when he nodded. "Yesss."

"You can go to a small restaurant just up the street," Mr. Mills offered. "Great chicken wings and chocolate shakes."

At the restaurant, I met Samson of the Islands, a giant guy adorned in gold. He called himself the most famous wrestler of the islands. I had a hard time believing that, because after joining us for several beers and chicken wings, I ended up having to pay the entire check. Antoine and I went back to our room after that and washed up, even though there was no soap. I used her handkerchief to dry off.

I thought to myself, "Ok, jerk, you have money. Get out of here, go to a good hotel."

But I could not do that. I was a hippie. I didn't want to embarrass Suzie/Antoine or look like some ugly American. If she could stay there so could I. Besides, I was really getting off on the adventure. I broke into my stash hat and took two quaaludes.

Then I brought up the elephant in the room.

"There's only one bed." Then I blurted out, "I'll sleep in my clothes." Suzie quickly replied, "Don't worry, I'll get you up."

What did that mean?

I had no idea, but I was now gone, out like a light. Next thing I remember, it was early morning. I woke up to the sound of roosters outside the broken glass window. I faintly heard Suzie's Caribbean accent.

"Cambo, get busy now."

I jumped out of bed and realized I was completely nude. I couldn't remember anything. On our way to the airport we didn't say much. I wondered why she was so silent.

Shit! I was raped! Anyway, that's what I tell everybody. I'm still not sure.

She gave me a note with her address and left for Montserrat. Still dazed, I took a small plane to Dominica. Landing at the rinky-dink airport, I put on my Frank hat and stepped off the plane. At customs, agents took one stern look at me, I broke out into a cold sweat, and suddenly I was surrounded as they started looking through my bags.

"Please, Sir, come with us."

They escorted me to a back room and I knew I was in for a strip search. I didn't care if these soldiers saw my dick but standing there naked but for my hat, long ponytailed hair, and long bushy beard, I thought I was screwed. I had weed and coke woven in my ponytail and I could feel one of the five joints in my beard falling out and poking me in the neck. Not to mention the drugs Tuna had hidden in his hat.

I was sure they could smell it, but they never checked my beard, hair, or hat, and when it was done, they looked confused.

"Nothing!" They shook their heads, puzzled, but an agent stamped my passport.

"No hippie type," he said. It seemed Woodstock had left its mark even down here in the jungle. "You can stay one day."

"One day? What the hell?"

"You must go Rousseau Town to get an extension." I could tell he just didn't like me or my hippiness.

As I left customs I finally met up with the Kornfelds, who looked great. We kissed and hugged, and I was glad to see little Jamie Jell-O all tan with bleached-out hair. She was as beautiful as her mom. Artie had rented this open jeep-type Range Rover that clanged and banged and looked like shit.

The ride from the airport was like a sight I had only seen in travel brochures. We drove through the most beautiful tropical jungle that suddenly parted to a blue and green sky. Transparent rain fell like crystal sunshine on the multi-colored rooftops of the village. I took a joint out from my beard.

"I told you, Artie, that he would figure it out. That's my Frank." Linda looked at me and smiled. "Wait till you see our house on the mountain, the beach, the sand, the jungle, the town, the lake, the view, the sun, the moon. It's beautiful—peace, love, calm, blue." At the time, I had no idea what she was talking about. I figured it was the joint.

Equally excited Artie said, "Wait till you see the natives."

I answered back, "I see them Artie. I hate them and they hate us. See those houses? They're full of natives with machetes who don't like hippies."

"It's not so bad." Artie tried to gloss it over. "They're just the local color."

That name stuck. From then on, to us they were the local color. We would soon learn I was right, though. Even in a tropical jungle, just like back home, we hippies would have trouble being accepted.

Artie kept repeating himself. "It's great, man. It's great they call us hippies. It's great how they keep saying that." I didn't quite agree with him. "What?" I exclaimed. "You're not paying attention. Their favorite phrase is no hippie, no hippie type."

Then came the rain. It rained all the time on the island and the local color was used to it, but in reality it got in their way. It turned the sand into mud and overflowed the 360 rivers that crisscrossed Dominica. The rain made it near impossible for them to catch the land crabs that dug deeper under the sand to avoid the water, not to mention the dangers of the giant snapping turtles that came ashore. You had to watch out for them, along with iguanas and the flying fish.

Artie's voice broke my trance. "Since we're halfway there, let's drive straight to Rousseau to get your extension."

It took forever, but we finally got into town. The wooden police station came right out of a movie set. We all went in.

"Good morning. I'm here to get an extension."

"What's your name?"

"Bruno Fataché," I said, straight-faced.

"Mr. Fataché. See Sergeant George."

The tall, thin officer at the desk pointed to the back room. I smiled, hearing him say Mr. Fataché. I walked back.

"Hello, Sergeant George. I'd like to get an extension." I handed him my passport. "I'm a writer. My pen name is Bruno Fataché. You can call me Bruno."

He looked up at me and freaked. He screamed at Artie.

"I told you when you came here! No more hippie type." He turned toward me. "And you can only stay three days."

I thought quickly.

"You're a racist!" I retaliated. "What?" he stammered.

This is another example of when it's okay to lie. Sometimes a lie is not a lie, but a super exaggeration with parts of the truth woven in it. "I guess you didn't know that I'm a reporter with the *New York Times*, did you? You want that kind of trouble, Sergeant?"

We went back and forth for a minute. He finally agreed that I'd check in every week. "No more than four weeks, Mr. Bruno."

I looked him in the eyes, pointing my finger at him. Shaking my head, I reached down and took a shark's tooth and matchbox from his desk. Keeping eye contact, I backed out of his office, still shaking my head.

"Thanks." That's all I said. He wasn't ready for Bruno Fataché. I stole his shark tooth from his desk as payment for his disrespect.

Free of the sergeant, we finally got to the house. Painted turquoise and white, it sat on top of the mountain with a garden overlooking the end of the world. The inside was simply decorated. It didn't need much because every room had a picture postcard view.

I was excited. "Charli arrives day after tomorrow."

Linda smiled. It was one of those female smiles, like they know so much more than us. "She'll love it here." "I better call her; tell her what to expect."

I wasn't talking about the views, the rain, or the local color. I was talking about drugs. I had been lucky that they never checked anything above my neck. But Charli was bringing in the motherload. I had to warn her to be extra careful and to under no circumstances tell them she knew us or use the words Woodstock or hippie. "I have to call Charli."

"We don't have a phone, man," replied Artie. "It's cool. I know someone who does."

We drove to a remote house near the village. Leave it to Artie to find a guy with supposedly one of the only private phones on the island. The guy, however, was a bona fide capitalist.

"Twenty-five dollars."

"To make a call?"

I knew the score. Money in hand, I just paid him.

After he put the money in his pocket, he told us, "No guarantees."

The process took over two hours. The call failed a dozen times. On the thirteenth, the phone rang. "Hello, this is cousin Linda."

"Hi, Linda. It's Frank. Can I speak to Charli?"

"Hi, Frank, Charli's away. The connection's funny. Where are you?"

"I'm in Dominica."

"Where's Dominica?" she asked.

"That's not important." That joke was getting old. I was starting to wonder if anyone knew where I was.

"Well, unfortunately this is an inopportune time. Can you call back? Thanks."

She hung up. I wanted to kill her, although we all laugh about it now.

No worry, though. Charli made it to Dominica without any problem. She charmed customs and arrived with the stash. She was given an indefinite visa, on account of her short skirt, I'm sure.

It was great to see her. We hugged and spent the night talking to the Kornfelds. Everything felt so natural with Charli.

In Charli's Words

Dominica was like being on an enchanted island with lush, beautiful, breathtaking views, pure white- and black-sanded beaches that led to turquoise water, surrounded by millions of giant palm trees. I loved being there. I was free for the first time in my life and realized I loved Frank even more.

The next morning, we dropped acid, got in the car, and drove to a secluded beach. We were now in a car instead of the Range Rover that had finally broken down. Luckily, Artie, in his peace and love way, managed to borrow a car from Derek Pernoud, a local banker. Only he could do that.

Artie took some roads that were not safe to walk, let alone drive. We got lost driving through the jungle and wading rivers with Linda, Jamie, and Charli in the car. I sat on the roof. I was up there guiding him through the brush and mostly taking pictures. Another wrong turn and we ended up in a village.

"Cool, Kornstalk."

"Far out, Cheech. Maybe they can tell us where we are."

We stopped the car. Still on the roof, I watched as people appeared in the doorways of the huts, stepping out into the center of the village to approach our car. I knew something wasn't right, but we were all tripping our brains out, so maybe it was a hallucination.

"Man, what's up with them?"

The people had bandages wrapped around their hands and arms. One man, or maybe it was a woman, had half her head covered. I thought one guy had no nose, but decided it was probably the acid. It wasn't.

Like a scene from some zombie movie, they approached the car. That's when it dawned on me. "Kornstalk, get the hell out of here!"

"Why?"

"They're lepers, man, real lepers."

Artie hit the gas. Mud flew from the back tires. He almost hit one of them, but we got away, drove over rivers and more rivers, and somehow found the beach. The shock of the lepers slowly faded as the Kornfelds played with Jamie in the black volcanic sand. Charli and I waded out into the warm, turquoise water. We were in paradise until I looked down the beach. I saw a group of local color bopping toward us, five of them, all wearing dungaree jackets and wool hats in the blazing 120-degree sun.

Shit, what is that? I thought to myself. Then Charli saw them. As the gang approached, we headed toward the Kornfelds. All of us converged at the same time.

"You must be Frank, the karate killer." Their leader looked me up and down. "I'm Fabian." He had "Love and Sex" written on his pant legs. I moved over to Artie.

"What's this all about?" I asked him.

Fabian looked at me matter-of-factly. Artie whispered in my ear. "We had some trouble with these guys hanging around."

I looked at Artie, and then at Linda, who was wrapped in nothing but a thin silk scarf. No wonder Artie was having troubles with these guys. And then he dropped the Kornfeld bomb.

"I told them you were coming," he continued, "and that you were a karate expert." "What? *Karate*? I don't even know how to spell that."

Fabian, all six feet something, had stripped down to his white underwear shorts, proudly displaying all of his very big shiny muscles. Barefoot, he proceeded to climb up a palm tree, shake off a coconut, climb down, take out a pocketknife, and rip it open. He scooped out the prize, a tender little fillet of coconut meat, and handed it to Jamie. She took one lick, "Yuck," and threw it in the sand. Not to offend, I quickly picked it up, washed it off in the salt water, and ate it. That's Brooklyn.

"Wow, that's great." That's when he hit me, planting an open-fisted blow to my stomach. Being from Brooklyn, my friends and I would do that to each other all day, trying to catch the other guy sleeping. Like I said: you snooze, you lose. You have to be prepared to react fast at any given moment. I tightened my stomach muscles, held my breath, and smiled.

"Yeah. I'm Frank, Karate Killer."

He wasn't impressed, and with a daring smirk on his face, challenged, "Show me."

Shit. I immediately clicked into survival mode and shot out my karate fist. I pulled the punch a half an inch away from his face and yelled in a deeply accented loud karate voice.

"*In karate . . .*"

I moved my fist even closer to his face.

"There are two blows." I sneered. "The Maiming Blow . . ." I raised my voice, ". . . *and the killing blow.*"

He still wasn't fazed.

"Show me the maiming blow."

There he was, standing at attention with his big chest and bulging collarbone, waiting to be maimed. I remembered a tai chi move I'd heard somewhere: when your opponent thrusts his fist at you, back up out of his reach. When he fully extends himself, move forward and hit him in the face.

But nah, that wouldn't work. He wasn't moving. In a flash, I thought of my mother trying to get my attention or make a point, tapping me with her clenched knuckle on my collarbone. I remembered how that little tap hurt like hell. This time I knew the ball was in the air and I had to grab it as fast as I could. I threw my whole body at him.

I hit him with all of my might, striking a closed fist to his collarbone, punching his kidney with my other fist, all while driving my knee into his balls. He fell to the ground, shaking in pain. His gang was shocked.

And so was I. It worked! My excitement was short-lived, however, when Fabian got up. "Now show me the killing blow."

My hand was bleeding. I had stabbed my own palm with my long pinky nail, the one I used to snort coke. I hid my hand behind my back, throbbing with pain. Blood dripped to the sand. My knuckles were probably broken, but through the pain, I answered in my karate voice. "Only when I have to, Fabian, only when I have to."

He was still dazed and confused, not quite convinced that I couldn't kill him. His gang gathered their things, probably wondering if there really was a killing blow.

Fabian backed up a step. "Next time."

"Anytime. I'm the hammer looking for a nail."

I glanced at Charli, my hand still bleeding. Fabian was scared, and Charli seemed relieved. We hugged and walked down the beach together. Frank and Charli—Charli and Frank.

One night a few weeks later, sitting in the kitchen looking out the window, I could see we had uninvited visitors. Two scruffy European-looking guys approached the front porch. I was suspicious, of course, wondering if this was another Artie Kornfeld surprise.

"Artie, who are they?"

"Far out," he opened the door. "Hey, man, come in."

The tall one with striped pants and a pointy nose spoke with an accent.

"Good evening. I'm German Mike me and my mate is John—saw your lights from our ship harbored in the bay. Thought we would say 'hello.'"

"Great, sit down, man." Artie sounded like they were all old friends. "This is my wife Linda and Frank and Charli."

We all swapped salutations. Linda, never shy, jumped in. "Hi German Mike, nice to see you."

Of course, I needed more information. "You came by ship? From where?"

"I guess you can say from everywhere. We run a pirate radio broadcast ship traveling around the islands, broadcasting free rock 'n' roll music and information, and whatever we can to keep it going."

Pirates, I thought. Charli moved closer to me.

German Mike asked, "Would you like to smoke a splif? Gunja, mon?"

And so he grabbed a large piece of newspaper and proceeded to roll a one-inch-thick, foot-long joint. I had never seen that before. I nodded approval at his artisanship. Turns out our visitors were cool. They were drug smugglers, sure, but we still hit it off. We bought a couple handfuls of weed and I can't even remember when the two decided to leave that night.

The next morning, I could see by Artie and Linda's attitude that something was up. Fatigue showed on both their faces and it was the first time I noticed that they were at the end of the line. After several weeks on the island, it had all caught up with them: Fabian, the local color, no money, eating only papaya, mangos, bananas, some other fruits, chicken wings, rum and coke, and mustard sandwiches. Pirates were the straw that broke their spirit.

With no more notice, two days later, the Kornstalks were packing it in, already having made plans to leave. We agreed to meet in New York. Charli and I drove them to the airport where, sadly, they said goodbye.

Charli and I stayed behind. To us, Dominica was special and the most beautiful place on earth—even with its karate death matches, lepers, and drug smugglers. It was still an adventure. We haunted the island, continuing to subsist on mustard sandwiches, fruit, and rum.

After the Kornstalks left, I assured Charli we would leave soon, but we had to wait for money from my father before we could get our return flight. It was a ruse. I had money tucked away. Dad always told me to keep some cash in my grandfather's pocket, the hidden pocket only I knew about; that same lesson taught to him by his father, and his father before him, to never show anybody all your money or drugs.

The local color, however, having had enough of us hippies, circled the house each night, chanting and flashing their burning torches. The flames were normally used to hunt land crabs, but we had a suspicion we were next. When my father's money arrived at the Barclays Bank, after eight weeks on the island, it was time to get out. My last extension was up. That day, we took our housekeeper, Maudlin, home to her house to meet her family. She made us a traditional Dominican lunch of rice and fried flying fish, the perfect ending to our time in Dominica.

Neither of us was ready for civilization. For two months all we'd worn were cut off dungaree shorts and sometimes a T-shirt. Never shoes. We needed a vacation from our vacation to slowly reacclimate ourselves back to civilization. The next morning, on our way to the airport, we climbed into Artie's car that he had borrowed and never paid for—one of the reasons he left. When I tried to start the engine, the key broke off, leaving one half jammed in the ignition. Charli freaked as some of the local color were heading up the mountain toward us.

"Shit."

Prying off the dashboard and tapping out the key, I stuck the two halves together with toothpicks and gum. The engine roared to life. With the dashboard hanging like a broken arm, I slammed my foot down on the gas. The tires screeched in a cloud of dust as we tore away, heading for the airport. When we got there I left the car parked on the corner of the tarmac with the engine running. We ran into the airport, bought our tickets, jumped on the plane, and flew to Puerto Rico.

CHAPTER 6

Tempo and the Family

The next morning, sitting poolside at a four-star hotel in Puerto Rico, our culture shock began. Charli and I were having a huge breakfast in the outside dining room when I happened to look up and see an American reading the *New York Daily News*. The headline read: "JFK Truckers Indicted." I could just about read the sub-headline—Tempo Trucking . . . that was all I needed to see. I bolted to the newsstand, bought a paper, and read the article. There it was in big bold letters: "Tempo Trucking owners, Frank Yandolino and organized crime members . . ."

Suddenly everything became a blur. *Shit!*

I called my father.

"Dad, are you okay? What's going on? You're all over the news."

"Don't worry, son, that's why I wanted you to leave. I had you listed as an employee."

"What do you mean don't worry? This article says Attorney General John Mitchell has personally indicted you, Tony, Hickey, and others."

"Don't worry, Mitchell will be gone. You can come home now. See you soon."

He hung up. My father was a man of few words, especially on the phone. Several weeks later in court, Dad pleaded to the charges with one simple phrase: nolo contendere, the legal plea meaning no contest. That was it, it was over. He was put out to pasture, as the saying goes, and just like he had foretold, John Mitchell was gone, forced to retire a short time later. The movie *Goodfellas* was based on this episode, but fortunately some names were changed to protect the innocent.

As we expected, arriving back in New York from Puerto Rico was an even bigger culture shock. After weeks running around without shoes, half naked in Dominica, simply adjusting to wearing clothes again was difficult. They were restricting and uncomfortable and I just felt like letting my freak flag fly.

The Kornstalks were staying at the St. Regis Hotel, having landed in Manhattan ten days before us. All of a sudden they showed up at the Chatsworth: Artie, Linda, Jamie, and their two Chihuahuas, Piper and Seeco. All that stimulation was too much for my best friend Bruno. Many nights Charli, Bruno, and I slept together. Bruno chased the other two little shits around the apartment. It was nuts. I swear the entire building shook, but not as badly as Piper and Seeco. Several weeks later, the Kornstalks had had enough. They moved into a ground-floor townhouse apartment on West 86th Street. When the dust and canine fur settled, I realized Charli and I were now living together, just the two of us and of course, our baby Brün.

In Charli's Words

Those days were consumed with great rock 'n'roll and amazing people. It was the beginning of a new generation—the me generation. Everyone did whatever they wanted, no rules, no guilt. Whatever you once believed suddenly became swept up in the revolution of change.

Most of us were all open to this new type of living and thinking right from the start, but it was something that I had to learn. Linda and Artie and Frank did not have to learn. It was already a part of them. They were the beginning of the freedom that was Woodstock. As for Jamie, when they stayed with us, she had no choice but to fit into the Kornfelds' lifestyle. She was just a little girl who spent a lot of time in front of the television eating cereal and twirling a finger through her golden locks. Linda was a woman most women did not like. Most men, though, wanted her and she not only knew it, but used it to the max. Her somewhat nonchalant attitude was foreign to me. Fortunately Frank, my true love, had two sides. He was still very Woodstock, going with the flow, and a very free spirit, but could also be more straight and traditional. When it came to me, for instance, he always was very Italian—protective and controlling.

I learned to live in both his worlds. To this day, I am married to a very responsible professional who is morally and ethically strong, an old-school Italian family man mixed with some very free attitudes to life. I called him my Italian hippie at times. We traveled the world with many amazing people, and they all remark that there are certain "freedoms" that do not apply to me, especially if it includes other men. No one ever disrespected me. They all somehow knew not to.

Soon Frank, Bruno (Baby Brün, as we affectionately called him), and I were living together, one happy family. Frank was a power-ful and influential force in my life, someone I respected very much. I suppose he thrilled me. He is truly a renaissance man. But one day he made some comment about my mother that upset me. I ordinar-ily would never fight with Frank in any way, but this time I amazed myself. I lifted my fist and punched him in the eye. He ran after me, but I ran and hid in the bathroom, slamming the door in his face.

He screamed, "You hit me!" and tried to kick the door down. When the dust settled on that one, he had a black eye and limped for a week. When his friends showed up to watch football that weekend, they were shocked; they saw a whole new side of me. Now we were equal. It was the last time Frank had anything negative to say about my family.

I still had never been to Brooklyn. Living in Great Neck we were such snobs that we would never date or even talk to anyone who came from Brooklyn. Before Frank I didn't even know where Brooklyn was. And yet Frank was so totally Brooklyn. In life there are always surprises, so the lesson learned is to just be free enough to take the ride.

Soon it was Christmas, which we would spend with the Pedones and the Yandolinos. That meant reaching two milestones: I would finally set foot in Brooklyn, and I would meet Frank's family. We drove to Brooklyn and went into his Grandfather James Pedone's house. I followed Frank into the two-story brownstone and straight down into the basement apartment. Everyone was there, welcoming beyond imagination: Frank's parents and brothers and dozens of aunts, uncles, cousins, nieces, and nephews. These were the family members that I would see for the next forty years at weddings, parties, and funerals. It was exactly like all the scenes in Hollywood movies, far from any gathering that I had ever had. My own family was a total of ten people, but Frank's family consisted of about two hundred who knew and loved you a lot. I was already crazy about Frank, but this family put the icing on the cake. They were so warm and truly loving to me from the start. It took me by surprise and I fell for the whole package, love like you could not believe. After being hugged and kissed by everyone (and that's a lot of kisses!), we sat down at a sixty-foot table filled with the most amazing food. Some of the men were in their undershirts, others in suits and ties, several women wore aprons, others all dressed up, young and old—a little bit of everything.

This meal was not a typical American Christmas dinner, but a very typical Italian Christmas. It was a surprise to me that there even was such a tradition.

Aunt Millie and her children started bringing out the fish. Christmas Eve is all about fish. No meat is served at this meal; just every kind of fish you've ever thought of and plenty I'd never heard of. Everyone in the room was a great cook and many of them brought their delicious special-ties. I love to eat so we ate everything—lobster, shrimp, calamari, filets baked and fried, exotic fish, and all kinds of pasta with fish and clams. And the specialty, pulpa, a kind of baby squid that takes several hours to clean and prepare. I ate it all and fell in love with this Christmas Eve tradition.

There were also a lot of children in Grandpa's basement. After about two hours of eating, all of a sudden Santa Claus came into the room ringing his bell and dragging large bags full of wrapped presents, adding to the mountain of presents already under the huge, elaborately decorated fresh Christmas tree. Many times my mother-in-law dressed up as Santa. She wasn't always so believable. Then cousin Donald Mazza took over. He was perfect. Each year the younger kids would sit on his lap, believing he was the real thing, telling him that they were good and deserved their gifts. Those kids had a great childhood, lots of love, a whirlwind of kisses, praises, hugs, and lots of presents.

After more than four hours of continued eating, drinking, exchanging gifts, dancing, talking, and Santa, I was sure it was time to go home. But no, the next surprise I will forever remember. Just after midnight, when I thought it must be about time to go home, Aunt Millie, such a great host, comes out and says, "Let's eat!" She really enjoyed feeding and making her family comfortable and happy. She loved my Frank and always called him Jun, short for Junior. Aunt Millie's little son Henry was also named Junior after his father, Uncle Henry.

After the announcement of "Let's eat!" I learned firsthand how after midnight, now Christmas Day, you are allowed to eat meat according to their Catholic religion. So out comes a parade of fresh ham, turkey, chicken, meatballs, Italian parsley and cheese, sweet fennel, hot sausage, and of course beef braciole with hardboiled egg, provolone, and pine nuts inside. All accompanied by salads, cakes, *cookies, candy, nuts, and fruit. And more wine. I was not sure I would ever get this opportunity again, so I ate everything. Again! We left at about four in the morning. Aunt Millie made everything look so easy and she made me feel so comfortable, and all of her family was the nicest people I had ever known. I loved them then and still love every minute I spend with them.*

I say this was the night Frank and I decided to get married, but to this day we argue over how we agreed to do it or who said what. Whatever the case, that Christmas was a special night. The whole family connection must have made these two hippies very romantic.

After several months of serious dating Charli was spending most of her time at my apartment and before I knew it my Afghan woman had moved in. We were now living together.

As far as I recall, the way Charli and I decided to get married was quite simple:

"Charli," I said. "I paid off all your credit cards. Now I'm paying all the bills. If we get married, I could claim you and deduct all expenses on my taxes." And she agreed. I like keeping things simple.

As I recall I never really proposed.

In Charli's Words

According to my recollections of that night, after our Christmas dinner at Aunt Millie's Frank said it: "Let's get married." He swears he didn't, but he did. Well, maybe he didn't say it per se, but I knew that's what he was insinuating with his actions. Either way, we decided to do it. Frank was such a hippie, but his family instincts and morals were really ingrained in him. The taxes played a role, I'm sure, but I know that deep down he'll admit that marriage was important to him. Besides, in those days getting married was really uncool, and now Frank had an excuse. So just like that, we borrowed his mother's car the next morning, drove to Baltimore, Maryland, where we learned we could get married in Elkton, and off we went.

When Frank and I arrived in Elkton, a small, lazy little town with no visible life, no one even walking around, we stopped at a phone booth on the street to look through a phone book for a place to get married. After we tore out the wedding chapel section I closed my eyes and blindly moved my finger across the pages before stopping and opening my eyes. My finger was pointing at The Little Wedding Chapel. We agreed it was the perfect place. I asked Frank to stop at the drugstore to buy us a ring, where we picked a thin one—two for eighteen dollars.

The Little Wedding Chapel was presided over by the Reverend Ruby Davis. We naturally opted for the cheapest, simplest, shortest, two-ring, standing ceremony. That option meant the two of us stood at the little altar, no kneeling (normally a wedding tradition). The reverend clicked a switch on a tape player and the wedding music came on, dum, dum, de dum. It lasted a few seconds and then shut off. He said something like, "Do you both take each other in sickness and in health, till death do you part?" Frank answered, "And even after." He knows just what to say. Reverend Davis ended with, "You are now married and joined together forever." Off we went to the reception across the street at the luncheonette. We sat at the counter. Frank ordered two grilled cheese sandwiches and a chocolate shake. He looked at me and asked, "Are you happy now?" I was. And so was he.

We drove home, now to our apartment, made dinner, and that was that, the best wedding ever. No stress, no cold feet, just two young kids in love. Frank bought me a spaghetti strainer and a hardboiled egg holder. I cherished them both, and still have them in my kitchen cabinets today.

Some men complain about married life, lamenting the loss of their bachelor pad. I must admit it was a bit of a change in philosophy and lifestyle for me, a new chapter in my free spirit counter-culture evolution. I had to adapt my habits to a one-woman existence. But Charli was worth it.

She had no problem adjusting, as long as my past girlfriends stopped showing up at my door and stopped calling all hours of the day. Not long after she moved in, we were in bed when the phone rang. Charli picked it up.

In Charli's Words

Hello? Oh, hi Marsha, this is Charli. You would like to speak to Frank? Marsha, you should know Frank and I just got married. I don't think you should call here anymore. Oh, you want to hear it from him? In that case, good-bye, Marsha.

Charli can't help it. Women smell other women's intentions, like cats and dogs. I never did hear from Marsha again.

With Charli, it was just a better layer of life laid over mine, a new emotional complexity that fit like a broken-in pair of leather Mexican huarache sandals.

This has become a phrase of ours, when we want to say do it simple: "Two rings standing."

CHAPTER 7

Dali

One sunny summer afternoon in 1971, I was walking up Fifth Avenue. Ahead in the distance, I noticed two people standing out as hazy silhouettes among the crowded New York sidewalk, slowly emerging from the glaring sun behind them. As they got closer, images from my days at Parsons became clear. I realized who they were. But could it be? Yes. It was Salvador Dali and his wife, Gala, and they were heading right for me.

He strutted like a bird, dressed in black, carrying a walking stick. She looked like a European cat, also dressed in black.

Before we reached each other, forces were at work. A connection was being made through the air, something pre-evolutionary. We were both sending out signals like radar.

That's when Dali and I danced. I tried to avoid walking right into him. So did he. Dali went left, I went right, I went left, he went right. Like post-modern ballerinas, we swayed left and right over and over again. Dali couldn't take it anymore. He put his hand out, two inches from my face.

"*Stop!*" Dali shouted in a distinctive voice, his strong accent so deep that it resonated from one end of the street to the other. It shocked the shit out of me. I'm sure people watched us as they passed. They may have seen his hand, still in front of my face, as if regally presenting himself, adorned with a big colorfully jeweled ring on his finger while holding an equally bejeweled silver-handled cane in the other hand. Dali captured my focus with such force that everyone else disappeared.

His hand remained inches from my nose. I didn't know what to do. My first thought was, *Should I steal that big, jeweled ring and run?* Or was I supposed to kiss his hand? I lost track of how much time had passed. Finally, I shook his hand like a wet noodle.

"Are you an *artist?*" he asked, although it sounded more like a command coming from him.

"Yes."

"Good. What is *your* name?"

"Frank Yandolino."

Then, he repeated it, as if tasting a fine wine.

"*Yan Doo Linoo* . . . give *me* your phone *number.*"

Once I did, he stepped aside, granting me passage, saying nothing else. Gala never spoke. She just looked right through me. I could feel it even though she was wearing dark sunglasses. We continued on our journeys down Fifth Avenue, neither of us looking back. Brief as it was, that chance meeting led to an amazing friendship. For me this became more like grabbing a giant beach ball.

I believe that Dali, in that split second, knew that art had always been the center of my life. As I walked away, my mind took in our short conversation, one that by all accounts should have been our only conversation. It transported me back to a time when I made my first dollar as an artist.

In 1963 my mother was working as an assistant to a dentist. One of the patients that came to the office was Tatyana Grossman and her husband, the Bohemian painter and sculptor Maurice Grossman. Mom got me a part-time job at their world-famous lithography studio on a small estate in West Islip, Long Island. During the week I studied at Parsons, and on weekends I was a stone grinder at the studio. After each printing, the image etched into the Bavarian limestone had to be worn off by taking two stones and grinding them together in a circular motion with aluminum oxide and water until the old image vanished and the artist had a new surface upon which to create.

Another job I performed for the Grossmans taught me much of what I know about color. I mixed ink for some of the world-famous artists of the day, such as Jim Dine, whose works included Toothbrushes and White Teeth, along with Jasper Johns, Rauschenberg, Robert Motherwell, Helen Frankenthaler, and Barnett Newman. Suddenly, I was hanging out with the painter Larry Rivers as he played trumpet at the Five Spot Jazz Club in the Bowery, in New York City. I actually ground the stone and helped mix the ink for Rivers's famous "French Money," which hangs on the wall at the New York Museum of Modern Art.

One night, while sitting at Tatyana's kitchen table eating a lavish homecooked Russian meal, listening to whichever great artist was there that weekend talk about their creations, I realized something: they always spoke about art, and what it meant to be an artist. A direction, as clear as the yellow brick road, opened up in front of me.

The time I spent at the Grossmans, ingesting the culture, art, the history, and the great artists I was working with, was a rare and special opportunity. If that ball hadn't been grabbed I don't know what would have happened.

I became someone with direction and a title. I was an artist.

Out of the Army, my life as a true artist continued. I went to work for one of my professors at Parsons, Richard A. Steinberg, in his studio at Carnegie Hall. I was responsible for location and studio sessions, and some printing. I took on this opportunity for almost no pay. One thing led to another, then another. Balls of opportunity were ready to be grabbed, and I had no intention of letting them go. I began to feel that I could take care of my assignments on my own, without more experienced people there to guide me. And it was a good thing that I could work on my own, since soon after taking the position, I often found myself up all night taking nude pictures of new aspiring models. The girls would pay me to get them high, take their pictures, and have sex. Sure beat the Army.

During one slow period, I sat alone in that giant studio with its high ceilings and oppressive emptiness. Richard came by to see how things were going. When he walked in, the phone rang for the first time that day. I reached for it and he slapped my hand.

"What the hell was that?"

In response, he grabbed the receiver, answering the phone. "Who's this?" he impatiently asked. "Hold on, hold on."

Richard put the phone down, holding a hand in the air, counting off with his fingers.

One . . . two . . . three. I had a momentary flashback from my Army days and instinctively reached for my gas mask. Richard ignored me and picked up the phone.

"Hold on one more minute, I'm in the middle of a shoot." Richard held a hand over the receiver and looked me in the eye. "Don't ever let them know you're not busy."

He returned to the phone call.

"Hey Massina, what can I do for you?" He paused. "A quick black-and-white shot? No, I can't, I'm set up for a color spread." Pause. "I can do black and white but I'll have to charge you for color."

That's when I learned Richard's lesson: *lie.* More specifically, don't ever let them know you're not busy or that you're down-and-out. And then charge more.

I learned a similar lesson a few years later in 1973 from the world-champion boxer Rocky Graziano. He and my father were long-time neighborhood friends from the Lower East Side of New York, 9th Street and Second Avenue. I went to lunch with the two of them at PJ Clarke's on Third Avenue. They were reminiscing, telling folklore stories, when Rocky offered some very profound advice.

"Remember, kid, never show your sparring partner all your punches. One day, he may become your opponent."

I thought of Richard when Rocky said that. It is a concept I practice all the time. You might think that in the world of an artist, such a harsh reality does not apply. But art, like any other business, is a shark tank.

Sitting at lunch with Rocky and his view on life reminded me of Moreton Binn. At that time, I had been promoted to art director by seizing an opportunity with his agency. When he entered my life, Moreton was a whirlwind of hype and energy. After joining his agency, MPA, working as salesman looking to secure clients, he made me an offer.

"If you work on my prospective clients for free, and bill that time to your real accounts, and those new clients sign on with me, I'll make sure you're the art director."

I went to work like my hands were on fire. Soon enough, his scheme paid off. I was art director and he was president of the agency. This was a boon for me beyond just the money. I now had copywriters who would correct my dyslexia-inspired misspelled headlines.

Moreton was a genius. One day, he walked into my office. "Come with me, Frank."

We went to the merchandise premium show at the Coliseum at Columbus Circle. Upon entering, he headed straight for the first booth, a sunglass company, and spoke to the man that looked to be in charge.

"If you give me one hundred pairs of sunglasses, I will put your company product and name in a full two-page spread in *Look* magazine."

On to the next booth.

"If you give me your motorbike, I will place a full-page ad for you in *Look* magazine."

On and on we went, hitting every booth in the place. By the time he'd hit every vendor, he had twenty-five different piles of products. These manufacturers could never afford getting an ad in a major national magazine themselves. I had no idea what Moreton was going to do with all that merchandise, nor how he'd get all those ads to run, until we got back to the office, where he immediately called his biggest account, Pine Sol.

"You should do a sweepstakes." When they stalled, he gave them the hard sell, ending with his true brilliance. "I lined up all the merchandise for the winners. All you have to do is run a full two-page ad in *Look* magazine."

It worked. I designed the two-page sweepstakes ad. Pine Sol gave away thousands of dollars of product, in return getting tens of thousands of people who saw the ad to try Pine Sol. And all the vendors got a portion of the ad, based on the value of their product. On top of that, I watched as Moreton kept one of every item for himself.

"That's how you barter."

Moreton went on to head up Atwood Richards, one of the largest barter agencies in the world. I visited him there years later. He was trading razors for brassieres and mayonnaise.

As art director, I was a big deal. I grew my ponytail and beard, wore tie-dyed T-shirts, and drove my motorcycle to work. I was known to smoke some grass in my office while surrounded by day-glow psychedelic images. Music posters covered my wall. The other people working at the agency were afraid to come into my office. Luckily, my clients and Moreton loved my work, although the head of the agency made me keep my door closed. I hung a sign up on it that read:

If you see Chicken Little around me, shoot him.

During those agency days I developed a campaign concept to launch a popular East Coast product to new markets in the Midwest.

HEBREW NATIONAL . . . IS NOT A JEWISH BANK . . .

IT'S THE FABULOUS FRANK.

For Eldridge and Co., a New York stock and bond house, I designed a full back-page ad in the *New York Times* featuring a beautiful blonde dressed in a sexy black dress. If you looked closely you could see the pearl necklace she was holding was broken and pearls falling to the ground.

GENTLEMEN PREFER . . . BONDS

The second ad for Eldridge featured a very young girl with arms folded under her very large breasts. It read:

MY BONDS . . . BELONG TO DADDY

It was about that time when I was turned onto a new project. My new client was the National Parks Commission, whose business was to run the government's summer vacation parks and camping grounds programs. Andrew (Andy) Wallcrest was head of the Parks Commission, which is controlled by the US government's Department of the Interior.

Smokey the Bear, who had been the commission's mascot and spokesperson, was no longer going to be the image that would represent the Interior Department's ecology efforts, which was becoming a hot subject in politics. Wanting to be more contemporary and reach a broader market, they came up with a new character—a cowboy named Johnny Horizon, who wore a cowboy hat and was a very chiseled, American, sly-looking man, with a handkerchief around his neck and a very big, toothy smile, although to me it looked more like a shit-eating grin. He was modern, hip, and intended to stand for more than just putting out forest fires; he was meant to promote ecology.

The ball was in my reach so I grabbed it. I took the opportunity to discuss a related idea with some friends in the advertising business and then was introduced to Mary Wells of the Wells Rich Green advertising agency. We became partners and agreed to pitch a television cartoon series based on Johnny Horizon, an ecological series with episodes about what you can do to save the planet. We took weekly trips to Washington, DC, and had meetings with Andy and other heads of various departments within the Interior Department. Funny thing about all of this is that none of the meetings were ever in offices; we would meet there just to formally say hello and then leave immediately. Most conversations were actually done on street corners and in restaurants where they couldn't be detected. The reason for all this was the paranoia that was raging through DC following Watergate. Everybody in Washington feared they were about to lose their jobs.

After we presented our storyboard to the government, we expected a favorable decision, not only because we were confident in our work, but also because of who was involved with what we planned to do. Specifically, we had Richard Green and Stan Dragoti, who were well-respected partners of Mary Wells. Plus, Stan was married to model and actress Cheryl Tiegs. We collectively pitched the Johnny Horizon television series, and we were feeling confident. But all of a sudden they told us they were instead giving the project to Hanna-Barbera, the famous animation studio. Wallcrest had worked it out so that Hanna-Barbera would offer him a job when his time in Washington ended. *What?* You could do that?

From that point on, whenever I made a deal with someone who had control over something that I needed, and they received little or no benefit by giving it to me, I made sure to offer them something on the back end—in many cases, a job.

I loved being the art director at MPA. It gave me an opportunity to make a statement. Ironically, my messages almost always went straight past my clients, even though they were right under their noses. My disguised statements were often political, but the clients only saw something they thought was hip and modern and that promoted their product. One client, for instance, was the Seagram liquor company. I was against the use of alcohol in advertising, especially in promotions that would be seen by young kids and old drunks. So I used my art to tell the truth. In one particular piece, I depicted a modern bar scene with stools that had American flag seats. People's asses sat on them while drinking. The bar countertop was also painted in an American flag motif. If you looked closely, you could see in the far corner a fallen liquor bottle spilling alcohol on the flag. No one at the agency or the client realized what I did. They all thought it was very modern and patriotic.

In other ads, even more subliminal—and truthful—advertising was included without the knowledge of the client. One such ad included a shadowed image of two people having sex, frozen inside an ice cube floating in a glass of alcohol. I always got off using subliminal images.

Today there is nothing subliminal about what we see in the media. Politicians and stars promote their messages and songs with images that openly degrade women, police, religion, and race. Some say this is a reflection of our time, a rampant freedom of speech. I say these unending contrived images that distort reality are the beginning of the end of America.

Some say you can't use the word "God." I say what's wrong with God? Words don't have the same meaning anymore, whether in standard conversation or when expressed in anger. The same people who angrily say "Jesus Christ this" or "Jesus Christ that," for instance, frown when the winter holidays are described as "Christmas time." The word "fuck" is used to express so many meanings, and often no meaning at all, while the term "nigga" is a word explained by some as a term of endearment, but for black people only. We have to reevaluate our relationship with vocabulary, and with it our morals and the images we project, to find some truths we can all agree on. Otherwise we can forget the Woodstock Nation and prepare for a world more like Sodom and Gomorrah.

Not too long ago, I was speaking to about fifty young students at Bloomfield Music College in New Jersey. One of the young ladies held her hand up.

"How do you get a job after graduation and get ahead?" I thought about Richard Steinberg when I answered: "Lie, then learn."

The class gasped. The faculty instantly regretted asking me to speak, but I finished my thought.

"First, you grab the ball. Without that, you have a problem of control and you're lacking risk. Without risk, there can be no reward worthwhile.

But how do you create that opportunity? When you graduate, find an entry-level job or even an internship, and stay at it for a few months. While you learn your job, learn the job from the guy next to you, too. Then quit. When you go looking for your next position, tell the person interviewing you that you did the other guy's job. For me, it was watching the assistant art director while I held an art mechanicals position. I went to the next company saying I was the assistant art director and that I was looking for an art director position.

"I kept doing that for about two years. Start a little at a time; the worst thing that can happen if you get caught in your lie is you get fired. So what? Your mother won't know, and you'll have gotten paid. You do this until, finally, you are able not only to do what you say you can do but much more. Once you grab the ball you can do great things."

I hope the young lady got the point. It's not entirely about "lying." As an artist, it isn't always easy to succeed in the world of business. We want to let our freak flag fly; we want to be open and creative. We hold the world to such a high standard. Combining that side of us with the cut-throat capitalism of America is like speaking sign language while wearing mittens. Art seeks to capture truth, and that truth comes from within the artist. And this pure sort of expression can be at odds with our culture, since exploring art in order to make truthful discoveries is not often a recipe for capitalistic success. Somewhere along the way, then, the "truth" gets compromised. My choice to lie up-front gave me a better opportunity to portray an undistorted truth in my art. And since I seemed to be highly qualified, the guys hiring me felt like they were producing art that portrayed a truth they wanted to sell.

In most cases in the distant past artists were bound to paint and capture the truth in their art as they worked for the noblemen, kings, and popes who commissioned them. Other artists have painted simply because they had to, and would do it even without payment. In today's world some artists paint strictly for the money and will distort the truth.

This holds true not only in art, music, and writing, but is actually most evident in the media and especially in politics.

My unforgettable relationship with the artist Salvador Dali sprouted from that single, chance meeting on the street. I like to think he realized that I, like him, was an artist grabbing that ball of opportunity, and that that's why he called us on that late Sunday afternoon shortly after our encounter on Fifth Avenue. Charli and I were home when the phone rang. It was that one-of-a-kind voice on the other end.

"Yan Doo Linoo . . . Dali . . . Tonight. Lutece, 7:30. Goodbye."
Click.

Dali hung up. I didn't utter a word. Charli and I met the Dalis at Lutece, a four-star French restaurant in Midtown. We stepped into a dining room adorned with crystal chandeliers and plush velvet, high-backed chairs. The atmosphere was crisp and white. Dali and his entourage of twenty people were already there, sitting at tables that had been pushed together. It was like walking into a surreal Fellini movie.

Dinner started with Chef Soltner's famous Alsatian tart. We drank bottles of wine as the room dimmed. With the giant Parisian mural behind us, I spoke to Dali. We debated the color red while Gala and Charli hit it off together.

In Charli's Words

When the first telephone call rang that Sunday, I could hear Dali's voice blaring through the phone from across the room telling us to meet him for dinner at Lutece. Excited, I got all dressed up. Frank and Dali had a magnetism, an understanding of each other right from the first moment that, to this day, amazes me. I was young. I certainly had not met anyone like Dali, or Gala. I must say, she had the power in that family. She was old to me, full of wisdom.

Dali suddenly decided dinner was over, and it was time to pay the bill. He waved his hand in the air and, as if on cue, the maître d' hurried over to present the check to Dali who simply grabbed it and signed his name. The maître d' took the check to a different table, giving it to a man no one seemed to know. Dali tipped his golden-handled cane at the man, put on his cape, and off he and Gala went. They must do this all the time, I thought. Gala and Dali went everywhere for free. Amazing, funny, inspiring, that evening was a life experience I will never forget.

The Dalis lived at the St. Regis Hotel. What little I saw of their apartment was cluttered with all kinds of things, new and old paintings, drawings, sculptures, flowers, artifacts, and bottles of champagne.

The truth is that the Dalis liked, no, loved me as much as I loved them. I think I made my biggest impression on Dali when I helped him with a TV commercial for a new product, a women's nylon stocking. He wouldn't tell anyone his idea; I called ahead to the photo studio to schedule Dali's arrival for the shoot, granting his wish: "*Yan Doo Linoo*, make sure there is a model there wearing only nylons."

Dali showed up with his entourage. He instructed the camera to roll. Without hesitation he approached the model and lifted her leg, placing her foot on a pedestal, signed "Dali" in thick black marker across her leg, and walked out. For this, he was paid $50,000 dollars.

From that day on, when anyone would present him with an idea or a project, he would look at them and say in his memorable voice, "Only if you can do what *Yan Doo Linoo* does. He makes the checks fall from the sky."

Dali and I met often after that spring afternoon when I made cash fall from the sky. Once, during lunch at the Plaza Hotel's Palm Court, we had just finished a conversation about whether or not we dream in color.

"Do you see the colors reflected from the light and shadows in the corner of the ceiling beams?" he asked. He was serious, as always, never wasting words.

"Yes, I do. Shades of gray, magenta, blue, and white."

"Do you not see the purple hues and shades of burnt umber?"

I thought I saw what he saw. We connected. I stared up at the corner. When something came over me, I blurted out, "I'm dyslexic."

Dali fingered his mustache while answering matter-of-factly, "I understand this problem. Art will set you free." The way he spoke and the look on his face gave me the impression he knew from personal experience. He answered sharply, looking directly in my eyes, sort of through them, to my mind, my brain, and beyond. "That's how I saw it," I offered.

"You cannot see exactly what I see." Then he schooled me as he began his lecture, "We are looking at the reflection from different angles, *Yan Doo Linoo*. We cannot see the exact same colors. That is why the artist is so important. It is he who captures the colors of moments, documenting visuals for others to see from his perspective."

I sipped my wine, listening to him as he continued.

"The painter must unlearn old habits of reason and thought. The artist sees things through his mind's microscope, then documents them one stroke at a time. Habitual common sense dictates reality. You see, *Yan Doo Linoo*, you must rethink and change that habit. You must see things as they appear only to you, and exaggerate them in order to make your point. This is the difference between appearance, reality, and interpretation."

I realized he wasn't just talking about the reflections in the ceiling. It was a lesson on why the artist and his art are so important. What I believe he was saying in a nutshell is that the artist must be creative and truthful and his art should come from within and never disappoint. I put this lesson of the importance of creativity into my own words in an analogy: Once upon a time, all bakers made and sold loaves of bread in the local market to everyone in their neighborhood. Then one day, a baker across town decided to slice his loaves of bread. Now people came from all other neighborhoods to buy his sliced bread.

The thing that separates classes of people is the ability to be innovative.

I'm reminded of a story in the painter Arshile Gorky's biography. He asked Dali how he could become famous, how he could get his art known.

"Meet me at the New York Public Library steps," Dali answered. "We will invite the press and you will piss on the lions."

I am sure Gorky didn't realize just how serious Dali was. Gorky wrote that he did not show up for fear of becoming famous and being deported at the same time.

Gala taught me just as much as Dali did, maybe more. She was a true character. I sometimes walked through Central Park with her. On one occasion, I thought she was hitting on me. As I flirted back, she was highly insulted.

"I can flirt with you. You cannot flirt with me. Who do you think you are?"

Gala gave Charli and me the greatest gift imaginable. She saved our marriage. On another occasion at dinner with Dali and Gala at the St. Regis, Gala interrupted our conversation as only she could, asking me to sit on her lap. I was embarrassed to do it. She insisted, so I did. There I was, a grown man sitting on her lap, not knowing what to say, everyone watching. I looked her in the eye, held my hand to my heart, and stupidly barked out:

"It does my heart good to be with you."

She immediately punched me in the head. "This is where your heart is."

Sheepishly, I slumped back to my seat. Charli sat beside me. As I started another conversation with Dali, I heard her talking to Gala.

In Charli's Words
While I was working at the Saks Fifth Avenue hair salon, I met a very attractive English woman named Kathy Keeton. She liked

me and I liked her. We talked about personal things—girl stuff, mostly. She was involved with magazines and was starting a new one called Viva. I told her all about my Frank and his new project—erotic sheets and pillowcases. Soon enough we met Kathy and her boyfriend Bob for dinner. He was an older, handsome man with very curly black hair, wearing a fluffy white shirt opened to mid-chest and what seemed like fifty gold chains and trinkets on his neck. Frank and Bob connected immediately, spending all their time together. At first I did not realize that Bob was Bob Guccione, owner of Penthouse magazine.

Frank called me one day and asked me to meet him at the St. Regis Hotel. I walked in and there they were, Dali, sitting in a throne-type chair, and Frank next to him, talking about the colors and the designs in the room. A dozen beautiful people and Penthouse Pets, Miss January, etc., surrounded them. I found Gala and we took a seat far away in the background, drinking vodka and eating caviar. I was upset, newly married with this Italian hippie who had Miss January draped all over him.

As Frank was knee deep in conversation with Dali, I asked Gala, my voice shaking, "How do you do it?" "What, darling?"

"How do you just sit here while all these beautiful women are around Dali all the time, flirting and propositioning?"

Gala reached across the table and picked up a cashew nut, her other hand taking mine and gently opening my fingers. She placed the nut in my palm and touched the nut with her beautifully unpainted fingernail, then closed my fingers around the cashew.

"If you hold a bird tightly in your hands, when it can, the bird will fly away. If you let the bird go free, it will always come back to you. You can never stop the artist. The bird must fly."

That moment was a lifelong lesson. I never interfered with Frank's work. If he went on trips, stayed out all night, anything. As Gala said *he would, he always came back to me. Gala's story really worked for me. I tell this story to most women I meet. I had many opportunities to worry about my bird. For a while Frank and Dali would meet at the St. Regis and the Plaza Hotel almost on a daily basis. On several of those afternoons, I would sit with Gala off in a corner sipping our vodka and as usual eating caviar on little filo pastries with chopped onion and egg whites, laughing and enjoying great conversation. Gala was a wise, tough, and very opinionated woman. She taught me many things, most importantly, to keep my own space and life, not just to follow Frank. To always tell him the truth, to trust him, praise him, and encourage him, and of course always show unity and unequivocal love. Just as she did for Dali and he did for her.*

They were not afraid or embarrassed to openly display their unwavering love for each other. As a matter of fact they enjoyed playfully teasing each other in public, reinforcing for everyone to see that neither one of them could be replaced.

Dali seemed to always be checking on Gala, looking over, more concerned with her in the background, sitting with me. Always asking what he could do for her. If you look in many of Dali's paintings you will see her, either as the main object or in the background. He was madly in love with her. It's the same with Frank and me. I'm in all the pictures, regardless of all those Pets, models, princesses, and ballerinas. And they know it.

Frank is truly an artist, working on many canvases at the same time. He has the guts to try whatever comes his way, as he says grabbing the ball of opportunity twenty-four hours a day.

Dali was my inspiration and my guiding light. He taught me to always be what and who I am, not what others want me to be. To believe in my convictions, trust my artistic talent, and be confident. He reaffirmed my own philosophy to grab the ball every time.

CHAPTER 8

Fritz

Ever since Charli moved into my life in 1971, the mementos of her life began to mingle with mine, things like her boxes of clothes, photo albums, some records, and lots of her credit card bills, which I paid off (she still tells everyone about it; it's great PR for me).

The most notable evolution occurred in my bathroom, as bath oils, makeup, fragrant soaps, hair and skin care products, rollers, and blowers invaded, all foreign to me. I've never spent more than five minutes in the bathroom. I do what I gotta do and I'm out, and the same goes for my bed. On the other hand, Charli seems to spend two hours or more, and when she comes out, she's still not ready.

Our apartment resembled an art gallery, with paintings and sculptures by artist friends of mine taking their places on the walls and within the nooks of our famous bookcase. Among them were my great friend Joe Lombardo from our time painting mess trucks in the army, and Fritz Moody, a modern abstract expressionist. Fritz was a wild man, with long hair that he never combed and a bluish-black long beard, resembling Blackbeard the Pirate. He spoke with a deep, slow voice, and whatever he said always sounded philosophic.

Joe and Fritz each painted one of our bedroom doors. Fritz's painting was intricate, complicated, deep, and dark. Joe's, on the other hand, reflected him: fun, light, and flowery. Eventually, someone, including me, had painted every door in our apartment. We also had a wall in the hallway that everybody who came to the apartment (it seemed like a hundred people a month) signed with their own unique signatures and colors.

In the early '70s it became the first graffiti wall in history. The entire apartment was like a psychedelic trip, smelling of incense and weed.

One night Fritz had a party at his loft on Canal Street. While there, I reciprocated by painting a modern abstract on one of his doors, not stopping to eat, drink, or sleep for two days. That's how I did things back then and still do today, to some extent. I hardly sleep. To me sleep is boring. I go to bed when my head falls down and the minute I open my eyes I jump out of it. To show his gratitude for my painting and my dedication to finishing the work Fritz gave me one of his paintings that he said represented me—a five-foot-by-five-foot, surrealistic, modern visual that from a distance looks like a series of lines, colors, shapes, and forms, but from closer up, those lines, shapes, and forms become parts of hundreds of human faces and heads. He called it Head of Heads. He was dead serious when he said, "You are Head of Heads. You should have it."

It has since hung on our living room wall, more than forty years. It reflects a time in my life when I was truly obsessive. Not that I have changed much: back then, there was nothing I wouldn't do or try. And if I didn't die, I would do it again with a reckless abandon. I had no fear. Taking the road less traveled has always excited me. Much of that character remains. The difference is now I approach all things with some skepticism, always, as the saying goes, keeping one eye open as I sleep.

Patti Smith

In the late sixties, before I met Charli, one of the early rock clubs, even before CBGB's, was Max's Kansas City on 23rd and Park Avenue, a two-story building that truly reflected the times and mirrored our generation—what we looked like, listened to, and believed in. It was the gathering place for New York's underground society, frequented by artists, poets, rockers, and punk rockers, like Patti Smith, The Sex Pistols, and The Velvet Underground. Bob Marley once opened there for Bruce Springsteen.

Max's had several areas to hang out in. The main room had the big round table reserved for special guests. Upstairs was smaller and intimate, and reserved for live music. Then there was the famous dimly lit, red-lighted, and very private back room, reserved only for the inner circle of very special guests.

I hung out at Max's at least once a week, when not at the Fillmore or other Village bars and clubs. The physical club was a living act in and of itself with its own personality, where people gathered to feed off each other, like a mob developing its own mentality and agenda that changed each night. I always went in ready for something amazing to happen.

I first saw the punk rock group The Senders at Max's. Not so surprisingly, years later I became their manager. They became the opening act for Mick Jones and The Clash, and Sid Vicious, Johnny Rotten, and The Sex Pistols. One night, just before the end of The Senders' opening set, I realized I hadn't seen Johnny. I searched and finally found him in the bathroom slouched over the toilet, semi-coherent. I tried to bring him around and worked on him for several minutes until he became more conscious. Suddenly he got up, calmly combed his hair in the mirror, walked out on stage, and did a great show as if nothing happened.

One of the great early performers at Max's was punk rock poet Patti Smith. Back then in the early seventies I didn't know who she was, but everyone who saw her knew she was destined to be a star. She had a unique style, not only what she sang but how she sang it. Years later, Michael Lang, or maybe it was Artie Ripp, I can't remember who—anyway one of them brought in some photos to the office for the album cover of a "new" artist the music industry was abuzz about—The Patti Smith Group. The same Patti Smith I had seen years before at Max's. The photo was black and white, Patti was dressed in a very large men's white dress shirt and black suspenders. She had short punk-type black hair and looked like she weighed about fifty pounds. I saw her again a few years later, in 1974, this time on line at the Ziegfeld Theater with her boyfriend Robert, waiting to see our movie *Ladies & Gentlemen: The Rolling Stones*. This was another ball I'd grabbed and ran with, but we'll get into that later.

In the pre-Charli days of the late sixties to early seventies I would often ride my motorcycle to raconteur promoter Bill Graham's Fillmore East, a narrow, brick-front building on Second Avenue in the East Village, near St. Marks Place. It turns out my father, as a kid growing up a few blocks away, was a stage hand/curtain-puller there before it was the Fillmore. The inside could have been a rowdy theater from the days of Shakespeare. Fans filled the rows of seats and pressed to the front of the low stage, always dancing to the music. Others stood on the balconies to the left and right of the theater stage, swaying and leaning over the railing. The upper balcony was straight up, so high you could get a nosebleed. But it didn't matter. The Fillmore was packed every night. Instead of sonnets, the walls shook with the top bands of the day backlit with Joshua's psychedelic liquid light show.

The Fillmore East was another incubator for our culture during the time of turn on, tune in, drop out, and sex, drugs and rock 'n' roll. I definitely fit the bill—very long hair tied in a ponytail with a long straggly beard, dressed in faded dungaree pants and hand-embroidered dungaree jacket (now called jeans; my kids laugh that I still refer to them as dungarees), standing in the back looking for the next opportunity. In those days, when invoking my natural sex, drugs, and rock 'n' roll, I almost always had a choice—color, size, and shape. Women followed me home, sometimes staying for several days, often with minimal food and water, unable to break the spell, never wanting to go. That's how I like to remember it, anyway. In any case I often met women who wanted to utilize my photographic skills, which I'd honed at Richard Steinberg's studio. Young girls, aspiring actresses and models, were once again paying me to take their photos and put together their portfolios and have sex. What a life. On one occasion, the police arrived in the middle of the night looking for the girl who had stayed over for two days. Her mother had called the cops, who had somehow traced her back to my place.

This short-lived but iconic Village venue was a special place for me. I had many extraordinary moments there in the late sixties, sometimes as a spectator in the audience, other times in a dressing room or hanging out backstage. One night in September 1970, I was standing on the backstage staircase talking to a girl.

Everyone seemed to acknowledge she was Jimi Hendrix's girlfriend. She leaned in close to me so I could hear her over the music. Suddenly the place erupted in a buzz like a disrupted hornets' nest. Jimi Hendrix was dead. The shrill went through the building, then, like a bolt of lightning, through her. She broke down and ran away. I'll never forget that vivid moment. Walking out of the Fillmore in a daze I somehow wound up in the Village at the Café Figaro. I had the same melting, dazed feeling while at Parsons when word spread through the halls and then boomed over the loud speaker that President Kennedy was dead.

On another occasion walking the back halls of the Fillmore I found myself drifting around and wound up in Bonnie Bramlett's (of The Bonnie and Delaney Band) dressing room. She invited me in and I fell in love. Bonnie was a true blonde bombshell with a Southern, deep, raspy voice. We just started talking like we'd known each other forever. I noticed little round red marks on her arm, some with scabs. She told me they were from lit cigarettes, some game, or something she played with the band. Just then Delaney stuck his head in the room, asked if she was okay and said, "Let's do it." The next time I saw them was in 1972, with Charli at Madison Square Garden, opening for the Stones.

My time at the Fillmore East can be summed up with one night. I parked my bike outside on 2nd Avenue. I was there to see Elton John's first show in New York. He wore a big yellow hat with a giant daisy stuck on top. I was standing in my usual spot in the back leaning on the wall just behind the last row of seats when a cute, curly-headed girl approached me. That's how it was then. Guys picked up girls and girls picked up guys. We were free.

"Hi, I'm Nancy."

"I'm Frank."

She smiled, "Great name."

We hit it off immediately. Nancy claimed she was at one time a girl-friend to Bob Dylan. Not only did she have a great smile, she had a seriously funny sense of humor. I told her my real name, which I didn't do most of the time. She was something special, Nancy Cohen. Now, she calls herself Lola Cohen, much like Suzy calling herself Antoine on the way to Dominica. I never did ask either of them why. We dated for a while until I met Charli. Nancy was cool about it.

When Charli moved in, I gave up looking for the grass to be greener. I knew I had something special. So did she. It felt and still feels right to this day. As I always say, the grass may be greener on the other side, but you have to make sure it's not Astroturf.

Nancy introduced me to her friends, two sisters, Carol and Barbara Rossenou. Carol was more of a bohemian, hippy type, with her silver and turquoise jewelry, beads, and silver earrings. She often traveled to the island of Ibiza. Her sister Barbara was younger and a bit less flamboyant. Both were seriously connected to the underground movement and intro-duced me to Neville Gerson.

Neville was six feet tall, a lanky guy, with longish, straight combed-back dark brown hair. He looked like a young Harrison Ford and prided himself in his preppy, expensive Brooks Brothers look. Neville and the girls considered themselves underground activists. They knew everyone: John Lennon, Abbie Hoffman, Jerry Rubin, Allen Ginsberg, William Kuntsler, John Wilcox. Neville had just been voted *Cosmopolitan* magazine's most eligible millionaire bachelor of the year. Invited as a guest on the Mike Douglas TV show, he showed up in snakeskin boots, long hair, and very tan skin. Through projects like our erotic sheets, we became great friends, like brothers. Still are to this day.

CHAPTER 9

Erotic Sheets

$\mathcal{L}$ife was good living at the Chatsworth. Charli became a constant partner, joining me in grabbing every ball that came along, always encouraging me to do whatever presented itself, especially when Neville visited and introduced his idea for the erotic sheets.

Even before he spoke, I could see his excited expression.

"Hey, Frank."

"What's up, Nev?"

"I'm good. In fact, I have an idea you'll be interested in. We should make and sell erotic sheets and pillowcases."

Understand this was 1971. The sexual revolution was at its height. Young people were experiencing a crescendo of sexual freedom that would not climax until the dawning of AIDs more than a decade later. At that time, the thought of naked people wrapped around you every night was as American as apple pie. I totally embraced the thought. There it was, another ball floating in the air, ready for me to grab. Immediately, I pictured pitching Neville's idea to *Penthouse* magazine. We had work to do. Neville and I created a company, first called Blueberry Hill, named after our favorite Fats Domino song. We then changed it to Yandolino, Gerson, Inc. Its sole raison d'être, at least initially, was to design and sell our creations. Neville had a lawyer friend, Dick Massina, whom we visited at his office at Kroll and Massina on Park Avenue. After revealing our idea, they gave us the entire office complex to work out of. For free. To make erotic sheets and pillow cases. This could only happen in New York.

After setting up shop our first order of business was to come up with a theme. I was not happy with calling them erotic sheets and pillowcases, even though it was that description that got everybody's attention. Instead, we focused on the elements—earth, air, fire, and water. The look would be classic exotic, not erotic, stylized after the famous masters: Klee, Renoir, Klimt, and Rousseau. Neville and I sorted through artist after artist, interviewing them until deciding on four that we believed could execute our vision. Then it was time for the important stuff: money. Neville convinced Barbara and Carol, who loved the idea, to invest, and then we presented the opportunity to Abbie Hoffman and Jerry Rubin, who agreed to do it too, as long as we never told anyone. The ultimate anti-establishment duo made a capitalistic investment; they collectively put up $10,000, a lot of money in 1971.

In Charli's Words

Frank and Neville were working on the erotic sheets. This was the first time for me to see Frank the art director really direct. I was home when Frank invited the four contemporary, well-known artists into our apartment. One by one, they showed their portfolios. They were great talents. He spoke to them with conviction; I could tell they respected his insight. He would tell them what he wanted and send them on their way. Once Frank has a vision, you can't stop him.

The artists would return the next week with what they thought was finished work. Amazing work. Then, without the slightest hesitation, Frank would change things, rearrange colors, facial expressions. You name it, he changed it.

I'll never forget what he said to Nicholas Paladino, the artist who painted air: "I don't like the way the legs are turned. Can you change it to the other direction?" Oh my god! Nicholas's face fell, but he returned the following week. Again, Frank directed a change to the position of the arms. I felt bad for Nicholas, but Frank did the same with all of them. The artists were like workers next to the art director. I was amazed when they each thanked Frank for pushing them to do a perfect job on their painting.

After all these years, I have seen a lot of artists come and go presenting many different types of work—paintings, photographs, stories, music. Whatever Frank worked on, if he didn't do it himself, it had to be done as he saw it, no matter whom he was working with. The keen eye and confidence of the art director, the captain, is what made him special. Frank was blessed with the amazing gift of a very critical eye and strong convictions.

Many years later, on December 10, 2012, Charli and I visited our old friend Barbara Rossenou at her apartment, and we were talking about her sister Carol, who had passed away several years before. We reminisced about a story that is now New York underground folklore, regarding a certain famous celebrity from across the pond, an English mega male songwriter, producer, singer, band member, legend, icon, superstar, who at the time of this tale ran in that underground circle that liked to get high. On a particular day in the early 1970s, his yellow brick road led him to a party at the historic apartment owned by Jerry Rubins, which Jerry inherited from the folk singer legend Phil Ochs. The same apartment was frequented by famous lawyer William Kuntsler, Paul Obst, Abbie Hoffman, Jay Levin, and poet Allen Ginsberg, who on that very day was witnessed making out with Julian Beck. As they say, all roads lead to Rome, and back then, Rome was drugs and the roads all led to Jerry's apartment, 6H.

As legend tells it, that night at the party this certain rock star and his long-time Japanese girlfriend showed up. Carol had been staying there for a while, and I believe Barbara and Nancy were there as well. It's been reported by several on the scene that the rock star liked Carol a lot. They shared the same drug of choice and disappeared into a back bedroom to score. He scored all right, with Carol. Everyone in the adjoining room heard it, too, including his Japanese howling singer girlfriend, who the world loved to hate. She was pissed as she waited at the door for her boyfriend (of course I'm talking about John Lennon) to come out.

As usual I was searching for a ball to grab. Neville set it up to meet in New York with members of Elephant's Memory, John Lennon's new band, who were recording and doing shows together. Stan, the sax player, and Rick, the drummer, were considering signing a management agreement with me, so I went to several of their rehearsals and studio recordings. On one occasion, there was John in the recording studio behind the glass window, surrounded by musicians. Soon after, John was gone, shot and killed outside on the street in front of his apartment at the Dakota. Dion's song says it best, but you can now add: Has anybody seen my old friend John, Bobby, Martin, Jimi, Janice, Michael, Whitney? And on and on.

While I was hustling up investors, manufacturers, and distributers for the erotic sheets, putting various balls together Charli once again performed her magic.

In Charli's Words

One day I showed Kathy the erotic sheets and pillowcases. She liked the idea and arranged for us to meet with Guccione. We met at the Drake Hotel in their multiroom suite. It was lavishly decorated with plush couches, sitting areas, flowers, photographs, paintings, and mirrors; crystal, gold, and silver were everywhere. Frank and Bob connected immediately, and later spent a lot of time together.

Bob Guccione was a handsome older man who reminded me of actor Victor Mature in Samson and Delilah, with very curly black hair, very

Italian eyes, and long eyelashes. Guccione always wore an opened to mid-chest fluffy black or white shirt, and what seemed like fifty gold chains and trinkets on his neck. He liked my erotic sheets and asked me what else I had done. I told him everything I could think of. He was impressed, saying, "Maybe you could help us with our new project." He then explained the concept of *VIVA* magazine.

It was to be an offshoot of *Penthouse* dedicated to couples—men and women, not just for men. But this visit was all business. I wanted their involvement in our erotic sheet venture. Guccione, though, was more interested in having Charli and I pose as a couple in the nude for *VIVA*. That was not going to happen. I did, however, grab the *VIVA* ball and run with it.

After several meetings, Bob asked me to come up with ideas for the look and logo of his new magazine. As I started work on the design, I knew *Penthouse* and everything it could offer me was the golden opportunity. This was a ball I would work till all the air came out of it and it looked like a Dali clock. Charli worked on Kathy like a true talent agent, talking up my skills and experience. She did a good job following this credo I always use: if I stick my foot in the door, my head will follow.

Generally, I follow this rule. But, as a rule, I don't always follow rules. So sometimes when I grab the ball, I go ahead and do it the other way around: I stick my head in the door, forcing my feet to follow.

In order to distinguish *VIVA* from other sex magazines, I designed it as a slick, glossy, oversized publication with a square book-like binding. I also created its logo and typeface. Guccione never paid me or gave me credit. I was too star-struck at that time in my life to do anything about it. This later became a habit with him, not just with *VIVA*, but also the erotic sheets and pillow cases, the Happy Hooker, Hells Angels, Penthouse Viva Village, and several other projects I presented and worked on. I was excited about *VIVA*, but I didn't want to move past our sultry sheets. I unveiled the finished presentation to Guccione. He loved them, and

to this day everyone I show them to loves them, proclaiming that when they are made they will buy them all. Yet after forty-two years they still aren't made. Some balls take years in between bounces. Guccione then dropped the bomb, suggesting that before he would get seriously involved, we should find a manufacturer.

This sent Neville and me to Vermont to meet with the president of Burlington Mills. We drove the seven or eight hours from New York City to Burlington in the snow. We checked in at the Burlington Mills reception desk and were quickly ushered to a holding area. Finally, the call came summoning us to the president's office.

The room was filled with people. We laid out our fancy box presentations and everyone seemed excited as I gave my speech. *Penthouse* would help promote, market, and advertise—on and on I went, till I turned blue. The response was enthusiastic, and mostly positive. "Oh, this is not what we expected!" "Oh, they are beautiful!" Oh this, oh that. Everyone seemed to have an opinion. The president's wife, secretaries, and just about everybody raved. I thought we were in.

I continued my onslaught. More responses: "No one's ever done this." "This could be huge."

The president, however, looked through our proposal as he spoke. "Did you say *Penthouse* would help market and advertise? We need some time to go over this. Let's meet again in the morning."

When he said that, just like my question of whether I could trace in drawing class I blurted out: "Let's talk turkey, not beef jerky."

The next day at our early morning meeting, though, the president talked beef jerky.

"Frank, Neville. We all like your concept and believe it could be a prosperous product. However, we here at Burlington Mills know about little flowers on our sheets. That's what we do. We love your idea and beautiful designs. However, let me put it like this. If you kill the Indians, we will sell them the Bibles, so to speak."

I'll never forget how he said it. What he meant was if we would do all the work to establish a market and find buyers, promote, and advertise—kill all the Indians, so to speak—then they would step in and sell them the Bibles. I immediately shot back with my closing line.

"If I'm going to kill the Indians, I will sell them the Bibles."

I know one thing: I'm not killing the Indians for anyone but me (metaphorically, of course). In my career as a personal manager and producer of entertainers, live events, and various businesses and projects worldwide, I've been proposed with "Could you just blah blah blah?" more times than I can remember. The problem is in most cases new startup clients don't have a product or a career yet, and they want me to do all this work to get them started, develop their business, and then they hope that by that point I'll be out. No way, Jose. I want to be paid for what I do for as long as they get paid for what I do, even if my contract is over. Perpetuity is my favorite word. In retrospect I would like to say to the president at Burlington Mills: "For your attitude, I extend my gratitude."

I must admit, however, that sometimes this self-centered attitude doesn't work and I lose the deal. Much to the chagrin of our investors, we never got the sheets and pillowcases made. Our most famous investor, Abbie Hoffman, went as far as saying in his book that we ripped him off. But his story is worth its own chapter.

CHAPTER 10

Abbie Hoffman and Jerry Rubin

Over the twenty-plus years Abbie Hoffman came in and out of my life, no two times were ever the same. We first met at Woodstock. A few years later Neville and I brought him in as a partner for our erotic sheets and pillowcases. Then we met again at a party after the 1972 elections where I told him I was working at *Penthouse*. A few days later he called to ask if I could help with an idea he had regarding an article he wanted to write and, since I was working with Guccione, we agreed to meet. We met for lunch in the village; he showed up looking like some preppy hippy, wearing dark sunglasses, a tweed jacket, T-shirt, and corduroy pants. He sat down across from me, sliding into the high-backed booth. I could see a smirk on his face even through the gloom of the dimly lit restaurant. Abbie, always the funny guy, opened with:

"Are you following me?"

I answered, "How could anybody follow you?"

He shot back, "Just look around. There's a guy in that bush."

"I'd like to interview you for *Penthouse*," I told him.

Abbie scratched his chin.

"Cool, man. I'll tell you all about my upcoming vasectomy."

He continued in great detail, painting a picture of himself high on nitrous, his legs up in stirrups. It was a great tale (no pun intended), but I suggested, "I don't think it'll fly with Guccione."

Abbie, however, was insistent.

"Don't worry. You'll be surprised," he said. "We can shoot it with Penthouse Pets dressed as nurses. Yeah man. I also can talk about my new book and I also have a screenplay." He talked and talked, on and on. He had a million ideas.

So off I went to present Abbie's vasectomy to Guccione. I laid out various angles to do the article in the magazine but Guccione wasn't going for it. He wanted me to do something provocative. What could I do, though? Abbie wanted to do a story about his vasectomy.

I dismissed Guccione's concerns. "It'll work out; don't worry."

He wouldn't sign off on the plan, so I called Abbie and we agreed to meet again. I had to try to change his mind. We met on August 28, 1973, early in the afternoon. He confirmed he would go back to his place then come over to our apartment around seven o'clock to have dinner with me and Charli and discuss what to do. That evening, while we waited for him to arrive, I thought up some ideas I could pitch to him, hoping to get him off the vasectomy topic. Before I knew it, it was eleven and he still hadn't shown.

As Charli and I were watching the news on TV, she asked, "What ever happened to Abbie?"

Then, just like that, right there on TV, we saw Abbie being dragged across the screen, arrested and in handcuffs. How could that be? Wasn't he was on his way to see us? Weren't his evening plans to sit and eat with us? I guess not. I could relate to that. After all, sometimes I myself go with the flow then turn left.

Abbie and three others were caught red-handed in a seedy Times Square hotel, the Hotel Diplomat, by several undercover agents. They were charged with possession and sale of three pounds of coke, with an estimated street value of $500,000—a class-A felony carrying a mandatory sentence of fifteen years to life. According to the news he would be eligible for parole when he was sixty-one years old.

Charli and I knew it couldn't be true.

I believe it was a setup. Abbie and I knew each other very well and we talked about everything; I would have known about a drug deal. The prosecutor, assistant DA Lawrence Herman, said Abbie's crime "was insidious and treacherous, equal to homicide," and requested bail to be set at half a million dollars. His decision caused great concern among Abbie's supporters, lawyers, and friends. We petitioned the special prosecutor, arguing that because of Abbie's fame he was being treated unfairly. Under pressure, Judge Hyman Soluiker reduced bail to $202,500. One of the defense attorneys, Gerald Lefcourt, proceeded with a new angle for Abbie's defense, claiming that the three pounds of substance wasn't all cocaine, pointing out that two-thirds of the so-called coke had been cut with sugar and, furthermore, that the bust was a setup to arrest Abbie in an effort to stop his anti-government antics.

Everyone thought that was a brilliant argument, but Lefcourt's defense was overturned and in order to avoid similar defense arguments in the future, the law was changed from charging someone with possession of a narcotic to charging for possession of a controlled substance. Now it didn't matter how much a drug might be cut—like pot with twigs, seeds, or parsley in it—it was all now considered an illegal substance.

Abbie could not raise bail on his own. To help raise the money, John Wilcox, Tom Forçade, and several other friends launched the underground marijuana magazine *High Times*. I designed the poster and helped create the silver-colored first issue with Neville.

Abbie already had a long history of arrests and troubles with the law. On August 24, 1967, he, Jerry Rubin, and other Diggers—a San

Francisco guerrilla theater group—barged into the New York Stock Exchange to make a political statement against the Vietnam War. In order to make sure their efforts received worldwide attention, they invited everyone from the media. As they entered the exchange, the stockbrokers greeted them with cheers and applause. The would-be Yippies proceeded to throw fists full of money in the air and onto the exchange floor. The brokers and traders ran and dove for the falling cash. Abbie and his entourage were finally thrown out, but not before making local and international news.

Abbie and Jerry were masters of getting free press for their cause, no matter the repercussions. The next year, in 1968, they formed the Youth International Party, espousing the nickname of Yippies. They focused their attacks on politicians and were totally anti-establishment. Their main goal was to mobilize a freak-out at the 1968 Democratic Convention in Chicago, hoping to gain additional worldwide exposure for their fight against the Vietnam War, big business, and government spending and control.

The Chicago convention turned into a beacon for social unrest, bringing together dozens of diverse groups, some against the war, and others for a better, more equal way of life. Abbie's Yippies were joined by the Black Panthers, the National Mobilization Committee to End War in Vietnam, and others. Everyone came together for change, to be heard, and to take advantage of the media coverage. As a promotional stunt, Abbie and Jerry announced their plan to present their own presidential candidate, bringing out a big, fat live pig they anointed Pigasus the Immortal.

That Wednesday, August 28, 1968, about ten thousand people showed up to the rally in Grant Park. Things got progressively more heated as they advanced toward the amphitheater near where the convention was being held. Police, some on horseback, all in riot gear, shot tear gas and swung batons at the demonstrators. All hell broke loose and as Abbie was protesting and rousing up the demonstrators he got himself arrested with the word "FUCK" written on his forehead. The police charged him with indecency.

That march and demonstration is now known as the Chicago riots. The U.S. National Commission on the Causes and Prevention of Violence called what happened after that demonstration a "police riot," leading a federal grand jury to indict eight police officers and eight demonstrators. The latter was first known as the Chicago 8 (later the Chicago 7), and comprised of Yippies Abbie and Jerry, Black Panther Bobby Seale, and activists Rennie Davis, David Dellinger, Tom Hayden, Lee Weiner, and John Froines.

After a few days of mayhem in court, Bobby Seale was bound and gagged for his continued verbal attacks at Judge Julius Hoffman, calling him a "racist," "fascist dog," "honky," and "pig." The proceedings got worse and the courtroom was turned into a circus, caused by the judge's decisions and threats and the defendants retaliating with insults to the court. Judge Hoffman then had Bobby removed from the courtroom, sentencing him to four years for contempt of court. The trial then became internationally known as "The Chicago 7 Trial."

Everything Judge Hoffman did backfired and played into the defendants' protests. The removal of Bobby Seale ignited public outrage. The trial and courthouse turned into a media calamity. Judge Hoffman did not lend any credence to the testimonies; he simply refused to listen, and cited over two hundred contempt charges to everyone involved—the defendants, witnesses, and lawyers.

Near the end of the five-month trial, the defendants were appalled by the judge's decisions to silence their testimonies. Jerry Rubin paraded in front of the judge, giving Hitler salutes and yelling at the top of his lungs, "Fascist," and "Tyrant." Everyone in the courtroom joined in on the assault, including the audience.

Abbie and Jerry continued to mock the trial and especially the judge, appearing in court dressed in judicial robes. When ordered to remove the robes, the Yippie leaders willingly took them off to reveal Chicago police uniforms underneath, making the judge look even worse and the trial even more out of control. Abbie gave the finger to the court, frequently insulted the judge, and blew kisses to the jury. Judge Hoffman became the courtroom goat.

At one point Abbie shouted to the judge, "You are a *'shande fur de Goyim.'* You would have served Hitler better. Your idea of justice is the only obscenity in the room." Jerry announced to the judge, "This court is bullshit." In later interviews he proclaimed, "Our strategy was to give Judge Hoffman a heart attack. We gave the court system a heart attack, which is even better."

Here is an excerpt from the Chicago 7 conspiracy trial, from December 23, 1969:

Direct examination of Abbie Hoffman by defense attorney Lenard Weinglass, the assistant US attorney Richard Schultz, and US Judge Julius Hoffman

Q. Where do you reside?

A. I live in Woodstock Nation.

Q. Will you tell the court and jury where that is?

A. Yes. It is a nation of alienated young people. We carry it around with us as a state of mind in the same way the Sioux Indians carried the Sioux nation around with them. It is a nation dedicated to cooperation versus competition, to the idea that people should have better means of exchange than property or money, that there should be some other basis for human interaction. It is a nation dedicated to—

The Court: Excuse me, sir. Read the question to the witness please.

(Question read)

The Court: Just where it is, that is all.

The Witness: It is in my mind and in the minds of my brothers and sisters. We carry it around with us in the same way that the Sioux Indian carried around the Sioux nation. It does not consist of property or material, but rather of ideas and certain values, being cooperation versus competition and that we believe in a society—

Mr. Weinglass: Your Honor, the witness has identified it as being a state of mind, and he has, I think, a right to define that state of mind.

The Court: No, we want the place of residence, if he has one, place of doing business, if you have a business, or both if you desire to tell them both. One address will be sufficient. Nothing about philosophy or ... *India*, sir. Just where you live, if you have a place to live. Now, you said Woodstock. In what state is Woodstock?

The Witness: It is in the state of mind, in the mind of myself and my brothers and sisters. It is a conspiracy—

Q. Can you tell the court and jury your present age?

A. My age is thirty-three. I am a child of the '60s.

Q. When were you born?

A. Psychologically, 1960.

Q. Can you tell the court and jury what is your present occupation?

A. I am a cultural revolutionary. Well. I am really a defendant—

Q. What do you mean?

A. Full-time.

On February 18, 1970, all the Chicago 7 defendants were found not guilty of conspiracy. Froines and Weiner were acquitted completely. The remaining five were convicted of crossing state lines with the intent to incite a riot. They were each fined $5,000 and sentenced to five years in prison. At his sentencing, Abbie wouldn't let up, recommending that the judge try LSD, and that he would make arrangements for him with a drug dealer he knew in Florida.

William Kunstler, the defense lawyer, appealed the case to the Supreme Court. After its investigation, the Court ruled that Judge Julius Hoffman used unscrupulous tactics in his handling of the case. The Court then reversed the decision of the lower court, annulling all contempt charges.

Abbie continued to have run-ins with the law. One of the most famous was when he was arrested for wearing an American flag shirt in the late sixties. At that time it was considered a crime.

Watching Abbie on the television that night, three years after the Chicago 7 trial concluded, realizing he was not going to make dinner, it dawned on me. I had my story.

A few days later, I met with Guccione, saying I now had something provocative for him to consider—an interview with Abbie in jail. I received a press pass from Guccione, made arrangements, and visited Abbie in "The Tombs."

It was chilly that day. I could see the Manhattan House of Detention for Men in bold type on the entrance door. I entered a very small, cluttered combination waiting room-hallway-office, feeling extremely nervous with my smuggled tape recorder and camera. It looked and smelled like a jail, something straight out of a movie starring Mickey Rooney or Mugsy Malone from the East Side Kids.

I'll never forget the sight as I walked into the holding area, where I presented my credentials and signed in. I was never searched. Two guards took me through two sets of barred doors to Abbie's cell. I was surprised to see him looking skinny in oversized green prison pants and a blue work shirt, his face unshaven and his arms covered in what looked like white chalk. I didn't know what to say. I felt terrible. This was not the Abbie Hoffman I had come to know.

"Hey Abbie." He never really looked up. He kept staring at the floor, but he tried to smile and be funny. I took out my concealed tape recorder and began recording.

Abbie Hoffman: This is not what I had in mind.

Frank Yandolino: What's that white stuff all over you?

AH: It's some sort of chemical to prevent skin disease, bed bugs, and rats. They are all over. Everywhere, more rats than inmates.

FY: You look like a ghost. Abbie, how are you?

AH: I don't know. I don't even have a number.

FY: I don't know what to say.

AH: If anyone thinks I just walked into a hotel room and presented some narcotics officers who I never met before with a pile of cocaine for a pile of money, you've got to be out of your mind.

FY: What happened, Abbie?

AH: Well I'm not exactly here on a field research. The case is so sensitive and the charge is so heavy that I can't really talk about all the events that happened in the case. There are other people involved. I need to know what roles they played. Freedom is such a fragile thing. It's easy to be busted when you're outspoken. This is my sixth time in the Tombs.

FY: But this is serious. It's not something you have done or said. This is something everybody understands—three pounds of cocaine.

AH: I never saw it. I don't even know . . . what does it look like? When I was busted there was at least two dozen narcotics cops, you're staring into a stream of shotguns pointed right down you. Very rough. Very heavy. It's like you're dead.

FY: You're talking like it's over. You gave up.

AH: It's heavy.

FY: What is?

AH: People are put in solitary confinement.

FY: Why are you in this section?

AH: For my own good.

FY: Have you seen anyone?

No response while staring at me.

FY: How do you spend your time?

No response; he looked to be daydreaming.

FY: What have you learned about living in the Tombs?

AH: There are guys here two years. Not tried yet.

FY: Do they seem friendly?

AH: Sure.

FY: What about the guards?

AH: I don't think I can answer that.

FY: How do you feel about the prosecutor?

AH: Men of ambition.

FY: You're not the same person I have met before.

AH: I'm not the same; I'm not the same man. I'm thirty-six. I mean I never had a suicidal thought in my life. The first three days in the Tombs, I mean, I took off my shirt and put it around my neck. I'm now an inmate in the Tombs. You're the first. I've not talked to anyone in the press.

FY: Do you feel isolated?

AH: I cry, I cry. This is the worst interview I ever did.

I now felt even worse. A guard came over and took Abbie by the arm. "Time is up."

The guard then looked at me as though I were also a criminal. "You have to leave now."

I discreetly put my recorder back in my bag and gave Abbie a hug, saying, "I'll be in touch." He nodded with a distraught look on his face, answering back, "Sure."

Even though he had been arrested forty-two times before, this time it seemed different. He wasn't the same old defiant, you-can't-stop-me Abbie. He looked bewildered and scared. We walked out of the holding area together. He was cuffed and guided down the hall by the guard. That scene burned itself into my memory. As we got closer to the exit, we were separated by a four-foot-tall concrete dividing wall. He was taken left, back to his cell. I continued right, straight out the door. Wow, I thought. The difference between jail and freedom is this little concrete wall.

Soon after our interview, while being transferred to an upstate prison, in true Abbie style, he escaped and went on the lam. Some of us saw him occasionally while on the run. He had plastic surgery to try to hide his famous face, but it didn't work; it was a terrible job. He looked like Abbie Hoffman, the prizefighter with a bent nose. He was going nuts, not being the real, one and only Abbie Hoffman. He spent the next seven years going by the name Barry Freed. He couldn't take it anymore. Anonymity was not his style. So in early 1980 he resurfaced and did an interview on Barbara Walters's show. Abbie turned himself in, pleading guilty to a lesser drug charge, did some time in jail, and then embarked on a new career as an organizer, activist, author, and lecturer. It never really worked. He wasn't the same; times weren't the same.

Some eight years after resurfacing, he tried standup comedy. Abbie, the comedian who wanted to be Lenny Bruce, was a changed man. In August 1988, Charli and I went to see him perform a few blocks from our apartment on the Upper West Side at the New York Comedy Club. The carefree Abbie was no more. Seeing Abbie standing there trying to be funny and relate to a non-responsive audience made him seem even more distant and spaced out than he'd been in the Tombs. Years before, Abbie had had a natural sense of humor. But his new comedy act didn't go well at all.

"I'm not connecting with the kids anymore. I can't even get arrested," he told me after.

The first time I saw Abbie was in 1968, at the first marijuana "Smoke In" that he organized in Central Park. Then, he was a modern-day social crusader, often called a radical, a political activist spreading his Yippie, Zippie, Hippy message. Not anymore. On Thursday April 12, 1989, Abbie killed himself at the age of fifty-two. He was found at 8:15 a.m. in his two-bedroom apartment in Solebury Township near the Delaware River, dead in his bed, fully dressed in a red flannel shirt and corduroy pants, under a quilt covering up to his neck. It seems Abbie prepared to check out, dressing for the occasion. His remains were cremated; his ashes spread to the wind.

Abbie had so much to offer, a born leader with boundless energy, full of wit and humor. Why would he just stop? The doctors found 150 doses of Phenobarbital, along with Valium and Propanol (the same drug that killed Michael Jackson)—enough to kill fifteen men—in Abbie's system. That seems about right. When it came to sex, drugs, and rock 'n' roll, it would take several men to equal one hippie. Fifteen is what it took to bring the leader down. He was no ordinary man.

But why did he do it, kill himself? To be honest, I'm not sure he did. He just didn't seem the type—not the great leader full of vim and vigor, Abbie Hoffman. People question where he got those drugs from. To this day, no one knows. No drug containers or prescriptions were found in his apartment. Was this another suicide like Marilyn Monroe's? Did any-body see Peter Lawford or Bobby Kennedy lurking in the halls?

Abbie had shocked the world for the last time. Jerry Rubin's fate, how-ever, was much different. He called himself an "entrepreneur" stock bro-ker, founding a Manhattan-based company called Network America—"networking" parties for business executives in posh nightclubs in NYC.

"My protest days are over," he announced. Unfortunately, he was all too right. On November 28, 1994, Jerry was killed jaywalking, hit by a car in LA.

I really liked Jerry Rubin and Abbie Hoffman. Imagine what they could contribute today in this politically divided mess we are in. But then again, their stories remind me that unless you stay ahead of the curve, make waves, and stay in the news, this can happen to you—you go out with a whimper instead of a bang.

Nothing has changed since they faded. Today we have Occupy Wall Street, stop big business and a bigger government, the war in Afghanistan, and other hot spots. As Yogi Berra would say, deja vu all over again, Abbie and Jerry. They did not know that the Festival of Life, a music festival they organized as a protest, would become one of the most controversial, polarizing, and investigated events of American history, right along with the assassination of President Kennedy.

Most of us hardcore Democrats who were part of the sixties' and seventies' movements against government intervention and big business, corrupt politicians, and war, still hold on to some of those beliefs. However today we have come to realize that you can't survive being a true hippy. You must camouflage yourself, blend and sway, in order to make a living and prevail in this current "politically correct" society. Protesting is not enough; you have to do something about your protest, infiltrate the enemy and tell little white lies. You have to become a hybrid, like me, a "Republicrat."

Several months ago I was in my literary agent's office delivering a draft of this book. In a moment of excitement, he called an editor at a prestigious publishing house to pitch him on my stories. After running down several events, he explained my life.

"This guy was kidnapped in Paris, hung out with the Hells Angels, managed Joe Cocker, was involved with Woodstock and Abbie Hoffman ..." He paused, then continued, "Yes, Abbie Hoffman."

Suddenly, he held his hand over the phone, looking at me for an answer. Repeating the young editor's question out loud.

"What did *she* do?"

Abbie, I'm sure, rolled over in his grave.

CHAPTER 11

Angels, Stones, and Pink Flamingos

On December 29, 1971, Charli and I were celebrating our one-year wedding anniversary. Just as I popped the cork off a bottle of champagne, the phone rang. It was my father. As soon as he called me "Junior," I knew something was wrong. My brother Jamie was on a commercial airplane that had crashed in Florida. The rest of the conversation was a blur.

The next day, Mom, Dad, and I flew to Miami. For what seemed like eternity we sat on an Eastern Airlines flight, the same company of the plane Jamie had been on. We didnt know any details. Fear and worry consumed us. Mom and Dad cried the whole time. All we knew was that my brother had been on his way back to college when his plane crashed in the Florida Everglades.

The Miami airport was a total chaos of hundreds of distraught crying people running in different directions. We were escorted into a private area. No one knew anything, who died and who didn't. The airline officials were totally unorganized. We were told to check into a hotel and that they would get back to us as soon as they had more information. The hours in that room were torture. Every minute took life out of my parents. Then the phone rang. I answered it, looking at my parents sitting, holding each other. It tore me apart. I was shaking all over as the words came out.

"They want us to go to the morgue."

Mom collapsed. Dad fell to the floor next her. They could not see their son dead under any circumstances. We agreed I should go. I'll never forget Mom's words on the way out the door: "Maybe it's not him."

I went to the address I was given. It wasn't a morgue like you would imagine at a hospital or city building; it was a large, makeshift holding and viewing area with doctors, nurses, and what appeared to be other family members standing around gurneys, viewing black body bags holding people who had died in the crash.

I was in shock. It was too surreal for me, a sight I will never get out of my mind. I still hear a voice in the distance saying, "Are you sure you want to see this?" I identified my brother.

James was a loving, great kid. There was nothing he wouldn't do for you and he only had good things to say. He was generous and happy and enjoyed cooking special family recipes. James couldn't wait to graduate college after studying marine biology, ready to save the world. I still cry when I think about him. Mom and Dad cried every day since that tragic phone call. It's hard to imagine the pain that fathers and mothers live with after they lose a child, whether by bad health, accident, or war.

Mom gave me a little three-dimensional piece of art that of course now sits on my mantel, bearing a quote that says "Do It Now."

It reminds me to make sure I do it now every day.

In Charli's Words

The telephone rang and it was the worst news anyone could hear. Frank's younger brother James was on his way back to college at Miami University with his friends when the Eastern Airlines plane he was on crashed in the Everglades. Frank grabbed the ball, leaving immediately to take care of his parents through the worst nightmare any parent could experience.

Now that I am a mother I don't know how they ever got through that time. Frank took care of everything. It was remarkable. When a tragedy happens you cannot think; you just act. Because of Frank, his parents were able to grieve. This was the first tragedy I'd had in my life. Although James was young, a lot of people knew and loved him. A great number of them came to the funeral. It was overwhelming, beyond anyone's imagination.

This was when I realized who I had married. I learned then and would find out over the next forty years just how strong a character Frank was. This book tells about his more charmed moments and the amazing people he met throughout his life, but he had another side that only I knew, and it gives me confidence that he would always take care of me. Through all those years I never had to worry about anything.

Over a short period of time he lost not only his brother James, but also his grandparents in a fire and later his beloved father to cancer. I think those experiences could make another book.

Frank's life was not all fun and games. There were many times when he had to rise to the occasion and take care of people in his family in extraordinary ways. My life with him was really easy. Many of my friends wish they had a husband and great father like I had, who enhanced my life. I always say how lucky I am because I got to take this ride.

Hells Angels Forever

After my brother James passed it took several months to get back to thinking clearly. I needed excitement, something dangerous to throw myself into. A photographer friend of mine broke the ice when he came by the apartment to show Charli and I photos he'd just shot: dramatic, up-close studies of behind-the-scenes moments inside the Hells Angels motorcycle club. There were shots of several bikers tied together on a pole while others included semi-nude "old ladies" (as they called their girlfriends) getting beer and who knows what else poured on them. Since I had connections to *Penthouse*, we thought it would be a good project for the magazine to do something with the Angels.

My friend set up a meeting. I'll never forget that hot summer day forty years ago. I pulled up in front of the Angels' enclave, a three-story, run-down brownstone apartment building on Second Avenue in the Lower East Side. I parked my 250cc Yamaha street scrambler next to over a dozen chopped Harleys. I was immediately surrounded by Hells Angels with sarcastic attitudes, laughing and making jokes, wondering why I had the balls to pull up in what they called a Singer sewing machine.

Even though I'm sure they knew I had an appointment I was asked in a polite but cautious, direct way. "What . . . can we do for you?"

"Hi, I'm here to see Sandy Alexander."

There was a man they called Tiny who was about three hundred pounds, with a long bushy beard, and totally tattooed. His very large belly peeked through his opened Colors—the leather or jean vest the Hells Angels wear that displays the name of the club and chapter, and various patches depicting rank and other things. Tiny motioned and whistled to the roof, and answering back with the same whistled code was Sandy Alexander, the leader of the New York chapter. I was escorted to the roof and had my first meeting of many to come. I have a knack for meeting people, many by chance, who I've seen on TV or in the news, and who eventually would wind up on my living room couch. When I met Sandy, I realized I had seen him before as a boxer fighting at the New York Golden Gloves just some weeks earlier. We talked for a while. He seemed to like me and invited me back to meet other members like Vinnie and a girl they called Mousey.

After hanging out with the Angels for several weeks, I got to know them and became a trusted insider. I even rode my sewing machine with them on several short motorcycle runs. Gaining trust was important to them, and once I had it I proposed doing a photo spread with Angels and Penthouse Pets. Guccione was a little nervous about that, so as an interim idea I convinced Sandy to allow Guccione and me to attend a Hells Angels inauguration of new prospects (that's what they call potential new members before they get to wear the Hells Angel patches on their Colors). The initiation is not usually witnessed by outsiders. Eddie Adams, the Vietnam Pulitzer Prize–winning photographer, was to join us. Sandy and I agreed on conditions. No photos could be released in any way until they were approved, along with any copy or story related to them. And of course a fee was to be paid to the Angels.

The night of the event, the street was very eerie. Dimly lit street lamps highlighted a hazy, dangerous vibe in the hot, smoky air filled with dozens of Hells Angels and their old ladies, with pot, drugs, booze, and bikes everywhere. The street was lined with sixty-foot-long mats of firecrackers that the Angels lit as they did wheelies with their bikes through the smoky blaze while others tossed lit cherry bombs and ash cans at them. They hooted and hollered in a jubilant bliss. I'm sure it looked and smelled like Vietnam to Eddie.

Then, through the smoke and haze, Guccione arrived in a white stretch limo. What a sight he was, wearing white leather pants and white leather loafers, no socks and his fifty gold necklaces and rings hanging around his neck over his white silk shirt with collar up, opened down to the top of his stomach. It was a bizarre contrast to the Hells Angels, who looked at him as though he were the freak. One thing I have learned about true stars and celebrities is they stay true to their character, and the Gucc was a perfect example.

Leon Gast, an award-winning cinematographer, was there as well with his movie crew shooting footage for his planned movie *Angels Forever*. Scenes were to include the block party, initiations, and the motorcycle run to Laconia, New York. Years later Leon won the academy award for *They Would Be Kings* on the fight in Zaire, Africa, between Mohammed Ali and Joe Frazier.

That night I witnessed things you only read about. Initiations included a piercing with a nail driven into a new prospect's ear that became an earring, while another had a tooth pulled out with pliers. Other things happened behind closed doors that no outsider could see.

I continued to hang out with the Angels, working on various ideas. Frankly, I was in awe of the excitement surrounding them. Early on, I was smoking a four-foot Indian peace pipe made of wood and large bird feathers with Al Swartz, a record producer who lived on the twelfth floor at the Chatsworth, shortly before he moved to LA. As I was saying good-bye, he gave me the pipe, which I later gave to Sandy Alexander in his apartment to celebrate the birth of his son. We then became actual blood brothers. Sandy and I got on great. I helped him get on the David Suskind TV show.

The strangest event was when my mother was visiting Charli and I at our apartment and several Angels showed up. Mom still talks about how the Hells Angels called her Mrs. Yandolino. Another night, while sitting with a few Angels on their outside stoop, a car drove by full of black men who suddenly opened fire on us. Bullets flying, I scrambled to my bike and never returned.

Around that time, I grabbed another ball of opportunity when I was introduced to Bob Shay, owner and head of New Line Cinema. Bob hired me for a project that he had in the works, the New York Erotic Film Festival. I helped design several promotional pieces and organized the premiere party. He was about to launch a new movie, and since he was looking for marketing and distribution, I suggested Penthouse Films. The film was *Pink Flamingos*, directed by John Waters and starring a relatively unknown cult actress, a huge transvestite named Divine.

This episode has become one of my favorite stories. After I'd presented *Pink Flamingos* to Guccione and he was considering the film for *Penthouse*, I arranged for a private screening at his apartment. I had it delivered with a projector and screen, because back then video didn't exist. I can still hear Guccione now.

"Kathy and I were in bed ready to watch a porn movie and you send me that shit."

Pink Flamingos was way beyond a porno flick. Divine, among many gross things, ate real dog shit in the last scene of the movie.

"That was the dirtiest joke anyone ever played on me."

Hard to believe that, years, later John Waters went on to make *Hairspray* the movie and the Broadway musical. Continuing the saga, some thirty-five years later my daughter Jaime, now an accomplished public relations executive at Turner Broadcasting, met John Waters while working on his new TV series. She told him her name and reminded him about our meeting at my apartment.

He said, "Say hello to your dad" and signed a copy of his new book, *Till Death Do Us Part*, which joined the corner space on our mantle next to a photo of Divine in *Pink Flamingos*.

During this time I was working totally freelance, and I met Stewart Shapiro, owner of International Harmony Films, a small, independent avant-garde film production and distribution company that had an underground library that catered to our generation both in content and music. Films like Neil Young's *Rust Never Sleeps*, the classic *Reefer Madness,* and Deborah Harry's (Blondie) first movie, *Union City.* Stewart asked me to help him with a new film he was about to distribute called *Effects*. He wanted to market, advertise, and build a campaign to launch the controversial film built around rumors surrounding the film industry that *Effects* was a real snuff film about the making of a snuff film.

I designed the ads and hired Barbara Neisem, the well-known artist-illustrator, to do the art. I still am not sure if it was a real snuff movie, but it sure looked like the actors were killed on camera.

Mission Impossible

If anything was a grab-the-ball opportunity, it was a phone call I got one summer morning in 1973, sitting in my apartment with Charli. It has become obvious to me I am blessed that after over thirty-five years my phone still rings with requests for me to work on one thing after another. And that I'm sure lucky to have had the same phone number all these years. People I haven't spoken to for years call and say, "Boy am I glad you have the same number." This time, Charli answered and handed it to me.

"It's for you."

"Hello?"

"Hi, Frank. My name is Sandy McCloud. I work for a company called Mission Impossible, you were recommended by a friend who said you might be able to help us with a project we are developing. We are hoping you could come to our office today at Mission Impossible. Rollin Binzer, project director, and Leslie Brooks would like to meet you."

Always ready to leap tall buildings in a single bound with ball in hand, I replied, "Sure, where is it?" The address sounded suspicious. Charli said, "If you don't call me in an hour I'm calling the police."

I jumped in a cab headed to an address the driver wasn't sure existed. We arrived to the middle of nowhere on the Lower West Side on 10th Avenue. The old brick building with steel doors seemed a strange place for a company, but there it was, a small hand-stenciled yellow sign that simply said "Mission Impossible."

There was no bell to ring so I opened the door and entered into a gigantic open warehouse converted into some sort of office. The walls and ceiling were painted black, hanging fluorescent and neon lights accented the walls, and modern, industrial-style big yellow desks and furniture were scattered around in no particular order. I had never seen a working environment like this. There were about a dozen people casually dressed sitting in groups, some on the floor, immersed in conversation. A young girl wearing black high-top Converse sneakers and denim coveralls greeted me at the door. She was a cute curly-haired strawberry blonde.

"Hi, I'm Sandy. You must be Frank."

As usual, when I'm presented with that salutation I answered with, "Always." She got my remark, answering "Great."

We were joined by two people. Sandy introduced them. "This is Rollin Binzer and Leslie Brooks."

Rollin was quite a character. He had on a pullover with a flapping ear-muff Tibetan-type burka tribesman hat and a handkerchief tied around his neck. His long black curly hair stuck out the back and sides, and you couldn't help but notice his colorful paisley baggy pants and T-shirt. He was like a modern-day Dr. Seuss. Leslie was quite the opposite—a tall, slender girl with very short black hair, like a boy's. She also wore a handkerchief around her neck.

It was then explained to me where I was and why. Rollin had been appointed by the courts to try to turn around dozens of Arlan's Department Stores that were in Chapter 11 bankruptcy. The stores were spread around the country, and it truly seemed a mission impossible. We discussed me joining the team as advertising media buyer for the chain. Although I wasn't too sure about the media placement part, I had knowledge of advertising, so I grabbed the ball and took the job.

I tried it for a few days but it was not my thing. Leslie realized it, but instead of firing me she spoke to my coworkers, who said I was much more capable of contributing in other creative ways. I became one of the appointed directors of designing and restocking the stores with contemporary, more appealing inventory. The working environment was great. Every day we added more people: a fashion buyer, painters, architects, writers and designers and, thank God, a media buyer. Charli became my assistant, answering phones and in charge of lunches and dinners, which were always an event, ranging from twenty-five pizzas to thirty hero sandwiches to mass amounts of Chinese food every day.

In Charli's Words

At Mission Impossible we would all sit around the floor and on desks discussing plans while drinking beer and smoking a joint. What a great job. From that point on the only hair I cut was Frank's, as I did when I met him forty years ago. The time we spent together on his projects taught me many things I apply to my job today at Weill Cornell Medical College in New York. As one of the directors of student relations, I take care of organizing college events, lunches, dinner parties, graduation ceremonies, travel accommodations, housing, Broadway and movie theater tickets, personal considerations, and countless other things. I am the person the students, scientists, and post-docs turn to for whatever they need. I have learned how to juggle many balls by watching Frank.

Our team would go to a town on the Mission Impossible plane, which was painted with huge glittering letters on both sides, "The Flying Zombies." Arriving at a store, we would paint the walls black and hang day-glow signs and neon lights and palm trees.

Santa Claus would drop out of the sky onto the parking lot, handing out presents to the kids. Hot air zeppelins with the Arlan's logo hovered above the stores. The local press loved it and we got tons of free publicity to complement our spectacular ad campaign. I was learning free publicity is worth more than paid advertising.

Illustrator Charlie White did all the artwork for the campaign. Leslie hired the most famous photographers and models, dressed them in creative combinations of apparel from the store shelves, and shot ads in underground and mysterious places throughout New York, choosing provocative locations and placing the models in bizarre situations like phone booths, pool halls, arcades, and public bathrooms. She and Rollin had assembled a great team of innovative, creative people.

My philosophy continued to work and reap benefits. Once you grab the ball, you can do great things if you say you can do it and then do it. At this point Rollin, Leslie, and I were basically calling the shots.

A fellow worker I will keep nameless had a similar philosophy, but not the greatest execution. He was hired to restock the music department's records and tapes. Little did we know all that new power went right to his head. For many reasons I would find out later, Arlan's was not selling the most current inventory. If the doll Chatty Cathy was advertised on national TV, Arlan's was still selling Chatty Irene. This strategy was especially evident in records for sale; Arlan's shelves were full of old cut outs—records no longer distributed by the record labels. The record shelves rarely contained anything in the current top 40. Wanting to change this overnight, our nameless friend ordered tens of thousands of new product inventory from the major record labels. But the labels had already committed that year's supply of polymer chips needed to manufacture vinyl records, and were not prepared to press and manufacture these unscheduled large orders with which this worker was planning to restock all the shelves in 150 stores. That wasn't going to stop him, though, so he agreed to purchase and guarantee the record labels all the polymer chips they needed from Romania or some foreign country his father allegedly had connection to. As you could imagine, the record companies were thrilled. He would have instantly become one of their biggest distributors. The problem was he never figured out who was going to actually pay and guarantee it. Not being able to pay for his plan became a huge issue. This is a classic example of grabbing a ball and not knowing what to do with it. It drove him off the edge, and by the time we found out what was going on he had to be restrained and was taken away in a straitjacket from our office at Mission Impossible to Bellevue Psychiatric Hospital. The last I ever saw of this friend was on TV. Charli and I were watching a Knicks and LA Lakers game when security guards jumped him and knocked him out as he attempted to walk across the court during the game.

One of the perks Rollin, Leslie and I enjoyed as directors was that after landing in our private plane, we'd hop into a white limo, pull up to an Arlan's store, check in with the manager, and then proceed to the safe, from which we would take out bags of cash to cover our costs and expenses.

Rollin taught me a key lesson in that period about the power of people working together. He was a true revolutionary genius, with a clear vision. He had strong appreciation for the strength of community, the utility of sharing the workspace, and working together on jobs and problems. The office was simple. You felt at home, everyone had the same desk; no one had a title on their business card. Everyone was a director. We all felt equal, like a family with instant access to each other. We all shared one another's work and ideas, and looked out for each other. It was really the beginning of social networking. Working in that environment, we spent sometimes twenty hours a day, seven days a week for four months, until we turned the stores around from losing money to making profit using our creative marketing skills.

One of the most innovative programs we developed at Arlan's was the "Jean Heap." These were huge piles of old jeans that were left at the exits of the stores so kids could take them and think they were stealing them. It was part of our word-of-mouth marketing plan, along with live llamas, goats, and other animals that walked freely around the aisles. The stores had a full-time nursery for children where parents would drop the kids off while they shopped and walked by potted palm trees and Astroturf mountains. Every employee wore a red T-shirt with a silver-glitter Arlan's logo. Beautiful girls dressed as angels with wings and magic wands roamed the store, randomly touching a customer now and again to grant them whatever was in their shopping cart for free.

Our campaign was working. Word continued to spread. Arlan's was in every local newspaper, filled with photos, stories, and funny and artistic ads. Then we got fired. When all was said and done and the project was over, we were called and visited by the IRS for an audit. During my investigation the auditor said, "Mr. Yandolino, you and several of your group have $1.2 million in cash to account for. Can you back up these expenses and claims?"

My immediate answer was, "No."

We never heard from them again. All I know is we had $1.2 million unaccounted for in petty cash. No one cared how we did it, since we turned the stores around from a deficit to a profit. I still wonder why they fired us, since we were doing our jobs.

Years later, when Charli and I were sitting at John Revson's pool, I was to find out why and learn a very important lesson.

Ladies and Gentlemen, The Rolling Stones 1974

After Arlan's, Rollin was hired to produce and direct a Rolling Stones film. His job required that he piece together outtakes from a just-finished film the Stones had shot of their latest tour. After viewing the completed film, which included very provocative behind-the-scenes footage and explicit carryings on, the Stones did not want it released. The original film was titled "Cocksucker Blues." Rollin changed the title after re-editing it to *Ladies and Gentlemen: The Rolling Stones*. He brought a few of us from the Arlan's crew in to help promote and produce the film's opening and coordinate a traveling road show to accompany the film's release. We created a total experience. The re-cut and edited film was presented as if you were sitting front row dead center at the Stones concert, with no backstage, no talking, just the Stones as big as life performing on stage.

The traveling road show was designed to add excitement to the tour-like experience, opening in cities nationwide. It was the world's first quadraphonic film with large, twenty-foot quad-sound speakers, stacked like a live outdoor concert in the four corners of the theaters. Blue laser lights and Rolling Stone–tongued glitter Frisbees flew. The 1972 Stones tour was their first North American tour since the Altamont tragedy in 1969 in California. The footage was shot at four shows just after the release of their *Exile on Main Street* album.

Our plan was to launch the film and street fair wherever the Stones live tour wasn't, enabling us to use the exposure of their tour advertising and press to help sell our tickets.

Ladies and Gentlemen: The Rolling Stones was developed as one of the first films to "four wall," meaning the producers—Dragonair Films, an independent distribution company—rented the theaters for a flat guaranteed fee and retained all ticket sales. The feature film launched in NYC at the Ziegfeld Theater and ran for a record-breaking eleven weeks. It came along with a controversial opening-day extravaganza that closed off 56th Street and covered it with white carpet, which was supplied by Charli's cousin Linda's boyfriend, Nassa Aftab, who was the Shah of Iran's brother- in-law. I hired my cousin Frank Pedone to secure several classic cars that we remodeled; one was a rubber duck car Mick Jagger would arrive in.

The street and surrounding areas were designed to look like a Fellini movie, lined with real palm trees, tattooed sword swallowers, Angels of Light, and a life-sized Balinese cow outfitted in gold and glitter, designed by Joe Lombardo and his girlfriend, Donna—the same Donna and Joe who'd made the Frank hat I wore to Dominica. The cow stood next to a giant, inflatable Rolling Stone tongue on the roof of the theater.

The night before the opening at a private screening for the Stones, Mick was sitting right in front of me and Charli. Charli was a mess. Mick Jagger was her favorite person in the whole world and she could sing every word to all of his songs. When "Jumping Jack Flash" came on the screen Mick went into contortions, moving and fidgeting with his hair. This song really affected him, and he always performs it to this day. He is truly Jumping Jack Flash.

After the screening, Mick was asked by a reporter if he was concerned with all the press the film and he were getting, and whether the Hells Angels killing a concert-goer at the Altamont festival bothered him. He calmly answered,

"Publicity is publicity."

That was a lesson I never forgot and I always apply that philosophy.

At that time word on the street and pre-publicity tended to cause concern and fear for New York's Mayor Beam and his administration. They were worried Woodstock or even worse Altamont would happen on 56th Street. Two days before our event we were asked to attend a meeting at police headquarters. We were instructed to bring our plans for the event, including evacuation and medical triage centers. We had all of that and more.

Our entourage entered the police staging area meeting room, where cops of all sizes and shapes adorned in various gold braids, hats, stars, and medals were already seated at the large mahogany conference table. We sat down in the five unoccupied seats. I sat directly across from the soon-to-be-announced chief of police as he bellowed out his demands.

"Okay, let's see what you got."

We sheepishly answered his questions and showed him our plans. Well, that was not good enough for him. He had to prove a point.

Looking directly at me, he said, "Let me tell you, if there is any problem at all, *you* will be the first person I arrest."

At that point he waved his baton directly in my face. Shit, he was dead serious. That was all my friend and personal protector August "Augie" Dela Pietro could take. He freaked and grabbed the chief and started to shake him, saying, "Who you gonna hit with that stick?"

It took all the cops in the room to get August off the chief. That was it for us, but we luckily escaped arrest. The next day the mayor summoned us to a meeting at Gracie Square. I sat as his desk drinking a beer while we waited for him in his office. When he entered I gave him the finger. As you can imagine that meeting did not go well.

We were forced to go on TV that night, telling everyone not to show up because our permits were pulled and the street fair party was cancelled. Well we all know what that means: Ten thousand kids came anyway, on Easter Sunday, 1974, causing the city to call out hundreds of police in riot gear, trucks, vans, and dogs, costing millions in overtime. The film ended up being nominated for a "Rocky" Best Music Film.

We got "publicity is publicity" all right.

In Charli's Words

Easter Sunday, the premiere of Ladies and Gentlemen, *Frank and I got dressed and took a cab to the Ziegfeld Theater. I could tell he was distraught, worried, and mostly disappointed. As we got close I couldn't believe my eyes. What was supposed to be a canceled fabulous street fair extravaganza was turned into an armed camp. Police cars with flashing lights were parked everywhere, bus loads of cops in riot gear were waiting to move in, motorcycle cops were buzzing around barricaded streets, and other bunches of police were scattered everywhere. It looked like Beirut.*

We got out of the cab. The street and theater were both totally decorated. Joe Lombardo and Donna's golden Balinese cow was on the roof. Above the theater the giant inflatable Rolling Stones tongue waved in the wind, and hundreds of people were waiting on line behind barricades. Frank pointed out Patti Smith and her boyfriend Lenny in the crowd waiting to get in. It was a very bizarre and surrealistic sight, 56th Street lined in white carpet and palm trees surrounded by cops and horses.

Inside the theater was another story. As you entered the theater lobby the walls were draped in red satin with silver and gold glitter.

Specially colored food of red pasta, green bread, purple cakes and multicolored cookies and other assorted items had been moved to the lobby. The Angels of Light, scantily dressed in wild makeup with four-foot lighted headdresses, who along with sword swallowers and tattooed women escorted guests to their seats, handed out Stones-logoed Frisbees and silk and glitter multi-colored scarves and T-shirts. As the lights in the theater faded to black, falling glitter and Frisbees flew in the air, the laser lights went on, flashing in sync to music from the quadraphonic sound system cranked up to a deafening pitch, and the Stones took center stage. The audience roared.

I know one thing: I love Mick Jagger, but not as much as I love Frank.

CHAPTER 12

Atlantis and the KKK

was still freelancing at *Penthouse* and Guccione was getting a little upset with my popularity. Everybody there knew and liked me, especially the new Pets who were mostly out-of-towners who were not accustomed to my New York style. I was full of advice on how to survive in the big city and assured them if they ever needed anything all they had to do was ask. I grabbed every ball I could and many of my projects and contacts were being considered by Bob at the magazine. Guccione was very diversified, not just a smut peddler or a porn king as you might think; he was involved with many outside projects like real estate, offshore ventures, concrete sales, and a plan to move New York City's massive garbage problem to South America, where he had connections.

Guccione asked me if I knew anybody who could help with that. I guess he thought all Italians knew someone in the Mafia or the garbage business. Well, I did indeed. That was right around when my father introduced me to the Ponte brothers, Joe and Angelo, who were owners of Ponte's Restaurant, a rare mob safe house, downtown just off the West Side Highway where all the New York families could come to eat without confrontation. I'll get into that later.

Although Dad was a silent, calculating type, he and I got into some adventures of our own, and I learned a thing or two. On one occasion he and I were having dinner with one of his associates, Paul Wald of J. S. Wald Trucking. After dinner, for some reason Paul invited us to take a ride in his car. While driving, a voice from the dashboard came blasting over a police and fireman radio scanner. It seems Paul was an honorary fireman chief, which explained the large brass medallion on his car.

"How would you guys like to stop off at the fire station?" Before we answered, he made a U-turn, put on a siren, and sped off to the station. As we entered the firehouse he introduced us to everyone he knew. I looked around and I could sense something similar to what I've felt in the Middle East, India, and the Adirondacks: this was a man's society. The firemen were cleaning, cooking, and sitting around the table eating and telling jokes. The captain invited Dad and me to look around the firehouse, taking us upstairs where they slept on cots overnight and in between fires. It looked and smelled like a boys' gym. All of a sudden the fire alarm went off and everyone started scrambling. Dad and I slid down the fire pole and were scurried onto a hook- and-ladder fire truck, and the next thing I knew we were on our way to a real fire. I looked across the fire truck to see Dad holding on for life as the lights flashed and sirens blasted, the truck speeding down the avenues and narrow streets, whizzing past red lights and through the parting sea of cars pulling off to the side to make way for us. As we approached the burning building the truck came to a screeching halt. Dad and I jumped off as all the other firemen rushed toward the fire fuming smoke, water hoses started spraying, and me and Dad watched them douse the flames.

One summer break from Parsons, Dad asked me to help him make a delivery during a workers' strike at the New York World's Fair. No trucks were allowed to make deliveries, and when we got close to the picket line he scribbled a little note and placed it on the windshield. As we approached the strikers, I was surprised to see them waving us through. I still have no idea what that piece of paper said.

That wasn't the only time I noticed his quiet way in action. On another occasion Lufthansa Airlines was giving the truckers a problem, and Dad drove over to the shipping cargo hangars and said a few words to this guy, and the next thing I hear is "Okay guys, shut it down," and all the truckers walked off. Lufthansa lost hundreds of thousands if not millions of dollars until the ban was lifted. It turned out Dad was the president of Air Expert, an organization he formed to organize the truck owners against the truckers union. Dad had a strong character, but was subtle and non-abrasive. He knew just how to use it to get what he wanted. I guess it also had something to do with his smile and that look in his eye, which I knew well from my childhood, that said, "Don't try it." As they say, the apple didn't fall far from the tree, except I am far from subtle.

One day at a meeting Guccione surprised me when he casually looked at me from behind his desk and simply said, "Frank, I can't take it anymore. *My cup runneth over.*"

After his comment a moment of deafening silence filled the air as I was trying to figure out what the hell that meant. Then I realized what he really was saying—I was too popular, too many projects were mine, I was grabbing all the balls. He had had enough of me and I was becoming too important, in his mind making him look bad.

Guccione wasn't stupid. Instead of throwing me out the door and jeopardizing the things I was working on he decided to get me out of the *Penthouse* office in a more discrete way.

"I need you to be my eyes and ears and help with a major project in Georgia. I'd like you to meet my partner, Ed Brown. He will explain everything."

He paused, looking up over his rose-colored glasses. "Can you go?"

I saw the ball and said, "Yes."

Guccione introduced me to Ed Brown. They were planning to develop a *Penthouse* "Viva Village" somewhere in Georgia, a *Playboy*-type mansion resort destination, a Plato's Retreat with Penthouse Pets.

Ed Brown was a tall, handsome, very tan guy, and Hawaiian singer Don Ho's manager. We agreed I would go to Marietta, Georgia, which I later found out was the home of the Ku Klux Klan. Charli stayed in New York with Bruno while I set things up. I wondered how she felt about staying with our Bruno while I went traveling with Penthouse Pets.

In Charli's Words

I must say sometimes at weak moments I did have several reservations about Frank being around all those beautiful women, but Gala's cashew story prepared me for it so I let the bird fly.

We arrived at the site where the new complex was to be built on 150 acres of undeveloped land, a multi-million-dollar real estate project outside Atlanta, Georgia, across from the Dobbins Air Force Base. That's when I first met Ken Partiss, another one of Guccione's partners, the Pecks Bad Boy of Georgia. Ken had dirty blond hair and blue eyes and resembled James Dean with his blue jeans, cowboy boots, and a jean shirt that exposed his not quite hairy chest. He also had a pet rabbit on a leash. Ken and I got on immediately. That's how it is with me from that first encounter: you either do or you don't. Ken put us up in a five-room newly furnished townhouse at his Sundown Apartment complex. Charli and Bruno arrived a few days later.

I set up an office at the site of the soon-to-be Penthouse VIVA Village in one of the trailers on the side of the just-cleared dirt road. Construction had just started. It was amazing to see how the land was taking shape. Several weeks later I heard a commotion outside my trailer. Someone was saying that the project was closed down and that all Penthouse people had to leave. Then Ken walked in with a big ole smile on his face and a cigarette dangling from the corner of his mouth. He looked at me, smiling.

"Hey."

"Hey, Ken. What's up? "

His smile quickly turned to a dead serious frown.

"The town and city officials decided they do not want any Penthouse Pets running around Marietta. They gotta go."

I looked at him as if to say, "What about me? I thought you liked me and Charli. You said you even liked Bruno . . ."

"I want you to stay," Ken said.

"Me? Why me?"

"Cause you're a good ole boy and the only one we like."

"What will I do? What about the plans?"

"Don't worry, I already got a commitment from the bank. You decide what to build."

Ken was no dummy. He was well read. Ayn Rand, the *I Ching, Mein Kampf.* A very savvy, smart man, he used the *Penthouse* name, got the money and commitment from the First National Bank of Georgia, and then got rid of Guccione. I didn't care. The hell with Guccione; at least Ken was paying me.

Days later it all fell apart. I was on the site looking out my trailer window when I saw six or seven cars and pickup trucks come roaring down the dirt road, kicking up a dust storm, sirens screeching with flashing red lights mounted on their roofs, speeding to a halt. This was Ken's crew of good ole boys themselves, who had been working around the site, and who I'd later learn were part of the KKK. Instead of white hoods they now wore baseball caps, along with badges and guns. That day it was officially proclaimed throughout the lands that *Penthouse* and its Pets were no longer welcome in Marietta. Ed Brown and all the rest had to leave except me, Charli, and Bruno. "Come on," said Ken. "Get Charli. We're going to a picnic to celebrate Charlie Mixum coming home."

Little did I know it was also a KKK celebration picnic. Charlie was Ken's right-hand man and foreman who had just been released from prison for tying his ex-partner to a tree and setting him on fire.

Off we went to a spot somewhere in the middle of nowhere, deep in the woods. Getting out of Ken's black stretch Cadillac, it dawned on me that this was a southern good ole boy redneck version of the Hells Angels. Charli and I looked at each other with the same thought:.

"Shit, what are we doing here?"

Ken introduced me and Charli to Charlie Mixum, who was standing over a whole giant pig roasting over an open fire pit, waving two fifteen-inch knives. Mixum was a surprisingly distinguished older guy with grizzled short black hair. He tipped his baseball cap.

"Nice to meech y'all."

Charli and I answered in unison, "Nice to meet you, too."

Mixum half-jokingly handed me the knives. "Why don't you make the first cut?"

I must admit his reputation coupled with a sinister grin and gleam in his eye scared the shit out of me, but in the end we all got along fine. I knew just what to say to these good ole boys. I even spoke and cussed with a mixture of Brooklyn and Southern accents.

"Fuuckyaall now."

I came up with an idea for a new project Ken loved. Having read many books about the subject, he decided to build what I called "The Continent of Atlantis." It would be built and designed around the theme of the mythological Lost City of Atlantis.

Months later, Charli, Bruno, and I moved our entire five-room Chatsworth apartment—I mean everything: every book, record, magazine, pencil, paper clip, piece of paper, painting, the bookcases and sculptures, all of it—to Power Ferry Road in Marietta, Georgia.

My first job as design and marketing director was to let everyone know we were here, so I had Ken put up a giant sign that I designed stuck in the middle of the Kudzu off of Route I-95, just before our dirt road, with a giant arrow pointing and saying Turn Here . . . This Way to Beach.

The sign was beautiful. It had palm trees on a white sandy beach and turquoise water. It looked just like Dominica.

If nobody sees it, it's not interesting

People actually drove all the way down our dirt road to our little construction camp looking for the beach even though we were smack in the middle of Georgia, in Marietta surrounded by pine trees and kudzu. Whenever one of the adventurous souls made it to my trailer and asked dead seriously, "Where's the beach?"

I would politely but with a Brooklyn sarcasm answer, "It's coming up from Florida. You see we are building a P.U.D. here—a planned unit development that one day will have a beach. It's part of the concept and plans." They would shake and scratch their heads and say, "Thank ya... kindly . . . we'll be back."

Over time I began to get it and I learned what that meant. It was a Southern thing. They never really say what they mean, like when they look you in the eye and say, "Y'all come back and see us again now, hear." But what they really mean is "I hope you don't."

I began creating Atlantis, an oasis in the middle of nowhere, complete with a sixty-foot pyramid with a fifteen-foot chrome ball perched at the top, similar to the pyramid and eye on the back of a dollar bill. The pyramid would replace the beach sign, and would rise above the trees where everyone could see it. I commissioned my old friend Charlie White to paint the original art. It was spectacular. Charlie is a true master.

Now I had grabbed the ball, so to speak, in many ways. I had to get the giant chrome ball made. The sixty-foot pyramid structure was being constructed. Ken used dozens of kinds of wood from all over the world and it matched Charlie White's painting exactly. But I couldn't find a fifteen-foot ball made out of anything, let alone chrome. It couldn't be done. No one could fabricate a giant round shiny chrome ball. Now what? How do I get the ball made?

All the naysayers poo-pooed me, gave me the icorno, the Italian jinx horns. Forget it, they yelled, make it without the ball. Who needs the ball?

"It's all about the ball," I'd say.

The chrome ball is the most important part, it fits in the pyramid, and without each other they are nothing. The ball must be at the top, reflecting the Earth and solar system. I had designed it so that when you stand at the bottom of the pyramid and look up to the ball, your image will be reflected in the ball as you become part of the universe as well. The Michelangelo in me ignited. And like Michelangelo had his pope benefactor, I had my pope too. His name is Kenneth. "I will produce the chrome ball." And I did, using my most important ability to innovate.

Innovation is the key to creativity.

We hired a carpenter to make the ball out of wood, hired a specialist to fiberglass it, then cut it in half, separated it from the wood form, sanded the fiberglass smooth, and sent it off to be chromed.

The day of the unveiling of the pyramid and its chrome ball became a media sensation. I was in control, creating the look and feel of the entire project, writing the copy, taking the photos, and designing the sales tools. I did it all. Plans included townhouse apartments, a restaurant, a motel and cabaret theatre, an indoor and outdoor pool, and the beach. The project was completed almost two years later. It was very successful and became Marietta's wonder of the world.

Ken Partiss also owned the Sundown Apartments. I became the advertising and marketing director, changed the name to "Sundown At at the Oasis," planted palm trees, and added ponds, waterfalls, and sand dunes.

The following is a lesson well learned: Always get all the facts. Don't assume anything. To commemorate the original launching of the complex, Ken wanted to hire Howdy Doody and Buffalo Bob Smith to perform. Buffalo Bob agreed to do it, and insisted Ken rent a giant baby grand piano for the show. It was a nightmare finding one and having it delivered to Marietta. But Ken figured why not, anything for Howdy Doody.

The night of the show the clubhouse was packed, as everyone waited for Howdy Doody and Buffalo Bob Smith. The spotlight was on, and out comes Buffalo Bob dressed in his Davy Crocket leather and suede outfit. He takes a seat at the piano and starts to sing and play the theme song, "It's Howdy Doody time, it's Howdy Doody time, it's time . . ." Then in the middle of the song he stops singing, turns to the audience and says, "I bet you're all wondering, where is Howdy? Well Howdy's not here. You see, I don't have the rights to Howdy, just me as Buffalo Bob." Well, everyone went nuts, threw things and yelled obscenities at Buffalo Bob, who ran off the stage. He didn't care, though, since he was paid up-front.

Charli and I witnessed the same thing years later happen to Stevie Wonder when he was still Little Stevie Wonder, opening for The Stones at Madison Square Garden. He came out and started to sing songs from his new album, later to become one of his greatest albums, *Songs in the Key of Life*. But the audience went berserk, throwing things at the stage, because they came to see Little Stevie Wonder sing "Finger Tips." Another lesson learned: You gotta play them the hits, the songs they came to see. You can slide in new stuff and hope eventually the new stuff replaces the old stuff but there are those rare songs, the ones that brand you forever, that you must play or die. Like "Jumping Jack Flash." Jagger must have sung that song a million times. God forbid he doesn't perform it at a show. His audience expects to hear it. They expect him to be Jumping Jack Flash.

After the launch of the Continent of Atlantis at our Journeys End Restaurant and all the press coverage, I became very popular among the elite of Atlanta. Others wanted what came easy to me—my creativity, marketing, and advertising skills. Some, however, resented my particular professionalism, and my intuition that gave me freedom to pick and choose what and how I would do things. Most people don't like free birds because they are not one themselves.

Charli went to luncheons and took horseback riding lessons with Ann Partiss and other wives of the well-to-do clan. I felt like a foreigner in a foreign land, the different guy.

Charli, Bruno, and I moved out of the Sundown Apartments and were now living in luxury in a large ranch-style house in the center of the most prestigious area just outside downtown Atlanta. We were on the Brookhaven Country Club Golf Course, a short distance from my office at the Colony Square Complex, where I decided to open an advertising agency, Chrome Ball Productions, named after the episode. I drove a 1966 classic maroon 4.2 Mark 10 Jaguar that everyone called Big Red.

My clients included Colony Square, Atlantis and Journey's End, Sundown Apartments, WLTA Radio, Ted Turner Communications, and several other establishments and personal companies like Mr. George, as I called him, who was a prominent real-estate tycoon well connected in the Atlanta business community.

Neville was now living with us again. He showed up at the airport with just one little suitcase and a straw fedora hat. Charli and I would constantly go back to New York and stay at the Plaza Hotel while Neville stayed in Atlanta with Bruno.

One thing I learned in Atlanta is you never entirely know what people are really about. Mr. George, for example, appeared to be a straight redneck with a wife and little kids living in a mansion, an estate with white columns, driveways and fences, and Dixie Flags. But secretly he led two lives; some days he was a straight Southern businessman, and others he was the owner, distributor, and producer of a chain of porno movie theaters in New Orleans: the Paris, Toulouse, and St. James. I became the advertising agency creative director to promote the theaters and coordinate the premieres and openings. Part of my agency's job was to write, design, and place the advertisements for the theaters and films in newspapers and magazines. I also wrote and produced the radio commercials, which were very provocative and extremely controversial.

I purposely placed some spots on Christian radio stations that ran them; how, you might ask, did they air? Well, simply because no one checked the content. As you could imagine, the X-rated material brought both commotion and promotion. Just how I like it. After outraged listeners called the radio station to complain, Chrome Ball Productions was banned from placing any more advertising on Christian stations. But as the master Mick said, "Publicity is publicity."

Ken wasn't done with me. He invested in and operated a strip coal mining company, Mako Mining, in Annville, Kentucky. We would go there a couple of times a month. I was a small partner and of course marketing director. Ken made sure I participated for my shares. He thought it would be funny to see me running around with coal miners. Whenever we went to Annville we all stayed in a giant, old wooden house just outside of town. Five of us: Ken, Charlie Mixum, two local coal miner boys, and me. "Town" consisted of four, maybe five streets that included a combination post office/convenience store, a small diner, a hardware store, and several homes next to each other with porches and unemployed people in rocking chairs.

The old wooden house we were living in was falling apart. Ken said it was haunted. One night while sitting around the kitchen table we heard sounds as if someone was running across the roof. I had no idea what it was and neither did Mixum or the boys. They believed Ken that it must be ghosts. They were truly scared to death. After two nights of this I went outside to see what was going on. Ken followed me. That's when we saw the apples falling from the tree onto the tin roof. Ken knew this all along, but Ken being Ken, he said, "Don't tell the others." I never did and I'm sure to this day they believe it was ghosts.

Annville, Kentucky, was quite a place, full of characters like the local crazy guy from town who would show up in my bedroom staring at me while I slept. The local boys said, "Don't pay him no mind; he does that to everyone."

Ken always liked to cause trouble. He wallowed in it. One morning we had to get up at the crack of dawn. Having breakfast at the local diner, Ken ordered eggs Benedict. The scrawny bleach-blonde waitress looked at him as if he was speaking a foreign language. She didn't know what it was. Annville was a small little town made out of wood, like a run-down Lionel Train Village occupied by the people from the movie *Deliverance*.

The waitress said to the cook, "He wants eggs benedick. What in the world is it?"

The other customers turned and looked at our table as if they thought we'd made a dirty remark. Are these wise guys were makin' fun at us?

The cook answered back sarcastically, "Yeah, scrambled or bulls eye?" Ken answered, paying no mind, loudly and very seriously, "Over easy."

The next day was my first working day at the strip mine site. Ken, again humoring himself and the other miners, gave me the most dangerous job of all. I had to fill the twelve-inch drilled-out holes in the mountaintop with dynamite charges that, when ignited, blew up the dirt and exposed the coal. Then the dozers would come in, strip the coal, and put it on large dump trucks to be hauled. After filling the holes I was to run as fast as I could to get out of harm's way before they would yell, "Fire in the hole!" then ignite the charge. The miners got a kick out of watching me scramble, not really caring if I was able to run away without getting killed. It was very funny to them. At any rate, now I could add coal miner to my résumé.

Ken was being forced to make changes with Atlantis. The bank was not happy with the way he was operating, especially the money he was spending. During that process the bank brought in a new operating management company, ASECO, whose representatives met with me under the guise that I would help them in transition, when in reality they and the bank were trying to get rid of Ken's team. ASECO was very cunning; they gave Chrome Ball a project to create and design a promotional brochure, a selling tool for their company that would be used to generate sales at the Atlantis complex. But it all was a scam to get information from me: how I did things in the past, who my contacts and vendors were.

Once I realized what they were up to, trying to get rid of me, I met with Ken. He suggested I consult with a lawyer since I was under contract with him and Atlantis. Per Ken's recommendation the lawyer I met with was Stanley Nylan, who was a quadriplegic, confined to a wheelchair. The only parts of his body that he could control were his eyes, mouth, one arm, and two deformed hands. He had to be wheeled in and out of the rooms, but he used his hand to write notes and smoke a pipe. Why I mention this at all is to emphasize that despite his condition he had tremendous drive and a brilliant mind. Stan Nylan had won several landmark court cases, wrote books, and spoke at seminars. At first I liked him a lot, even though I thought it strange that he videotaped our first meeting. Later it came out that the bank was paying him; he was working for them and ASECO, not me. It was their way of finding out even more information and building a case against me. Ken gave me a copy of ASECO's and Nylan's report. Their conclusion was I had too much power and that I should be fired. Just like with Guccione. I have since learned to camouflage what I think and do, and instead of protecting my position I am learning to share it with those who give it to me. Number one: I don't trust anyone but my kids and of course Charli.

In late 1975, Charli, Bruno and I were sitting on our veranda looking out at the lush golf course dotted with weeping willows, a small lake, and greener-than-green grass, the same grass I'd never even stepped on once since we'd moved there. Although Bruno did take a dump on it occasionally. As we sipped our coffee all three of us looked at each other and I said what I'm sure we were all thinking: "Charli, what the *hell* are we doing in Atlanta?"

CHAPTER 13

Riviera 76

s if sent by the Gods, the next day Ray Paret called from New York rambling on about a new project he and Michael Lang were doing, and he asked me to join them. He would not take no for an answer, and his last words to me as he hung up were, "I'm coming down. I'll see you Friday."

Ray came to Atlanta, laid out the plans for the Riviera 76 Festival, and I agreed to do it. A week later, I gave my ad agency Chrome Ball Productions and all accounts and clients to my agency staff. Charli and I split, headed back to New York, and checked in to the Mayflower Hotel.

Michael Lang had decided to produce, this time without Artie Kornfeld's involvement, another day Woodstock-type festival, called Riviera 76. He moved the party to the French Riviera at the Circuit Paul Richard Racetrack in Le Castellet. Along with Ray and several other investors, I was his partner and coproducer. Our office was at the old Gulf & Western building on Columbus Circle. Right from the start, I realized the plan had problems. Michael was spending most of his time in Paris while the New York office tried to keep up with his fast pace and always asking about the details. I began to question whether the artist lineup was strong enough.

I set out to make some changes. Charli now worked with me on every-thing I did. We truly became, as everyone referred to us, Frank and Charli. You couldn't say one without the other. She answered the phone, greeted everyone at the door, made the initial calls, and sent out the contracts to add some acts to the festival like Jimmy Cliff, Eddie Palmari, Ray Barretto, Gil Scott Heron, and Joe Cocker, who had performed and recorded with Stuff, a band Sunshine had signed to a recording production agreement, and who were already booked to play. I knew Lang didn't want Joe there. When I brought Cocker up earlier, he'd told me, "He doesn't fit the show theme." Michael was all about jazz-rock. He decided it was the new com-ing in music. That vision came and went, and never really materialized.

Ultimately we lined up two hundred musicians from across the globe. Somehow, Michael forgot to book and secure the passenger and cargo planes to get all of the acts from New York to France. Luckily, my father was in the shipping business at the airport. He set it up. Two weeks before the festival, I flew to Europe and had to pay World Airways for the planes. I came back to New York and then was ready to fly on to Paris.

Most of the acts not from France met in New York and boarded our chartered plane bound for the Riviera. Picture a plane full of musicians and their entourages, our staff and support people, over two hundred people, all smoking pot, drinking, and snorting coke for ten hours. With amazing foresight, we arranged for the plane to land without hav-ing to go through customs. Thanks again, Dad.

Our first emergency occurred before the festival even started. When the planes landed in Marseille, about twenty-five miles away from the town of Bandol, near the site, all hell broke loose. Michael had hired his assistant Ticia, who worked on Woodstock '69, to be his event travel planner. He thought she was a genius and put her in charge of transporta-tion and accommodations.

This logistical guru decided to color-code everything. Each musician was assigned a color to match a colored hotel where they were booked (red, blue, yellow). Luggage was marked and color-coded accordingly. Matching color-coded buses were parked on the tarmac ready to put her plan into motion.

The miscommunication started as the planes landed, when our French liaison told all the bus drivers to leave. I have no idea why or what he was thinking. The color-coded buses were gone. The musicians stood on the tarmac not knowing where to go. We had to call in taxis and car services. Problem was, when they got into the cars, the drivers asked them, "Where to go?"

The bewildered musicians answered with the only information they knew. "The red hotel." "The blue hotel." "The yellow hotel."

Half the drivers told them to stop being ridiculous. The other half drove around the city looking for colorful, phantom hotels in blue and red, all happening while the taxi drivers only spoke French. What a mess.

Somehow it all came together, just half a day late. On the first day of the festival, it rained. The weather, unfortunately, was not the worst of it. The next day I asked Michael for an update on crowd size and gate receipts. His answer surprised me.

"There are no significant gate receipts."

"Not again," I thought. Just like Woodstock '69 and as a matter of fact all the future Woodstocks to come, not only did it rain, but there would be no significant gate receipts.

To make matters worse, we were having trouble just paying the bands, and then twenty French security guards demanded more money. When they did not get it, they quit, just walked off, leaving me and five security guards from England to secure the stage. I can still see this image as clear as yesterday: standing off to the side of the stage, discussing our problems with Michael. I looked at him as the rain drenched the crowd. They were emulating '69, beating drums, chanting, and dancing nude in the mud.

Understand, I'm an opportunist. Actually, it's more than that. I will prostitute myself, just as long as I'm getting paid. As Charli always reminds me, I'm no Moses or the Pope. It's not for me to tell someone what they can or can't do to fulfill their dream, however: I don't want other people's dream to become my nightmare.

As far as I'm concerned, as long as they're paying me, that never happens. However, I also add to that philosophy this credo: If I piss in the wind I don't want it to hit me in the face.

During this episode, it literally did. I did not trust or have faith in the French. As I stood with Michael talking about it, a fine mist fell all around us. I looked back and saw a latrine on the rise above us. Piss was actually spraying on us as I spoke. From my experiences, whenever the French are caught fucking up, they cry, hiding behind their tears, saying how can I deal with the problem when I'm crying?

Anyway, the ticket problem started because Michael had arranged to have the Bank of Bandol armored trucks pick up the gate ticket money and deposit it into our bank accounts. What he did not know was that he had actually made the deal with the Corsican mafia. They took the money from the gate box office straight to their bank, not ours.

We did not have enough money to pay all the acts or most of the bills or to ship equipment back to New York. I had to call my father again. He, my mother, and my younger brother Robert flew to the festival site from Italy where they were vacationing. Somehow, they got to the stage. I explained the situation to Dad. He asked in his quiet, sort-of-to-the-point way, "What do you want to do with him?"

I knew he meant Michael. Dad, born and raised on the Lower East Side of Manhattan, could deal with the Corsican mafia no problem. He disappeared and came back an hour later. It seemed he had cleared everything up with the mafia, arranging to have the bands and their equipment return to New York. I would run into the French mob again, but that's for a later story.

With everything seemingly taken care of after the festival, Michael, Charli, and I went to visit Albert Gertner, our financier and producer, at his castle outside of Paris, to discuss plans to begin assembling the parts for editing the sound recordings and film footage for the Riviera movie. Unfortunately it never got made. There also was no film of Woodstock '79, '94, or '99.

In Charli's Words

At Gertner's castle outside of Paris the surrounding countryside was beautiful, with more than a mile-long tree-lined driveway leading to a moat and bridge. Right after we arrived, someone on staff came up to me, asking what I would like for lunch. He offered chicken, veal, or lamb. I chose the lamb.

Albert Gertner waited for us in the parlor. As Frank and Michael talked to him, I looked out across the grounds. A servant appeared from one of the out buildings, dragging a freshly slaughtered little lamb.

That night we ate on the bridge over the moat. When our meal was served, we realized every part of that lamb was used in the preparation, inside and out. I pretended to eat some of the more exotic cuts and when Gertner wasn't looking I'd throw the bloody parts into the moat.

From Gertner's castle, Frank and Michael evaded the threats and bill collectors that hunted them after the festival. Renting an expensive Peugeot, the three of us drove from France to London, stopping at every famous chateau and vineyard along the way, drinking and eating the best food on the menu.

My favorite memory of that time, one that started a tradition that continues today, has to do with duck. No matter where we went, we always ordered a duck. It became a kind of inside joke. We decided to compare and find out who made the best duck in Europe. Sitting down at our next feast, someone would say, "Let's order duck for the table."

It was an amazing time in our life, one full of lavish adventures, like something out of a fairytale. Our journey led us to the Hotel de la Post. Once settled at our table, the waiter eloquently explained the hotel's history in combined English and French.

"Bonjour, Madame, Monsieur. *Welcome to the Hotel de la Post. Did you know, Emperor Napoleon extraordinaire visited here* tres beaucoup? *As you can see on the menu, we have in stock his very personal brandy,* ça va, *the* exactement bouteille *from which he actually drank."*

He pointed it out, $45 a shot. I don't think he ever expected Frank to order it. It was for show only. That waiter must never have run into anyone like my Frank before.

"We'll take the whole bottle."

I think he almost fainted. When that poor young man returned with the bottle, his hands and knees were shaking. After dinner, the bottle came with us to the room. The next day when we checked out, we left a small amount in the bottle for the maids along with some francs as a tip.

After our cross-country drive from Bandol, France, to London, we returned to New York. We were staying with Michael Lang at his loft on Broome Street in SoHo. Frank and Michael were putting things back together after the festival in France. We'd abandoned our life and home in Atlanta, so I spent my time searching New York City for a new apartment. I searched the city every day: East Side, SoHo, Greenwich Village, everywhere. Ultimately I found myself back in our old neighborhood on the Upper West Side. Finally I found the apartment, a great one, on West End Avenue and 81st Street, huge, eight rooms. The owner and manager of the building had no intention of renting it to me, though. The entire building was filled with nice Jewish families and they wanted another one in this apartment. I went every day to visit with the landlord, Bushy Friedman, a big, bearded, burly, bully of a man. He could not get rid of me. I was there all the time, until he actually said, "Give me a few days." What he was really doing was stalling until he could find a family that would fit in with the rest of the tenants. Eventually, he said he wanted to meet my husband. I knew that if he met Frank, ponytail and beard, and especially Bruno, he would not rent the place. He finally agreed to rent me the apartment. Then he met Frank; that was something.

There we stood, two hippies and our German Shepherd who seemed to terrify everyone, the last possible tenants he ever dreamed of renting to. It was too late, though; he had already given me the lease. Bushy was in shock, especially when Frank told him he wasn't sure if he could live in a building that didn't have a synagogue across the street, recounting to Bushy his Shabbos boy experience growing up in Borough Park, Brooklyn. Bushy was amused by Frank's story and said not to worry: there is a synagogue in the lobby. Frank is convinced that even though we didn't know then that I am partly Jewish, Bushy somehow instinctually knew and that's why he liked me.

Frank says, "Everyone who meets Charli loves her, not me." At that time, no one in our building would talk to him and he didn't even know the names of the people who lived on our floor. What they didn't know but soon found out was that he was perfectly happy to avoid them. Well, all of them except for the infamous Bergmans, who lived across the hall.

In the early 1980s Rabbi Bernard Bergman's family was on the front page of the newspapers everyday, mired in a huge scandal. He had been convicted in the late seventies, accused and sued for cheating Jewish Holocaust survivors who were living in his many nursing homes from their Social Security and savings, and depriving them of their medication—truly a shameful act, much like what Bernie Madoff did a few decades later to his countrymen, friends and family.

We had just moved in across the hall from the Bergmans. I met the daughter-in-law, Frieda Bergman, a stunningly beautiful young woman with three young children. She seemingly led a very affluent life. Even when she would go to the grocery store she went in designer clothes and hats and always wore very expensive blonde wigs of various shapes. Frieda was interested in my life, and would constantly ask me questions, her inquisitive green eyes full of interest, thinking that what Frank and I were doing, leading a charmed life at a young age with no children, was very exciting. It seemed she married her husband without knowing him, having grown up a rich girl in Switzerland who was introduced to her husband days before their arranged wedding. Frieda gave the impression that this orthodox life was not for her. Maybe she was too young. She told me how she would get all dressed up with her cousins and drive to Studio 54, sit in the parked car, and watch the people go in and out, wondering and dreaming of what it would be like to go inside.

One day our elevator man said someone was found dead in the back alley. Suspiciously Frieda's husband remarked to the elevator man, "It must be my wife." Why would he say that so fast? Without knowing for sure.

Well, very sadly, it was Frieda. She had climbed the stairs to our rooftop, sixteen flights, then took off her clothes and her wig, and jumped. I will never forget her.

It is a sin to commit suicide in the Jewish faith. Some people from her world came and took her away, very quietly, and then immediately the next day her body was flown to Israel to be buried. Somehow this never made the news, but one neighbor, I won't mention who, telephoned the Daily News *and let them know what happened. It was then printed in the paper and the world found out how a Bergman had committed suicide. I just really thought that she should not be snuffed out like that; it was so sad. The press seemed so insensitive. A few weeks later in the trash outside of our apartment we found all of Frieda's photographs of her and her children, just all thrown out as if she never lived. I had to take these photographs and save them.*

154

Frank Yandolino at Camp Drum, Watertown, New York, "Special Forces War Games" during the war in Vietnam.

Producers Artie Kornfeld (L) and Michael Lang (R) at Woodstock '69.

Inside Bert Sommer, album cover designed by Frank Yandolino.

Erotic Sheets designed by Frank
Yandolino with Neville Gerson.

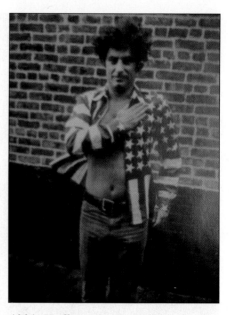

Abbie Hoffman: modern-day
revolutionary and social crusader who
began the Yippie movement.

Atlantis sixty-foot pyramid at the entrance of a theater, hotel, apartment complex in
Atlanta, Georgia. Total design by Frank Yandolino.

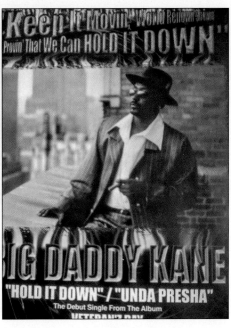

Bert Padell: Frank Yandolino's business manager and friend.

Big Daddy Kane's *Veteranz Day* was released by Frank Yandolino's The Label Records.

Album cover for *The Legendary Paul Butterfield Rides Again*, designed by Frank Yandolino.

Beach Boys concert on the beach at Atlantic City.

Poster for Woodstock '69.

Frank and Charli in Paris.

I save a lot of things, and Frieda deserved to be remembered, even if just by me.

Only a few months went by before her husband remarried. One day I saw him and his new wife in front of the building. She was the exact duplicate of Frieda, with all the designer outfits and wigs and Frieda's three boys beside them walking in front of my building as if nothing ever happened. I will never forget beautiful lonely Frieda and her sad story.

All my life, I was told by my mother that we were Norwegian and that she was born in Oslo in 1918. My family, my three sisters, and my brother were brought up Lutheran. Just a few years ago, in 2008, my brother Robert informed me he heard there was proof of our heritage that had been kept secret for several decades in a little black box in the attic of my Aunt Elsa's home in Lubec, Maine. Photographs and documents in the black box showed that our grandmother, born in 1900, and great-grandmother, born in 1880 or so, were Jewish, and that they had originally lived in Austria.

As the story developed, it seems my great-grandfather was a count whose last name was Van Geisler. He had owned a confection company in Austria. It is said that because he and his family were Jewish, they were persecuted and had to leave Austria. They fled to Oslo, Norway, and when they settled in my grandmother married my grandfather, Peter Egeland, a Norwegian engineer. They had three children: my mother, Erna; Elsa; and Peter. My grandfather became a sea captain and was encouraged by my grandmother to smuggle Jewish Norwegian children on his ships at night down the Black Sea to Germany. At that time, Germany was somewhat safe for Jewish people; it was just as Hitler was launching his plans for them. One day a neighbor, a Swedish man, reported to the authorities that my grandfather was smuggling the children to Germany, so my family had to flee from Norway to America. My grandmother had some money and opened a beauty parlor in Howard Beach, where her two daughters, Elsa and Erna, worked for her. My grandfather remained a sea captain on merchant marine ships. My mom eventually married my father, George Miller, also a Norwegian, but they never told us of our true heritage. I told my story to my neighbors and then the word got out about my grandmother being Jewish and then suddenly, the world changed. We were invited to Friday night Shabbos dinners. We were in.

Good Shabbos!

CHAPTER 14

Stuff

*A*fter the Riviera festival and our amazing car trip from France to England and back to New York, Charli and I moved in with Michael for a few weeks at his loft in SoHo while we searched for a new apartment. Charli eventually found a place on West 81st Street. We then made arrangements to have all our stuff packed and shipped from our house in Atlanta back to New York, moving every single thing we had brought with us, including Big Red. Returning to New York's hustle and bustle was as much a culture shock as returning from no-clothes-required Dominica had been. Ray Paret had arranged to move our office out of Gulf & Western into a four-story brownstone on East 61st between Park and Madison Avenues. A lawyer had a small office on the ground floor, Paul Simon and his company occupied the second floor, while our company, Just Sunshine Productions, had the two top floors.

Michael and Ray felt obligated to pay me back since I lost my investment in the Riviera Festival. They offered me the opportunity to become the sole manager of the band Stuff despite knowing full well that I didn't know much about what a manager's job was. Our first meeting was in our townhouse office with all six members of the band. I was scared to death and that was the beginning of a worldwide roller-coaster ride. The obvious ball was in the air. Although I'd never managed a band on this level before, it never really occurred to me at the time that I couldn't do it. Taking the risk with a careless regard, I just said, "Hi, I'm your new manager." They looked at me and said nothing. I took it to mean it was okay and from that point I never needed a management contract to represent the band. I just took care of business. The biggest task was keeping these guys from killing each other. I was the glue. We recorded and toured the world for ten years, and the band never really questioned me. They even called me STUFF. Somehow these streetwise musicians felt my honesty and Brooklyn vibe.

Stuff was composed of four black players—Cornell Dupree, Eric Gale, Gordon Edwards, and Richard Tee—and two white members—Chris Parker and Steve Gadd. These guys individually and collectively toured and recorded for everyone from Aretha Franklin, Paul Simon, James Taylor, Van McCoy, Quincy Jones, to Joe Cocker and many others. They were the best studio musicians in the world and everyone knew it.

Saturday Night Live 1975

Our connection to the New York music scene was at its peak, culminating around our almost weekly presence on *Saturday Night Live*. Stuff was basically the Saturday Night Live Band, and if they weren't, whoever was the band that night wore Stuff T-Shirts. It was very prestigious to have a Stuff T-shirt; they were very rare. I made them hard to get—you could only get one from management or a band member and only one at a time.

We began to work with Chevy Chase, John Belushi, and Dan Aykroyd—I might add mainly because of our partner in Just Sunshine, Ray. We were in the middle of what was happening in the city for years, constantly invited to shows, private parties, recording sessions, TV and radio shows, concerts, events, and many written stories and articles. The *SNL* after-parties were something movies were made of. We were unstoppable.

Stuff was the band all musicians respected. We played with and backed up everyone who was anyone that appeared on the show, or played and recorded in New York. We were by far and acted like the best band in NYC, bar none. No one could touch us. Others lived in fear of Stuff performing or opening shows for them, since even major acts could not compete with what Stuff did on stage.

As the new manager, I put together our personal cash machine, booking shows and tours for cash only. Charli came to every one. We would go out to do a little tour of six or seven clubs every two months or so, make a quick thirty, forty thousand cash in clubs like The Lake in Woodstock, New York, Mykels on 96th Street in New York City, My Father's Place on Long Island, and At the Bottom Line and Kenny's Castaway in Greenwich Village. Whichever musicians were in town made sure they stopped by to see or sit in with Stuff. We would headline or open for major acts on New Years Eve every year such as Ashford and Simpson, The Average White Band, and others.

There were several other venues and big shows—The Montreux Switzerland Jazz Festival, The Beacon Theater with Joe Cocker—and aside from other concerts and festivals worldwide we would go off to Japan two times a year where we would tour for two to three weeks. We would always travel first class and pick up a couple of hundred thousand dollars in cash along the way.

Charli always traveled with me and kept me and the band grounded. The band's wives and girlfriends and our crew—at times as many as sixteen or more people—were all considered Stuff. Nothing I did was ever enough, though. The problem with Stuff was their enormous egos. If they would have concentrated on the band instead of taking every offer to tour or work with other musicians, they would have been more of a success. Instead they felt more comfortable taking every studio or live gig and working for other acts that came their way. As they said, a bird in hand paid better. They didn't and wouldn't commit to their own careers.

In the long run it backfired; they remained very talented studio musicians but never became millionaires. They never fully understood that you have to believe in yourself and your craft, and work hard at your own life, not others', and then you will be free.

A perfect example was when we were all in Los Angeles. Stuff had been nominated for a Grammy. At the awards, Chaka Khan approached me and asked if Stuff would be interested in joining her to make an album and then join her on tour. When I brought it up to the band their reaction was, "We don't need that bitch." Many months later, I got a call from Quincy Jones. He wanted to use members of the band to make a record for him. He knew Stuff had a unique sound, especially when at least three members played together. Quincy wanted that sound, so he offered me something like double scale for each member to record. Single scale is a minimum fee per three-hour recording session set by the musicians' union—at that time about three hundred bucks per session, per man. His initial offer was for Richard, Steve, Cornell, and Eric. Quincy knew he would get the sound he wanted without having to pay the whole band. I told Quincy that as their manager, I couldn't accept the offer and I explained that if three or more members of the band were hired to perform or record, it constituted the sound of the band, and in that case, I would have to charge him a $25,000 fee. He laughed at me, saying, "Then I'll call them directly." You see, he knew they wouldn't see what I was trying to build. He knew they would take scale payment and run. Well the end of the story is Quincy hired them, paid them nothing, maybe triple scale, a few thousand dollars, recorded with Chaka, and not only got their sound, but called the song "Stuff Like That" and sold millions of copies. The other band members and I got nothing.

Grandpa Yandolino told me this story when I was a young boy, and ever since then I have repeated it many times to every girl I ever dated, never more important than when I repeated it to Charli.

Grandpa told it to me as if it were a matter of fact, taking my little hand in his, looking me in the eye very seriously and saying, "Back in the early days it was a measure and symbol of wealth and prestige to own a horse. Not everyone had one. My father's father—your great-great-grandfather—had just gotten married to your great-great-grandmother. On that very day he took her out to the barn to show off his fine stallion. He was carrying a bucket filled with water, and she wondered why her new husband was doing this. When they entered the barn Grandpa looked the horse in the eye and, making sure the horse and Grandma were paying attention, he placed the bucket in front of the horse. Pointing to the bucket filled with water, he commanded the horse not to drink from it. 'Do not drink,' he said. The horse was just a horse, though, and was thirsty to boot. Paying Great grandpa no mind he drank the water. In a stern, serious tone, Great-Grandpa shouted at the horse, 'That's *one!*' Then, taking Great-Grandma by the hand, he exited the barn. Great-Grandma was surprised by his actions. What did it all mean?

"The next day Great-Grandpa took his wife to the barn again, repeated the same thing, presenting the bucket of water to the horse and again directing the horse, 'Don't drink.' Well the thirsty horse again didn't listen and drank the water. Grandpa stood back and said to the horse, 'That's *two!*' Grandma was now even more confused by Grandpa's actions. What was the point? What is he saying? What did he expect from the horse? Still it wasn't over. The next day the same thing, off to the barn, putting the bucket under the horse's nose. Grandma looked on in wonderment. When will this end? Grandpa commanded the horse again, 'Don't drink.' As you can imagine, the horse paid Grandpa no mind, and sure enough he drank the water. Grandpa stood back, looked his prestigious horse in the eye and said, 'That's *three!*' This time he took out his gun and shot the horse dead. Great-Grandma was shocked by this knowing the value of this horse she was horrified, asking 'Why did you shoot the horse?' Great-grandpa looked her in the eye, proclaiming, 'That's *one!*'

"The lesson here is don't ask too many questions as to how and why I do things, especially if you don't know how to do what I do better."

You can lead a horse from water but they still drink.

Joe Cocker

Joe's character was exactly like the horse. You can lead him from water but you couldn't stop him from drinking. Stuff, having toured worldwide and recorded with Joe, became the official Joe Cocker Band. The music and the shows they played together were spectacular; there will never be another "Stingray" album, or another "Catfish" performance. Since I am a Yankee fan, one day I questioned Joe, "Why did you do that song about Catfish Hunter? It feels like you really know him." His answer surprised me. He said, "I don't know, Franco." (For some reason, to this day, he introduces and calls me Franco Zeffirelli, the Italian director.) He didn't know anything about Catfish, only sort of knew he was a Yankee baseball pitcher, but you would never know it. Joe was great. He always sang a song with complete soul and believability, always gave a great performance of a new song or a covered classic, like "Whiter Shade of Pale," which was originally recorded by Procol Harum. Joe covered the songs and he always performed his way, on any song he ever sang, like in the special Beatles song "A Little Help from my Friends," or "Feeling Alright" by Stevie Winwood and Traffic. In fact, Joe never wrote a song himself. He created his own style and put his own spin on songs. He would only sing songs he felt personally connected to and would never do a song if he couldn't relate to the lyrics.

Drunk or sober, he sang the shit out of it. No two days or performances were ever the same. They were all experiences. You always held your breath for his last scream, hoping he would hit the high note. Later on in his career, the audiences didn't care if he could hit those notes or not; they sang the high note for him. It became a thing for the kids to try—if they could hit it with him they had rights to say they sang with Joe Cocker.

In October 1976 everyone in New York was talking about the big event coming up on *Saturday Night Live*. Joe Cocker and Stuff were going to perform together live with the *SNL* cast. Thursday, the day before the rehearsal for the show, we flew Joe into New York, put him in his hotel room at the Essex House, and secured the two adjoining rooms.

I did the same thing for Brian Wilson of the Beach Boys for the event I produced at Caesar's in Atlantic City in 1983. There, too, we locked Brian in his room, with a doctor next door on one side and a nurse in the opposite room, but he still got out.

I suppose I shouldn't have even bothered with Brian, since I'd already learned with Joe that the idea doesn't work. Joe not only got out, he walked all the way to the Statue of Liberty and back in a torrential rainstorm. How did we know he did this? The phone in his room kept ringing from girls that Joe met along the way. He invited them all to the show and he showed up hours later, completely soaked from the rain. We rushed off to rehearsal at Rockefeller Center, NBC Studios. At this point we are live on TV, show time, with host Eric Idle from *Monty Python*. Imagine, Stuff is on stage, Joe is introduced, and he comes out wearing a Stuff T-shirt. Joe starts to sing "A Little Help from My Friends," it's going great, then out of nowhere, John Belushi comes out. Unlike rehearsal, this time he's dressed exactly like Joe, who was very surprised but kept his cool. Belushi's hair was all messed up, sticking up and out. He was holding and sipping from a beer can with a crazed look on his face.

Unbelievably, he looked just like Joe at Woodstock. He even mimicked and exaggerated all of Joe's moves. Even though Joe was taken aback and surprised he kept right on singing as Belushi sang back to him sounding and looking like Joe Cocker. Then Belushi threw himself on the floor in a spastic fit. Joe finished the song and Belushi offered Joe the beer, which he graciously refused.

Strangely enough, even though Joe loved to drink, especially beer, he said no to any offers we had for him to endorse or do a commercial for any alcoholic product, no matter how much the offer. He did not want to promote or condone a drinking lifestyle to kids.

It was during that time that we realized John Belushi could really sing and so could Dan Aykroyd, who also played the harmonica. They both performed regularly at Aykroyd's blues club. The Blues Brothers Band was born, and records and movies were made. One night Belushi asked to borrow some money. I wrote him a personal check for $175. I found out he then used the money to buy drugs. John Belushi died a short time later, after a speedball injection in Los Angeles. Several people I know have died there. I call LA the elephants' burial ground of creativity.

John Adam Belushi. Died: March 5, 1982. Shit. Location of death: Bungalow #3, Chateau Marmont Hotel, Sunset Boulevard, Hollywood, California. Cause of death: accidental drug overdose of the combined injection of cocaine and heroin, called a speedball. Catherine Evelyn Smith, described as a groupie, backup singer and—at the time—drug dealer, was with him in his final hours and, later, in a *National Enquirer* story headlined "I Killed John Belushi," she talked of injecting him with drugs. As the *Times* reported in 1985, Smith told the *Enquirer*: "John supplied the coke. I was Florence Nightingale with the hypodermic." She was known as Judy Silverbags because she kept her drugs and dealt them out of a silver bag. The $175 John borrowed from me that day was to pay her. I still have the canceled check. I had no idea what he was into.

I'm the line between love and hate; when I walk into a room it parts like the Red Sea.

The Rolling Coconut Review: Save the Whales

In early 1977 we were helping to organize one of the first major benefit concert tours in Japan along with Green Peace and the Seas Must Live organizations to celebrate whales and dolphins and to stop their illegal killing in Japan. The Rolling Coconut Review tour was presented by the Dolphin Project, headed by Rick O'Barry and Mark Lavelle. The concert was held at the Harumi Dome in Tokyo, with acts including Jackson Brown, Richie Havens, Stuff, John Sebastian, JD Souther, Fred Neil, Country Joe McDonald, Paul Winter, Terry Reid, Mimi Farina, Danny O'Keefe, Warren Zevon, Eric Anderson, and several other famous Japanese performers. Stuff was the only group paid a fee, the only act paid to do a charity event. That's how they are. How embarrassing. When we told the band they were chosen to do the tour and that it was for charity their answer was, "We are the charity." That was the attitude I had to work with for fifteen years.

I see that same attitude today in those who have been trained to believe they are the charity and always will be no matter how much they're given. They have a sense of you-owe-it-to-me entitlement. I have found this attitude in most musicians I have worked with and that it's more prevalent in today's society than when I was young, when we were taught you had to work hard to make money for your future and especially for your family. My father had two jobs when I was growing up before he finally opened his own business. When it failed he tried it again. I can't help but think this sense of you-owe-it-to-me is partly the fault of our government and many governments worldwide that give you guarantees and money for doing nothing, feeding into the "poor me and my ancestors" mentality. General laziness also has a lot to do with it.

It must be this same attitude that created "a'kees," a saying and belief from my youth in Brooklyn. If you said "a'kees" to someone who just found or bought something, anything at all, you were entitled to half of what they have. I grabbed that ball as fast as I could. I always said "*no* a'kees." Saying that allowed you to block them before they could even have the thought. I think I will produce a T-shirt with a message to the

51 percent of you who don't work or pay taxes, those who expect entitlements and to get half of what I worked hard for and expect me to give what I have. It will read in big letters: No A'kees.

Anyway, this was the same bunch, Stuff, who wanted someone to pay them for their band rehearsals. Imagine wanting to be paid to write and rehearse your songs. "Nothin' for nothin' is nothin'." The word got out on tour that Stuff was paid to perform and it didn't sit well with Jackson Brown. His crew, especially, was pissed. After the tour was over, at a post-celebration press party, their road manager hit Michael Lang in the face with a whipped cream pie. Not one to forget anything, Michael retaliated. On the return trip he hid a cream pie on the plane, and once back at the airport in New York, he smashed the pie in the face of the same crew guy, who was six-foot-six, three hundred pounds, and now more pissed than ever.

As luck would have it I happened to be standing next to him. He thought I did it and started to choke me to death. Charli was trying to pull him off me when Wavy Gravy slid in between us and began licking the cream off his face, defusing his anger. Only Wavy could do that.

CHAPTER 15

Japan the Tour

"**P**aid for It, Didn't I?"

During the Rolling Coconut tour Stuff became very popular and got a lot of press. I had made a few Japanese contacts, both in New York and Japan, and I saw the opportunity to grab the ball and take Stuff back to Japan and the Far East. When I presented my idea to our record company, Warner Brothers Records, to pay for a promotional tour of Japan, they laughed at me, saying there was no market in Japan. I was dreaming, they said. If I wanted to take the band to Japan I would have to pay for it myself. Well, I knew I wasn't dreaming so I put it on without them. I was free to do it all myself, including touring fees, ticket sales, merchandising, advertising fees, sponsorships, endorsements, recordings of live shows and records, and booking all the tour dates. We kept all the money. Charli as usual took care of transportation, accommodations, and domestic disputes.

The immediate scent upon arriving in Japan was jet fuel vapor and car fumes. The airport is two hours away from Tokyo, on a totally congested highway packed with cars, limos, trucks, vans, motorcycles, and taxis. We had six private limos that took us everywhere.

For our first Japan tour, I designed tour jackets for the band, special guests, and crew, a classic fifties baseball jacket retro look with white leather sleeves and blue cloth, adorned with a Stuff logo, New York Yankees emblems, Japanese and American flags, and embroidered personal names. We looked like a gang from Brooklyn, and that we were. The first-class flight was a movie in the making. All thirteen of us took over the entire first-class section on the upper level of a 747. Some of us were playing cards, drinking champagne, smoking cigars and joints in the bathroom. It was so intense the stewardesses were reluctant to come near us. During one card hand, I noticed two members of our crew—my road manager and his brother—were cheating. I don't like cheats. Without exposing them, I clicked into attack, determined to teach them a lesson. By the time the game ended, they'd lost all the money they were to get from the tour. We arrived after a fourteen-hour flight and were greeted on the tarmac by hundreds of people, mostly kids with banners, signs, photos, and every album cover the members of Stuff had ever recorded on, screaming and yelling, waiting to take pictures and get autographs. I was in shock, having no idea for sure except my gut feeling that there was even a market in Japan for Stuff. My dream and inclination came true. I was not just dreaming. The Japanese respect real talent and they truly love Stuff to this day.

The first Stuff press conference was packed with one hundred media outlets. During the interview, Steve Gadd was asked on national live TV and radio how he felt about his first trip to Japan. He looked right in the camera and answered, "Remember Pearl Harbor," a saying used by Americans after the Japanese attack. That set the tone for the tour. Stuff now had a bad boy, tough reputation, luckily backed up by great performances to sold-out venues.

We returned to Japan two times a year for ten years. On the road with Stuff was always an experience. During the second time we toured, I realized the promoters were selling a ton of merchandise—posters, programs, photos. Before our next trip, I negotiated so we would receive a commission on all merchandising sales, and that we must approve in advance what the product would be. I had come to learn you can't trust promoters of venues when it comes to being paid, especially after your final show. They always get tricky with creative bookkeeping. So I developed my own payment plan with advances and guarantees. We were to be paid an advance—one half of our fees plus airfare and all travel expenses—up-front before the first show, then after every three shows we'd receive additional payments, with all payments paid prior to the last two shows.

As an example, after receiving a very small amount from the merchandise sales of the first three shows, I questioned the promoter, Mr. Sato, on why the payment was so small. His answer was sales were not good. So for the next performance, I bought a Polaroid camera and took pictures. I showed him at least 75 percent of the audience holding posters, photos, and programs. Trying to swindle me, he said not to be fooled by this. In Japan, he went on, people don't have money, so many of them buy the used merchandise from the people who sell it from the last shows. What an ingenious answer. But I did not buy it.

He then gave me a few more bucks to shut me up. It didn't. Days later we were in Kyoto, shopping at a small shop, when I noticed Stuff merchandise I hadn't approved or ever seen before. I purchased a few things and brought them to my hotel room as evidence.

At the venue, I confronted Mr. Sato, who adamantly denied my accusations and refused my demands for more money, no matter how I threatened him.

"Okay," I answered. "Then Stuff won't go on and I will cancel the last three shows." I knew we'd been paid for them in advance, and of course the band couldn't care less about skipping some shows. He threatened me back, saying prove it, and agreeing to go to my hotel to see the product, hoping to bluff me out. I held a meeting with the band and crew to explain what was going on, instructing them not to go on stage until I got back and gave the OK. They loved the drama. On the way to the hotel Sato and I almost came to blows. He fought me all the way to my room, saying the band must play now or the crowd will riot because the trains would stop after eleven o'clock and they will be unable to get home. He was relentless, calling me crazy and telling me I'd be held liable. I showed him my evidence, to which he coolly replied, "Oh, these." I've learned the Japanese will go to the end no matter what the consequences in order to save face.

This guy was like others I have come across who will go all the way, risking everything, and, as the old saying goes, cutting their nose off to spite their face. He finally agreed to pay me more at the end of the shows, but I wasn't going for that. "No," I replied, "Let's go to the box office now. I'll take yen from sales." He had no choice. When we got there, I began to fill a large bag with handfuls of yen I took from the cash registers, not knowing or counting how much, just stuffing it in until I couldn't put any more in the bag. I ran out and as I left the room to head down the hall to the backstage area, I couldn't believe my ears. I heard the band playing. I began running, yen falling out of the bag, and Sato was chasing me to get it back.

By the time I got backstage and locked the door behind me the band and crew were there for the intermission break. I went berserk. "What the fuck? Why are you playing? I told you not to until I got back." They were surprised and explained our road manager said I called to say it was "OK to go on." I hadn't called anyone. Chris the road manager explained how he was threatened with the same things Sato said to me and he decided to have the band play. "Really, you decided? Do you have the money to pay the band? I don't think so. By the way, you owe me money from the card game you were cheating at." I fired and sent home the whole crew and finished the tour myself with Charli's help. Stuff was impressed and rarely questioned me again.

In Charli's Words

Once, during our several weeks in Japan, the Japanese promoters and Warner Brothers/Pioneer Records invited all of us to a lavish banquet dinner. By this time, after several successful tours, Stuff in Japan seemed as popular and as famous as the Beatles in the United States. Wherever we went there were hundreds of people waiting to greet the band with flowers, signs, records, and photographs, all wanting autographs. The band had girls everywhere, like sailors in every port, in addition to their wives.

The band members demanded private limos everywhere, and refused to share them even among themselves in order to invite the girls they picked up. Six or seven limos, each costing around $200 an hour, was a lot of money in 1978 Japan.

On this night there were a lot of people in the beautiful and classy restaurant waiting for the band to arrive. Many sat around a fifty-foot table decorated with bouquets of flowers, crystal, and hand-painted Japanese dishes, some filled with huge platters of sushi and rare cuts of sashimi. It was a truly beautiful banquet. And then the band arrived with what looked like several hookers, except this band went for the heavy-set, bowlegged girls of Japan. I swear, somehow they found the worst girls in the country. Although Eric Gale did marry a very nice educated young girl, Myoko, who never got in the way like other hip-hugging members' wives and girlfriends.

The promoters were not used to a band like Stuff. One of the executives politely said to Frank, referring to the girls, "Frank, for this we need limos? These are not nice girls," to which Frank answered, "These are not nice boys."

Eric looked at a strange-looking piece of sushi served to him and said "Frank, what is this?" Frank answered, jokingly, "Scalp." Eric said, "Will it get me high?" Frank said yes and Eric ate it. These guys were like no one I have ever known.

We traveled first class all over Japan by air, bus, and bullet train. It was spectacular. Whenever we would arrive at a hotel (usually four star), the band went directly to their rooms and never left, ordering room service and watching American basketball and Sumo wrestling. No sightseeing apart from the few minutes spent outside before arriving to the venue. They never rehearsed, never spoke about music, they just went on and played. They were naturals, really great musicians who could play anything. The Japanese bands and famous musicians tried to copy them but they never could. They all acted like children around Stuff, standing in awe.

The Japanese knew they were among great talent and had the utmost respect for Stuff, and deservedly so. I know Richard Tee was a Julliard student, a true musical genius. Any time you heard him, you could recognize his distinct sound. You just knew it was him. The same was true for all the members of Stuff. Steve Gadd, for instance, was the most amazing drummer of all time, with no practicing. They just knew what to do. Jazz, rock, rhythm and blues, pop. It just came out of them. Cornell Dupree and Eric Gale were untouchable on guitar. They had the respect of all musicians anywhere in the world. If I said I was touring with the band everyone would say I was so lucky, and I was. I lived a charmed life, handed to me by Frank. Other women would have done anything to be among these guys touring the world. At the time I never fully appreciated what was going on, but I do now.

At one point in Hiroshima the press was interviewing Steve Gadd, who was a little out of it. The reporter was missing his arm, and Steve said, "Where's your arm?" I will never forget that.

Later that day, Gordon, Frank, and I visited the bombsite of Hiroshima. It was quite a place.

As far as the eye could see it was flat. They say there were seven rivers there before the atom bomb fell. Even today people walk around with masks on their faces praying.

As I said before, these were not nice guys. Frank had tour jackets made for the entire band and crew with American Flags on the front and on the back a Japanese flag, which looked like a target with its *red circle. Gordon stopped directly on the spot they say the bomb hit and took a drink from a water fountain. Frank said, "What are you, crazy? That's where the bomb landed." Gordon freaked out and he would not stop spitting all day.*

China

Charli and I took a brief vacation from Japan and left Stuff on their own. Landing in China in the middle of the night was spooky. It was dark and looked like every Charlie Chan movie coming to life. The immediate sense I got when arriving to Hong Kong was the density. *Wow*, I remember thinking, *look at all these buildings and houses stuck together, just filled with people.* We were excited to be there even though it was three or four in the morning. Charli and I decided to leave the Excelsior Hotel and go for a walk to check things out. Once on the dark streets, we realized you could not simply make a left and walk a few blocks to leave Chinatown and end up in Little Italy like you could in New York. No matter where you turn, you see what seems like millions of Chinese people, laundry hanging everywhere, accompanied by the pervading smell of fish, salt water, seaweed, garbage, cats, and dogs. It's all Chinatown. No matter how far you walk you can never get out of Chinatown.

A few days later we took a boat trip up the river to Aberdeen, a large floating city where all the people live on the water in boats and never go on land. Some inhabitants have never been on dry land and believe something really bad will happen if they do. The entire city is a giant web of small and large fishing and houseboats, barges, and walkways, with bamboo bridges connecting the thousands of floating boats that include a very large restaurant and shopping markets that sell everything you could imagine, all on the water.

Charli and I kid about that first night walking around Hong Kong every time we go to New York's Chinatown.

Moreton Binn, John Revson, Eddie Gilbert

As I have said before and will say again, I'm lucky to have had the same phone number for over thirty years. Another ball was on the line, this time from my old advertising associate Moreton Binn, the Barter Baron. He invited me to the ballet at Lincoln Center in April 1977. That night he also invited and introduced me to John Revson, heir apparent to Charles Revson of Revlon Cosmetics. I must say I was impressed with who John was. He and I became friends instantly, having something in common: getting high. John invited Charli and me to spend July 4 weekend at his house. We took a limousine to New Bedford, Connecticut. The long, winding driveway was perfectly manicured, with huge apple and pear trees and a greenhouse. John's gardener once worked in China for the Chinese Emperor, Chiang Kai-Shek. From the terrace at "North View" you could see several states. All in all, the estate was magnificent.

At the time, Revson's beard and long hair were fairly new to him, as he had always had a very straight collegiate look. Now he styled himself a symbol of change and development after the death of his father. On several occasions we would meet at his office or his apartment on Fifth Avenue, and then go out for dinner. The young heir was eventually fired from Revlon. Apparently his newfound freedom and work ethic didn't conform to their plans.

The first time Charli and I arrived at the North View Estate, white-gloved servants escorted us to the breakfast dining room and served us coffee and biscuits. Then John came down the winding stairs, looking and acting strange in this environment, sort of playing a part. This was much different than sitting on our living room floor getting high. I still have an audio tape recording of a spaced-out Revson reciting his acceptance speech for when, as he prophesied, he would become mayor of New York.

He always seemed to be on fire, running to play tennis and then running from tennis to somewhere else, disappearing and reappearing, always in a huff.

Weekends at North View were interesting. Everyone did whatever they wanted. John took absolutely no responsibility for anyone. He had a style that made everyone feel at home. He had several personalities and always presented different versions of himself, so you were never quite sure who you were talking to. In spite of that fact, Charli and I thought and still think he was a great guy; he was lots of fun, enjoyed life, and very generous.

One weekend during one of our rages we decided to take apart the engine of one of the many vintage cars he owned. There we were in the middle of the driveway disassembling the entire engine piece by piece and placing them in no particular order on the ground. After several hours houseguests began coming by, wondering what the hell we were doing. We didn't know either, but the one thing we did know was that we had no clue how to put it back together. We ended up just leaving the parts scattered around, and the last image I have is of the white-gloved servants picking up the parts from the driveway and gently putting them randomly back under the hood.

On another occasion, while sitting far away from the pool, wearing a jacket in ninety-degree weather, I was working on the treatment for the Broadway musical Neville and I were writing, "The Pink Teacup." I was sitting in protest of Revson's lie: he promised that if Charli and I would come for the weekend he would not invite other guests. The place was full of people, though—young, old, kids. Then a short, stocky, middle-aged mustachioed man dressed in a white short tennis outfit with knee high socks and dark sunglasses, swinging a tennis racket, walked over and sat next to me.

"Hi, what are you doing?" he asked. "Sitting alone with your jacket on?" I answered flippantly, "Writing a hit Broadway show!"

I was prepared for that question and the one to follow. I don't do so well at parties or among crowds of strangers who ask a million questions and force me into small talk conversations. "Where are you from, what do you do?" I'm not good at hiding my true feelings, especially when drawn into dialogue about politics, philosophy, art, or religion, but other than those issues I have nothing to else to say, so I generally don't start conversations. It keeps me out of trouble. And I've never been good at staying in touch with people. Some people work their phone book, but once I finish a project like a painting I'm on to the next. I'm trying to get better at it.

I'm also not a social networker, even though I'm well aware in today's world it's expected and I don't recommend or condone what I do. Today you must use all the tools available to succeed. I do look at my social networking sites just to spy on others and see what they have to say or what they are up to but I don't Tweet or Facebook. When I'm asked about it, I say I have "no face page." It is a similar answer I give when asked what sign I am. I usually answer with "I'm a *stop sign*," although sometimes I make one up just to hear them say something silly like I knew you were a Cancer. Actually I'm a triple Scorpio and on the rare occasions I tell the truth it often scares the shit out of them.

I don't exactly know what my problem is and I'm not saying anyone should have my attitude or react the way I do to people, but I suppose I generally just don't like them. Over the years of meeting a variety of characters it's mostly been incompetent bullshitters who don't have what they say they have or can't do what they say they can. So I have become somewhat tainted, mainly because I am the opposite—looking back at what I have accomplished I can say I am what I say I am and do what I say I can do. Now that I think about it, my attitude must have something to do with my artist mentality—I don't feel a sense of entitlement and I don't like to beg for candy, sex, or money. I guess when it comes to most people, you can say I drop the ball. But luckily some bounce back later.

Back to the guy at the pool's next question: "Do you play tennis? What's your name?"

Aha. I was ready. I whipped out from under my
trophy that was tennis pro John Newcomb's. I ne
working on an ad campaign for his tennis school in

"I'm Ilie Nastase," I said.

He smiled and seemed entertained by my answer. ....
Your hit Broadway show."

He seemed genuinely interested so I told him the plot. After listening
to my story he asked, "What is your Yellow Brick Road?" I didn't know
what the hell that meant so I made something up until he cut me off.

"No, what is it that winds through the story that guides you to the
end, holds it together, and delivers the moral of the story? Think about
it, and when you figure it out come by my office."

I had no idea who he was, so I asked John. It turns out he happened
to be Emanuel (Manny) Asenberg, who had just produced *A Chorus Line*
and *The Wiz* and he was about to produce *Ain't Misbehavin'*.

The next day, having learned my lesson, I tried to be friendlier, realizing now there might be some balls in the air here. We were having a
poolside breakfast, sitting at a table with a man who had a large scar on
his chest from open-heart surgery. I had never seen that before and now
today, thirty-five years later, I have the same scar. He tried to cover it
with gold chains and a giant mezuzah during the conversation. Max, as I
believe he was named, described one of the worst deals he was involved
in, a chain of department stores in chapter 11. He wanted them closed in
order to get back the real estate, which had become more valuable than
the 150 stores' total inventory.

"I couldn't stop them," he said. "I chased these guys all over the
country. They kept turning the Arlan's stores around. Cost me millions
. . ."

At that point John interjected, "Hey Frank, wasn't that you?"

I sank in my chair. Max looked like he was having another heart
attack. "You're Frank Yandolino?" He then said, "Listen Frank, I'm

t to do the same thing with the Savarin Coffee chain. This time I'm
onna hire you to keep you away and make sure you don't fuck that up."
We all laughed. I wondered if he meant it.

Soon after, I was in John's office, where he introduced me to his
partner. I had no idea that he was the same seemingly nice little man
I had once met at John's pool wearing a cowboy hat to cover his bald
head. It was the notorious Edward M. Gilbert, John's partner in crime.
Eddie was a known crook who had embezzled millions of dollars from
investors via fraudulent stock manipulations at Conrac Corporation.
He'd gone to jail for two years, made a deal to pay back a few bucks to
investors, and kept millions for himself stashed in the Cayman Islands. I
bought into their hype and their job offer to work at their failing companies and loaned John $100,000. I never liked the idea of putting Eddie's
name on the loan agreement, instead of it being a personal loan to John.
But I thought, *How could I go wrong, here?* He is the heir to Revlon, after
all, and he owns a multimillion-dollar mansion and Park Avenue condo.
Boy was I naïve. John had told me he needed the money personally and
would pay it back in a couple of months, but it ended up being used
for his and Eddie's TV production company, Mobile Video Systems
(MVS). This was a sign John could not be trusted. As part of a pay-
back arrangement I accepted a job as marketing director for their three
ski resorts in Aspen, Colorado, and their MVS facility in Los Angeles.
Charli, Bruno, and I temporarily moved to Beverly Hills, where I drove
a convertible sports car.

As a director of the company, I had the opportunity to purchase a one-
of-a-kind piece of mobile editing equipment called the Squeeze Zoom.
I made a deal to purchase it for $90,000 and built in a clause restricting
the company from selling another one for nine months. Thanks to that
move, we got a slew of TV projects. We produced the Winter Olympics,
Grammy Awards, Tony Awards, various HBO and Showtime TV spe-
cials, and early rock videos. Just like with Guccione, though, my success

didn't matter to Eddie; he had a big ego problem. One day he called me into his office.

"You are fired," he said. "I can't take any more. No one knows who I am. I own this place. All the restaurants know you, not me; you get all the press, not me."

"Are you kidding?" I shot back. "I don't get it. Isn't that my job? If not, let's switch. You be me, I'll be you." He fired me anyway, that little five-foot short bald cowboy-hatted shit. With the help of my father and his convincing way of explaining why it would be a good idea to pay me, I did eventually get my money back. I was happy to hear their business folded soon after. I never saw Eddie or John again and have no idea what became of them. Again the lesson was reinforced that sometimes you may have to placate your employer and let him be king. Or at least let him think he is.

In Charli's Words

John Revson was the heir to the Revlon cosmetic dynasty. He had a certain charisma about him. His father, Charles Revson, started the business from his basement. John's mother came over to America from Europe without a passport, on a private yacht, and was considered to be one of the most beautiful women in the world. John was married in his early twenties to Ricki, whose parents owned Restaurant Associates and were jet setters at Hippopotamus and other discos. John and Ricki grew up very spoiled and their families hated each other. Charles Revson once caused a scene at the Four Seasons, which Ricki's family owned, annoyed when he did not get a discount. John and Ricki had one child, a daughter, Jill.

Their marriage didn't last. Ricki, who had emotional problems, took Jill to Las Vegas and lived with one of the owners of the hotel. Sadly when Jill was five, Ricki died, supposedly in the bathtub. Why do so many people die in bathtubs? Linda Kornfeld, Whitney Houston, Surratt. I'm not sure.

I thought Jill really needed a mother, but that seemed to scare her the most. Jill felt threatened by any woman that got between her and her father. Having lost her mother already, she was afraid she would lose her father as well. It's a terrible fear for an eleven-year-old girl to deal with.

That winter John had fallen in love with his new girlfriend, Valerie, after his failed affair with actress Jennifer O'Neal. Jill stopped eating, just as her mother did. It developed into hepatitis. On one occasion John was away with Valerie, leaving Jill with the nanny and maids. I liked that sweet little girl so I called her to see how she was doing, and she sounded so sick I ran over to their apartment on Park Avenue and made her chicken soup. I didn't realize at the time she wasn't eating because it was her way of getting back at her father. She must have been very lonely because John seems to always be on fire taking care of himself.

Jill was curious to hear the music from our musical, "The Pink Tea Cup," which Frank described as a totally different type of musical, one that Broadway had never seen before. Eleven-year-old Jill's blunt response was dead on.

"Is that good or bad?"

We had to step back and think. I never forgot that innocent comment. I ask that question many times in analyzing opportunities.

The Revsons were a perfect example of what you see is not always what you get. They appeared to be a wealthy, deep-rooted, loving family— the American dream, coming to this country with nothing and building an empire. As in most American dreams it is the founder, in this case the father, who builds the dream, and usually their kids screw it up. Or maybe the dreams of the parents just aren't the dreams of their children.

CHAPTER 16

Mode International

Shortly after the Riviera festival, in 1977, Ken Partiss from Atlantis fame invested in an avant-garde, hard-core French fashion magazine, *Mode International*. His plan was to bring it to America for distribution and hire me as marketing art director. Charli and I met with Ken in New York and he showed us the latest issue. At that time *Mode* was a great-looking, extremely innovative black-and-white publication without any color pages at all except for the provocative cover. Gunner Larsen, Ken's partner, was the original creator, owner, editor, publisher, and chief photographer. Gunner was great at all jobs, especially his choice of models and the clothes or lack thereof he posed them in. He would concoct combinations of designer clothes with bizarre accessories like wool embroidered leg warmers, jeweled jean vests, military gear, gas masks, and combat boots, along with waffled and braided hair, eye and face makeup with glitter and painted colors you'd never seen before, and plenty of exposed breasts. This was coupled with his distinct style of erotic photography: positioning extremely sexy, provocative, vulnerable women in unlikely positions. I thought Charli would take issue with this project, what with the models, Paris, and Ken, but as usual she didn't show any concern and she welcomed my next opportunity to do what I wanted and sent me back to Paris.

Arriving in Paris this time around was a bit more flamboyant than when I came for the Riviera festival. I was now living in a large, three-bedroom penthouse apartment on the Champs Élysées, with at least three models at a time. I would go out to clubs like Le Preve at two in the morning and stay out till dawn. Life was great. I designed the Cat Girl Campaign to promote the new look of the magazine and announce its arrival. I rented eight giant billboards on both sides of the Champs Élysées and several newsstands and magazine street kiosks all over Paris. The billboards had a large photo of the Cat Girl biting the magazine with a block of type in French that read "Mode International—The Fashion That Bites The Fashion. Our Magazine is 182 pages and now in color and only 80 francs." Then in bold letters, "If You Don't Like Our New Magazine stick your fish in it."

The campaign was a success. Everyone was talking about it. You could not help but notice the Cat Girl, whose image was everywhere. After two weeks the first posters were replaced with a new poster, just a color photo depicting a dead fish on a plate wrapped in a *Vogue* magazine. No copy, just that image. That visual told the story and I won a French Art Directors Award for that campaign.

Charli and Ann Partiss, Ken's wife, decided to surprise Ken and me by coming to Paris for a visit. The girls moved in to our apartment on the Champs Élysées. After a week or so in that environment, surrounded by the Paris nightlife and sexy models, I began to worry about Charli and how she felt about all this. I was hoping she realized there was nothing I would ever do to embarrass her or put her in an awkward position or, more importantly, jeopardize our relationship and the love we have. I couldn't help but wonder, though, if doubt were creeping? Are the other women taking their toll on her? I wanted her to know that down deep I would never let anyone replace her. She sits on the throne and wears the crown. Charli doesn't have to prove her position to other women; they feel it from both of us. She is a proud and confident woman, but still I knew it was key that I send her a message. That no one could ever take her place. I always try to include her in whatever I do and whomever I meet and make sure she doesn't feel left out. Dali taught me that. Always invite her, he said, and then she will pick and choose when and where to go, knowing she doesn't have to go to protect her position.

In Charli's Words

Ann Partiss and I decided to go to Paris, where Frank was designing Ken's new project, a magazine called Mode International. *We arrived and surprised Ken and Frank at the* Mode *office. I think I was more surprised than anyone. What a sight! Frank was spending all of his time with French and European models, probably the most beautiful women in the world. Even today, thirty-five years later, if you look at the photographs in the magazine you would say they are the most innovative pieces of art you have ever seen. I must say I could not blame Frank and I told him so. I spent my days in Paris with Ann shopping, sightseeing, eating and drinking wine in fabulous French bistros, and we all stayed at Frank's magnificent apartment near the Eiffel Tower.*

Kidnapped

At that time, when I was entrenched in the magazine, word on the street was the French security company from the Riviera festival believed they had still not been paid. Someone must have told someone that a Yandolino had made reservations to leave France, and, thinking it was me and not Charli who was leaving, they took action.

Throughout France, especially in Paris, underground gangs were prevalent. Groups of unemployed men who banded together formed different factions of terrorism, with ideologies based on fear and power. One evening shortly before Charli was scheduled to leave, at about five, several men in leather jackets broke into my office at *Mode* on Rue St Anne. They kicked everyone out and held my secretary out the window, threatening to throw her out of the building. They were serious. One guy, Claude, put a gun to my back, demanding $7,000 cash. They forced me into a car and took me to our apartment. When we arrived there were more of them guarding the lobby, elevator, and roof.

The guy holding on to me kept jabbing me in the head with his gun as we headed up to our floor. I was on edge but knew I had to stay cool, especially after I called Ray Paret and Michael in New York, my partners in the festival, who didn't believe that the French mafia was holding us hostage for ransom. I made an arrangement with Claude that they would go away if I paid them $5,000 dollars, and then called Michael and Ray again. They still didn't believe me. I was worried about the girls and so enraged inside I could kill. I was losing it. They put Ann Partiss, who was with us at the time, in one bedroom and forced Charli into a small maid's room bathroom. We were still negotiating when the doorbell rang. I opened the door a little and saw more men in leather jackets with guns drawn.

"We are looking for Frank Yandolino."

I freaked, saying, "That's not my name. You have the wrong apartment. He lives across the hall." I slammed the door, furious, then turned to the guys in the room.

"I thought you said if I paid you, you would protect me and guarantee that no one else would bother us." They looked around the room, seemingly more confused than me.

Suddenly the door was pushed open and about ten guys rushed in. "I'm inspector so-and-so of the French Shandon," one of them said. It was all a blank to me at that point. Charli, it turns out, had crept under the vanity in the bathroom and telephoned Leon Albert Gertner, the producer of the festival film and a very powerful man in Paris. During World War II, he was a leader in the underground

French Jewish resistance. Charli had explained to him what was going on. Gertner wanted to know who the men were in order to determine what political faction they belonged to before he reached out for help, not wanting to call the wrong group, thereby avoiding the possibility that they may be in cahoots with our captors. Everyone was speaking French and very confused, when in walked Gertner and his two German Shepherds. The kidnappers were arrested and we were freed. Gertner took us to his Greek friend's restaurant to celebrate a very terrifying experience that could have gotten much worse.

Several days later back in the *Mode* office something else happened I will never forget. After witnessing what I do best and knowing how much I enjoy creating, Charli again let this bird be free in spite of the fact I was surrounded by beautiful women, she looked around, then looked in my eyes, and simply said something not many women could say.

"I don't blame you." I was speechless.

Two days later Charli went back to New York. I stayed a few weeks more. Her words continued to resonate in my head. "I don't blame you." "I don't blame you." How stupid could I be? After finding Charli, my Afghan woman, I couldn't jeopardize this. I was out there like a rocket ship exploring galaxies far away from her, and I needed to come back down to earth.

Charli knows what and who I am, and how I do things. She goes with the flow and more importantly knows I am there for her despite my little escapades, always protecting her. She truly is the gatekeeper. In Paris I was a free bird, but after Charli left and I couldn't forget what she said, I realized my time was up. I knew it was time to come back to my cage. So I flew back to her and to New York where I belong.

In Charli's Words

After the Riviera Festival, the security guards who were not totally paid, according to them, were angry and demanding more money.

Frank explained to them that his partners who went back to New York, Michael Lang and Ray Paret, would be giving them their money soon and he had no way of paying them at this time. They were very aggressive, watching Frank and following him everywhere. Well I had had enough of the whole thing; first models, now French terrorists. I wanted to go home so I booked a flight, and the security guards somehow found out that a Yandolino was flying to New York. They obviously panicked, thinking they would never get their money, so they went to the Mode office with guns and proceeded to hold Frank's secretary out the window, upside down by her feet. Frank told them he was not leaving and that they would be paid. He called Michael and Ray, saying the security guards want their money now, that it's an emergency, but they just started laughing. Later they explained their actions with the excuse they thought Frank was making up the story to get money to stay in Paris. There were several men with guns, seemingly desperate men. They brought Frank to the apartment where I was staying with Ann, and barged in, all of these crazed men with guns yelling threats. They put me in a small room and I was terrified.

Hiding under the counter, I found a phone under the table and telephoned our producer of the Riviera Festival. "Monsieur Gertner," I whispered. "You must help us. We are being held in the apartment by these gunmen." He said, "Don't worry. I got the Nazis out of France once before and I will come and save you."

No one knew I made this phone call, not even Frank, who was in the living room with a gun held to his head. A little later, the doorbell rang and they told Frank to answer the door. He did, and in rushed a dozen men with German Shepherd dogs and more men with guns. Frank did not realize it was Monsieur Gertner and his group of men. There was a fight, the men pushed the mafia security out of the apartment, and it was finally over. A few days later, I went back to New York and Bruno.

The Real Bert Padell

After about a year of turmoil over the Riviera and *Mode* episodes, Just Sunshine Productions broke up and left our office on 61st Street. Ray Paret, Michael, and I divided up our clients and projects and went our separate ways. I was working from home; Michael, his two children, and his wife, Ann, took a place on the other side of our building on 81st Street; and Ray went back to Connecticut and eventually to LA. Before I went on to Atlanta I first met Bert Padell in 1973 at his office on Park Avenue. Bert later became an accountant for Alicia Keys, Puff Daddy, Prince, several New York Yankees, Mike Tyson, and more than one hundred other acts.

In 1979 I rejoined Michael, working out of an office at Bert Padell's half-a-city-block-long complex at 1775 Broadway on the seventh floor. Aside from about one hundred of Bert's employees, half of the space was occupied by some of his choice clients: other companies and managers like Gary Kurfis, Shep Gordon, Sam Lederman, The Talking Heads, Meat Loaf, The J. Geils Band, Luther Vandross, The B52s, Ben Vereen, Alice Cooper, Crush Records, Run DMC, Peter Frampton, Blondie, Earl "The Pearl" Monroe, and others who came and went. The office was the place to be, especially at every Christmas party. Bert would get dressed up as Santa Claus and hand out gifts to everyone and their kids. I am still working with Bert thirty-seven years later. Michael has since moved on. All I had to do on any given day at the office was answer the phone and just sit and wait for a ball to arrive. Being in the center of the entertainment business, eventually something would happen or someone pop in.

This was true at any one of Bert's offices, including later at 156 West 56th Street: a sprawling, two-floor complex that had a huge reception area equipped with a piano, pool table, spiral staircase, giant fish tanks, a full-service restaurant on the second floor, and walls filled with hundreds of platinum and gold records. Nothing was more impressive than a New York Yankees and sports museum conference room equipped with a twenty-six-foot conference table, adjacent music room, and projection screen, with every wall and corner filled with signed memorabilia. Other areas of the office were adorned with life-sized mannequins of Madonna, Prince, and Alicia Keys.

Bert was and still is a terrible closer and follow-upper, and I would tell him all the time that he needed a manager. He is a funny guy and in many ways quite the opposite of me. Bert waits for the ball to come to him and fall in his glove. Rarely will he go after it or grab it on the run. As a professionally trained ballplayer you are taught to charge the ball. With his longtime experience with the Yankees, you would think he would do that in his business as well, but he is an example of someone humble to the point that he feels he doesn't need contracts with his clients. In fact, he constantly boasts that it allows him to leave if he decides not to represent someone anymore. I tried that, but it doesn't work for me; my experience tells me that in such an arrangement the client feels they can leave you when they want to, especially if they owe you money. That happens to Bert most of the time, and over the last fifty-plus years, clients have owed him millions.

Woodstock '79

Bert Padell was hired to be our accountant and bookkeeper for a tour we were planning, billed as the Woodstock in Europe '79 Tour. No Artie at this one. After Linda's death he was gone emotionally and physically. Michael booked Woodstock '69 artists and their bands, including Joe Cocker, Richie Havens, Country Joe McDonald, and Arlo Guthrie. The traveling show was presented throughout Europe. Michael just knows how to do it. He booked rooms in The Haag, Netherlands, at the Kurhaus Hotel, a magnificent complex on the beach right on the North Sea. In the early 1900s the hotel was considered a getaway destination for the rich and famous, the Coney

Island playground of Europe. The sprawling, just-renovated building had a round lobby surrounded by a five-star restaurant with three-story-high domed ceilings and stained-glass windows that reflected multi-colored rays of light. The waiters were dressed in gold-buttoned epaulet uniforms and white gloves. The whole thing was dazzling.

Whenever I travel I don't go to the bathroom for days, sometimes many days, and it became a standing joke on the tour. Someone would always say "Did you go yet?" One morning standing in the lobby, a guy dressed in a black trench coat and hat right out of an espionage movie approached me. He very cautiously looked all around, seemingly embarrassed. Then in a thick Nordic accent, "Mr. Yandolino, I have something for you." He reached into his coat and took out a plastic bag filled with white powder. Thinking it was coke, I grabbed the bag and ran off to my room, stuck a tablespoon in the bag and shoved it up my nose. I immediately shit my brains out. It turned out to be baby laxative. Someone thought I needed it.

On another occasion, while waiting to be seated in the restaurant, Charli and I noticed Joe and BJ Wilson, who was the drummer for the group Procol Harum, sitting and talking across the dining room against the far window. Then out of nowhere, BJ sank in his seat, head back and cigarette in hand, while Joe, across from him, fell over face forward with his head now gurgling and drowning in his soup. Immediately six or seven waiters picked them up in their chairs and table, moving them out of the room, never skipping a beat. I will never forget that sight.

Backstage at an open-air amphitheater somewhere in the boondocks of Germany, during rehearsal, the producer of the show approached Joe and took out a folded piece of aluminum foil. He asked Joe if he wanted a hit, who looked at me and Michael and said, "What do you say, Franco?" I answered "I don't think so." BJ joined in with a "What about me? Just a little hit," so I agreed they could take just a little hit. Back in the car, heading to our hotel, Joe looked at me with a funny look in his eye. "It's getting a little bricky in here," he said. I thought it was some sort of English slang for something. The only bricks I saw were the bricks on the old buildings lining the streets. Then I realized it wasn't coke he took a hit of, but LSD. He and BJ were tripping their brains out, and that trip carried on into the show while on stage with his band. He began to mix and sing all his songs together as one. The band walked off, the kids threw bottles on the stage, and we ran for our lives.

The next day Michael Lang, Joe Cocker, Charli, and I were flying over Belgravia in a small plane on our way to do a radio interview for our shows in West and East Berlin. While looking out the window of the small plane, I couldn't help but notice the sense of nothing down there. We were flying so low, barely above the trees, but there were no people in sight. Everything was all brown, just a lot of dirt with nothing on it.

I asked one of the people who were guiding us through this interview, "Where are all the people?"

"Inside," he answered.

"What are they doing?"

"Waiting."

"What do they do?" I asked.

"They grow potatoes," he answered. "Except this year, because of the bad weather there are no potatoes, so they stay inside and wait."

"For potatoes?"

He shrugged his shoulders and looked at me as if to say, "So what's wrong with that?"

Some cultures go out of their way to not grab the ball, like those in the world who are starving, who live by the sea but don't fish. Or others who cut down all the trees to use as fuel and never plant new ones.

This reminds me of a story. Peter Saile and I were having lunch with our attorney, Andreas Khoelar, in Berlin, when the subject of him leaving for a month to go to his farm came up. "The farm? Where's the farm? I asked.

"It's in Namibia, South Africa," Andreas answered. "Near the coast. Several hundred acres of prime jungle and grazing land on which we have a small modest farmhouse made out of an adobe-type brick and mortar. The house is surrounded by a two-foot fence to help deter the animals; it's full of animals of all sorts, and trees and vegetation." As he explained, it sounded like a truly beautiful place. He continued to say that he employs local natives who patrol and protect this property from poachers and thieves. He told us he goes down there with his wife and his son, and mentioned that his farm and his neighbor's farms are miles apart. Then came the mind blower. When I asked what's in between the farms, I assumed he would say barren wasteland, which he affirmed. But when I asked why that was, his answer didn't exactly match my expectations.

"Because the natives ate all the animals," he said, "and cut down all the trees to cook them. Now they try to get to my animals on my land, so I hire the armed patrol guards to protect my property." He then concluded that in most cases people are paid with meat. It's like a trust barter system. In extreme cases you will see natives missing limbs; you may think *How sad. A lion must have eaten it.* Wrong. I was informed most of those people sold whatever body part was missing.

The next day we did our show in West Berlin and afterward we were invited to go over to East Berlin. Michael had put out the idea to East Berlin officials to do a show there. I will never forget the site, arriving at Check Point Charlie, crossing over. It was a scary feeling. You got the sense that you were surrounded by the enemy and we were.

We left Berlin and flew to Milan, Italy, where I felt much better being around my ancestors. Then we all traveled in buses to Bologna and did a show. Several days later we arrived in Florence, staying at the classically decorated Hotel Cavour, the oldest hotel in the city. Whatever hotel we stayed at didn't matter. It was always the same: meetings all night, discussing the show with the production people, the promoters, members of the band. Sometimes Charli would be off with Joe, keeping him out of trouble. Other restaurant guests would send over several bottles of wine and booze to Joe's table even when he was just eating dinner. Every night he, BJ, and Charli would drink two or three bottles and there'd be three or four more left at his hotel room door. I was always at some production meeting putting out the next fire.

One particular night, I left Charli, Joe, and BJ having dinner in the restaurant. They were already gone dead drunk, laughing, singing, and eating. After my production meeting ended at about four in the morning, I went looking for Joe, who was nowhere to be found. I gave up and went to my room to crash. Wouldn't you know, Charli had double-locked the inside double door. This European safety device sucks; you cannot get in unless the person in the room who locked it opens it. I had exposed one major problem here: you can't unlock it if you're sleeping.

So I rang the bell a lot, called her on the room phone and delivered many long loud knocks on the door. After several more bangs on the door, the hotel manager and several security and other help butted in, telling me to stop causing a scene and demanding my identification as I tried to explain the situation. They insisted I stop; other guests were sleeping, they said. I was getting scared and paranoid, beginning to wonder whether Charli was even in there, and if she was all right. Then I kicked and banged and yelled.

"*Charli! Charli, unlock . . . open the door! Let me in Charli! Open the fucking door!*" I kicked the door down. By now the police were on the scene and as I entered the room there was Charli, out cold, sprawled across the bed. She never even woke up.

In Charli's Words
Frank, Michael, Ann, and myself, along with a busload of rock stars from the original Woodstock festival, were traveling through Europe.

When we were in Florence, Italy, we were staying at the oldest hotel in the city. Frank was busy and he asked me to stay with Joe Cocker until he got back from this meeting. I guess you could say one of my jobs was in a sense to babysit Joe. So, one night Joe and I went to a pizza place and had some pizza. The owner came over, offering us some wine that had just been made in the vineyards of Florence. Joe said no, he only wanted a beer, but I said, "Okay, thank you" and I must say it was warm, delicious wine. I must have been really thirsty, and I really enjoyed it so I drank and drank. Well, who would believe that Joe Cocker, who we were always worried about, always having to make sure he was safe and didn't get drunk or anything, even though producers and promoters were always trying to get him crazy so he would behave like the original Woodstock festival Joe, would switch roles with me. What people don't realize is that Joe's seemingly drunk motions and actions at Woodstock during his performance had nothing to do with the effects of alcohol.

His spastic performance in reality was just his natural way of expressing his emotions, although on other occasions there were times he was performing dead drunk as well.

Anyway, after drinking that delicious wine like grape juice, Joe Cocker had to babysit me. He carried me upstairs—imagine that—brought me into my room, and dropped me on the bed. I don't remember anything, but later on that night, Frank apparently came up to the room, knocked on the door, couldn't get in, knocked again, and again, and since the room was small he wondered why I was not answering, and eventually he brought the concierge up with the police and then he broke down the door. I kind of woke up and asked, "What are you doing?" Then immediately fell back asleep. I still have the lock from that door on my mantle with all our other memorabilia.

In the hotel lobby in Florence you had to walk past a quaint little well-stocked bar dead center as you entered, and you could not get past it without having a drink or two, sometimes three. Who was counting anyway? One afternoon I entered the bar area and there was Joe sitting alone talking to the bartender when he spotted me and summoned me with his hands, followed by a soft, quiet, "Franco, Franco, come over. How about a little taste?"

I walked over to Joe and requested a Myers Rum and Coke with extra ice, please. Anywhere outside the United States they treat ice like gold; you're lucky if they give you two cubes. The bartender held up what looked like a bottle of rum and motioned with his face and hands as if to say I had to try this. Joe then told him to make it a double. I'm sitting on a stool and I down the double rum and coke like a kid at a candy store. This drink was smooth and tasted like dessert. After my second double I asked for another, but the bartender refused, holding up the bottle again and pointing to the label with a big "80" printed on it. I thought, *What's the problem, 80 proof? Why, I had 120 proof on Dominica every day.* So I again asked for another drink. I was served reluctantly and by the time I was halfway finished I realized I was now slouching way down in my seat and my legs wouldn't move. I asked to see the bottle. The label read Stroh Rum. Made from potatoes. 80 percent. Not 80 proof. 160 proof. What I drank was like having six drinks in three minutes. I was gone, out there floating, but not before I bought three bottles of the stuff from the bartender. What a trick I could play on anyone I gave a rum and Coke to back in New York. And I did. I even had my local liquor store import a case for me, and when it came in, a sticker was added to the label in red letters, Flammable.

After the '79 Woodstock tour and then Stuff's performance at the Montreaux Jazz Festival, Charli and I decided to spend time at home in New York. We were not thinking much about whether we wanted to have children or not, just going with the flow, running around the world together, never practicing safe sex. Then one day out of nowhere I was changed forever; one of my greatest pleasures: Charli was pregnant.

Several months later my daughter, Jaime, was born. I was ecstatic. Imagine I am a father. Wow. She was born on 8/8/80 and we were thrilled. I sort of took a sabbatical from work for the next year and I still bask in the joy.

By 1981 I was gradually getting back to work. That's when I met Tommy K, a crazy, out in space, very creative guy connected to New York's underground club scene and actively involved in the city's most happening discos and dance clubs. I was working with a band, VHF, with Richie Fliegler, Rich Tetter, and composer/keyboard player Bruce Brody. At that time we were in search of a lead singer and holding weekly auditions, often thinking we had found the right one but for various reasons they never lasted long, one reason being the core members were busy working on other artistic projects. Similar to Stuff, these guys were extremely talented musicians. In the late seventies they collectively recorded with Genya Raven, John Cale, Peter Bauman, and others. Bruce was Patti Smith's keyboardist in 1978, recorded with Tom Verlaine, and he wrote the score and the band re-recorded the soundtrack album for Barry Levenson's movie *Diner* in 1982. In 1984 Bruce performed with the band on John Waite's multi-platinum song "Missing You." But as a band VHF didn't happen. Another classic case of doing more for other acts paying you rather than working on your own careers only to eventually end up as side men for life.

In late December Charli was on her way to the doctor complaining of a cold and aches and pains that would not go away, but the doctor said, "You don't have a cold. You are pregnant." *Wow*! Seven months later, 2/18/83, we had the second greatest moment of my life when our son, Frank Yandolino the Fourth, was born. Charli and I took the kids everywhere. Whatever I was doing, Charli and the kids were right there.

CHAPTER 17

Bahrain

Over five thousand years ago the leaders of the caravans of nomads first settled the Island of Bahrain. In 1783 the al-Khalifa family, descendants of the Bani Utbah tribe, captured it from the Persians and ruled over the land. Initially, in the 18th century, they primarily traded silk on what is still called the Silk Road, which links Mesopotamia to the Indus Valley. This was later the road that led to the sea and the discovery of pearls, which transformed the Silk Road into the center of the pearl trade. At that time, the traders ruled the land. Now that road leads to oil.

My first trip to the Middle East in the early eighties was, as with all my travels, an event. Charli was a little nervous about this trip since I arrived to Kuwait City a few days after a terror attack destroyed the city's stock exchange. Special agents who were waiting for me met me at the airport, swooped me up, and walked me through without stopping at customs. I never showed a passport to anyone. I wondered how anyone would even know I was there. The next stop was a short flight to the Island of Bahrain off the coast of Saudi Arabia.

While driving to Manama, the capital city, I couldn't help but notice the smell. It was very distinct, a dry, hot air mixed with scents of the sea and crude oil. It was everywhere. The country had a barren feeling, with no color. Everything was sand-colored. I was on my way to meet my new partners, who were family members of the emir of Bahrain, Sheikh Isa bin Hamad al-Khalifa. We were meeting to negotiate and to discuss forming a company to produce and present live tours and music events throughout the Middle East, featuring major universal celebrities and recording artists.

I was excited to travel to countries in Asia, Africa, and the Middle East, with their histories dating back thousands of years. When I travel, especially to ancient cities, I get a sense of being a part of their history. I see myself standing there and wonder how it might have been back in time, what it was like to stand on the same ground looking out at the same land as others thousands of years before me.

During our first formal meeting I began to realize that this well-connected family was full of wealthy Sunni Arabs who didn't actually work, at least not the ones I met. They never had to grab the ball. It had been handed down to them for thousands of years. They were all figureheads in charge of some division of power in government, important businesses, or private enterprises. Most jobs in their way of thinking were beneath them; they would never consider doing anything that was labor intensive. And of course the dirty jobs they left to foreigners and the Shia Muslims who represent two-thirds of the population but have no political voice or future. They are owned like serfs by the king's monarchy and ruling party, who are the minority Sunni Muslims, yet keep most of the money. In fact, none of the Sunni Muslim women work or do anything. I never during my several visits ever talked to one woman. I can't help but wonder that these guys and others like them still control countries—how long will it last without equality and freedom for the people? World history tells us this will someday fall and crumble that the people eventually win. A perfect example: while traveling abroad I visited Portugal, a country that once was a major leader, a conquering nation that ruled the sea. But today if you ask someone where Portugal is, most couldn't tell you.

On the way to the Ramada Inn Hotel, while looking out of the limousine window, I could see the flat, dreary landscape, no trees or green anything, hardly any color except the most royal turquoise sea I have ever seen. My driver was quick to proudly point out the newly constructed modern Gulf Hotel. As we approached, I noticed an abandoned building resembling a large hotel right next to the new hotel. This, as it turns out, was the original Gulf Hotel, only a few years old. According to my driver, the first Gulf Hotel had begun to crumble and rust away. It seems the contractors, in order to save money—as if they needed to make more money—decided to cheat the hotel owners by using seawater in the concrete mix instead of more expensive fresh water. The salt water rusted and rotted the steel structure, so the building had been condemned. Not to worry. That didn't stop the Bahrainis. They built a new Gulf Hotel right next door. It's the same mentality as the Kuwaitis, who, just before I arrived in Kuwait, lost all their files, records, and documents after their stock exchange was bombed and blown to smithereens. One would think a financial disaster, but not so. They immediately built and started a new stock market and exchange across the street. These actions prove if you have the resources and lots of money, you can do what you want. So I say to those of you enslaved in self-inflicted bondage caught up in your entitlement mind and lifestyle, take off those shackles you've complained about for hundreds of years, get a job, make a lot of money, and set yourself free, and never get on those death trains and ships again. Fight and work hard for your freedom.

By maintaining this drive and coupling it with consistency and creativity, as I have personally experienced, you will find your phone will always ring, as mine has, with new opportunities and balls to grab.

Make Sure the Light at the End of the Tunnel Is Not a Train

Bahrain was a special place in the early 1980s. They were still in the 1950s, totally a man's society. It was the only Arab country where you could drink alcohol. Somehow they decided even though alcohol was banned in all other Arab countries, in Bahrain it was OK to get drunk, pick up foreign women, and do whatever you want. You could even act as a Westerner, and act as if your Gods weren't watching. There were private bars, dance clubs, and all-night restaurants, each one dedicated to a different clientele. In some locations, all the different cultures would converge: Bahrainis with Saudis, Brits, and Americans. Not a night went by that a fight didn't break out between the power of the princes along-side their entourages and the foreigners and ex-patriots, who were maintaining all of the oil facilities and wells. The atmosphere reminded me of Vinnie's Happy Landing, a bar in Bay Shore, Long Island, where there was a fight every night as well.

When Charli read this she told me she actually went to Vinnie's Happy Landing in the early sixties. Who knows, I might have even seen her there, subconsciously spurring me to look for her until we met again at the Chatsworth.

After the fights, the little princes would drive off in their white—I mean white—Mercedes, Rolls Royces, and Bentleys. I never saw this before; everything on the cars was white, no chrome at all; everything painted white: headlight wipers, air scopes, wings, and stabilizers. The sheiks would stop their cars wherever they liked, sometimes in the middle of the street, not even closing the doors, just stop and get out and then go off to an all-night restaurant where the now-very-drunk Arabs and ex-patriots would meet again and continue to fight. Both cultures resented the other; the ex-pats who worked hard in the oil fields for their pay, living away from their families, versus the young, privileged sheiks who had many wives and never worked for anything.

One night I was invited to a well-known Arab-only private dance club. Unbeknownst to me, I was the main attraction. The club was an amalgam of parts and pieces, the merging of New York discos and American Bandstand with a DJ. It happened to be Michael Jackson night, and since I was an American. I was assumed to be an authority and have great knowledge of Michael Jackson. So who better to judge the karaoke singing and dance contest? All the contestants were dressed like Michael Jackson, gloves and all. It was a sight to see, thousands of miles away in the desert, everyone dancing to and acting like Michael Jackson. That's when you know you're a huge star.

The emir of Bahrain—my partner and owner of the Bahrain Cinema Company—turned out to also be one of the largest movie and music pirates in the world. My first meeting with the Royal Family in Bahrain was with Esam Fakhro. We were meeting to draft an agreement for our new endeavor. At that encounter the same image kept entering my mind over and over: that my shoe soles kept sneaking out to be exposed. Back in New York, I was warned by so-called experts not to show the soles of my shoes as it was considered disrespectful, along with several other customs I immediately forgot. But I never forgot the shoe soles. We Americans are ignorant and were never told or taught anything about Arabs, Muslims, and their traditions or beliefs. Most Americans don't know shit from shine-o-la, nor about anyone except American movie stars and athletes who walk the Red Carpet; we are truly the leaders of the Red Carpet Society.

Then I met Prince Fahrouk Nonoo, a direct blood relative of the ruling king's family. We met at his office to discuss the terms and conditions of our contract to form a new entity that would organize, produce, and present live music events throughout the Middle East. In the middle of the negotiations, he paused dramatically and declared, "You are a very strong negotiator, but not strong enough. You see, we are here more than five thousand years. You Americans are only some 250 years old, with limited experience and knowledge. Mere infidels."

I thought, *Who does this . . . this . . . desert camel-herding nomad think he is? They didn't land on the moon.* He must have felt my vibe.

He got up from behind his desk, dressed in his whiter-than-white Arab dress, with his little gold-braided veiled head turban and black-and-white checkered scarf. I don't know how they do that, get it and keep it so white. The Indians do it too; it hurts your eyes. While he's giving me a braggadocio's history lesson on communication skills relating to our negotiations, he walks over to unlock a glass cabinet, and continues, "You see, we Arabs . . ." He takes out a clear glass box, shows me its contents, boasting and prancing around like a proud rooster.

"This is a four-thousand-year-old letter from my great ancestors negotiating the sale and fixing the market price for pearls. At that time we were one of the richest tribes in the world, trading goods and pearls we harvested. So you see, I come from a long line of strong negotiators, so we will split the company 60 percent for us, 40 percent for you."

I almost shit myself. Forty percent, wow. I grabbed the ball. "Okay, plus all cost and expenses," I answered.

You know, he never finished the whole story. Yes, at one time they cornered the pearl market. But then along came the Japanese, who developed the cultured pearl, and that was the end of the Arab pearls. For a long time, many, many years of poverty followed, before they got lucky and found oil, just a relatively few years ago, and because of that no Arab of wealth and class to this day does any kind of physical labor. They hire others to do the actual work, and there aren't many Bahraini bag ladies or homeless sleeping on the streets. The king pays all the citizens from the sale of oil and gives out key government posts and appointments to family members. So I let him win; it made him feel better to save face and all that jazz. They like winning. It gives them a sense of control and power; they are the winners, they are the conquerors.

Two occasions strike me as good examples of this. The first one happened while I was there. I was invited to attend a royal family outing at the horse racetrack. When we arrived, there was no one there but the royal family, relatives, a small group of other close friends, and of course armed security. The racetrack was closed for the day to allow the royal family to bet and enjoy a private day at the races. After a few races, I realized something was strange. No matter which horse won, they would cheer. Why? Because all the horses in the race were theirs. They always cheer because they always win.

The second occasion, years later, was while producing the Beach Boys Concert at Caesars Palace Casino, in Atlantic City. I noticed a commotion at the roulette table surrounded by onlookers fascinated at what was going on. Several Arab men were placing bets, but what's so special about that? Well, they were placing chips on 75 percent of the numbers, then seconds before the croupier would say no more bets, they paid no attention to him or the rules, and placed more bets to cover as many numbers as they could in a feeding piranha frenzy, so that lo and behold, when the ball stops in a numbered slot, they cheer with glee. And they kept cheering because they kept winning. Never mind the cost of it all.

These are traits we Americans must realize when dealing with the Arab mentality. If not, they will pick up their marbles, go home and end the game. I've noticed that other cultures have their own versions of this kind of attitude. The Japanese, for example, don't like to be backed into a corner when in negotiations, especially if it looks like they are going to lose. You must let them, as they see it, save face. Give them a hole to wiggle out; let them think it was their idea for you to win.

During that initial trip to Bahrain, at a meeting with Mr. Nonoo, I requested to buy something gold for Charli and the kids. He recommended I visit his brother-in-law, a well-known money changer/washer and gold dealer in the Suk. The Suk hasn't changed much in thousands of years. It's an indoor/outdoor sidewalk market with narrow cobble and dirt streets, with no trees or vegetation at all, where they still slaughter lambs; you can see the blood stains on the ground. Most buildings are made of a combination of wood and cement. Many shops are filled with jewelry and gold displayed in giant Macy's-type windows, full of gold bracelets, belts, chains, and necklaces. I walked past what seemed like hundreds of windows with more gold than you ever saw in your life.

As I approached the store, there was a line of people around the block, all carrying some kind of bag or attaché case. Europeans, Parisian Jews, South Americans, all waiting to change and wash currency. Once inside the shop, on the left side were little cubby holes with desks and stations, each manned by a person who would take the currency being exchanged and give it to a clerk who would put stacks of currency in various automatic money counter machines—one for every type of money being exchanged—after which the accountant would take it to a back room and return with gold or whatever currency requested, with no paperwork ever exchanged. On the right side of the shop were the gold salesmen. I was next in line. Next to me were three women dressed in full black burkas and veils covering their faces, talking to a salesperson, picking out several large gold-linked belts made of rows of gold chains. One woman lifted her burka blouse exposing at least ten belts she already had on. That's when I realized that's where they keep the gold. She bought five more. I bought three little gold coins.

I must say amidst all their bragging and boastful storytelling there is another story worth mentioning that they don't brag about. During one of my visits I was invited to the grand opening of the King Farad Causeway, an enormous undertaking that was built to link the mainland of Saudi Arabia to the island of Bahrain, offering Saudis a faster route to the high life. The plan called for both countries to begin construction at the same time on each side of their land, to culminate with both sides meeting and joining together at a big planned celebration. Unfortunately, it didn't turn out that way. The two sides didn't meet; there was a gap, so the emir had to be flown by helicopter to the other side. Not exactly something worth celebrating.

There is a remarkable difference between me and my family heritage and the emir and his. The kings, princes, and sheiks are not close to each other. They live in a formal, separated world of men, women, and children and in most cases are only exposed to the Arab world. From my experience most countries in the Middle East are the same, where outsiders are not welcomed; they just tolerate you, especially if they can make money.

The Shabbos Boy

Our family lived with my mother's father, James (Papa) Pedone, in his two-story brownstone with a full finished basement, on 42nd Street between 13th and 14th Avenues in Brooklyn. There were no zip codes at that time, in the early fifties. Brooklyn was divided into postal zones, identified by numbers; ours was nineteen. It was an Italian and Jewish neighborhood. Our house was on the same street as three Shuls, the Labor Laicism, a Hebrew school, and Dottie's corner soda fountain candy store.

At nine, I had my first paying job as the Shabbos Goy of 42nd Street. I always referred to myself as the Shabbos Boy, not Goy, not knowing its true meaning at that time. If I had realized I was the Goy, I would have been pissed. Before I got the job, my friends and I once used the heavily overgrown tree and bush-lined back yard of a nearby shul to hide a live turkey that we stole from the 13th Avenue poultry market. We called him Tommy. Several days later the Rabbis caught us hiding in our makeshift camp, and they tore down the little hut we'd made for Tommy. Then we sold him to them for one dollar.

Despite our neighborhood antics, the head rabbi of the Shul directly across the street liked me. He hired me to put out and turn on the lights every Friday night during Shabbos for several of the neighborhood Rabbis and to help their wives with the mitzvah of kindling the Shabbos lights while they recited the Beracha. The reason I was asked to do this is mainly because I wasn't Jewish and because after sundown on Fridays, observant Jews are not supposed to touch money, electricity, and who knows what else. In our neighborhood, a story during this era became folklore. It has been said that I held the Rabbi up for more money. The real story is, after walking up two flights of steps to the Rabbi's apartment, I refused to put on the lights, complaining it wasn't worth the five cents they paid me to do this job anymore, since they kept adding more Rabbis without raising my wage. So I rebelled, demanding an additional nickel. The Rabbi and his wife panicked, spoke to each other in Yiddish, and at the same time directed me to follow her to the bedroom to her dresser drawer, where she motioned me to open it, take out her purse and get the additional five cents. Little did I know this event and ensuing reputation would follow me throughout my life.

After my grandmother died, Aunt Millie, Uncle Henry and my five cousins (four girls: Bea, Angela, Camille, Linda, and little Henry Junior) lived on the first floor, while my Mom, Dad, little brother Jamie, and I lived on the second floor of our walk-up. The steps had a large mahogany winding banister that I slid down every day.

My dad is Frank the Second, so I am Frank the Third. He always worked two jobs, and tried everything to be his own boss, to be independent, and to provide well for his family. That mattered more than anything to him, to be a great father to our family, and he was the greatest.

Mom, Mary Pedone, preferred to call herself May—she hated the name Mary as much as she disliked her real name, Rebalta. She ran the show, at the center of everything family—cooking, cleaning, decisions, philosophy, medicine. You name it, Mom was right in there. Since Dad died several years ago she is more independent, just like him. Now she is both of them.

Dad was a quiet, silent-type guy who rarely volunteered information and loved his kids and family more than anything. Everybody loved Uncle Frank. He was also the handiest guy you ever met. There was nothing he couldn't fix, later on earning him the title, conferred by my kids, of "Mr. Fix It." He grew up on the Lower East Side, Ninth Street and Second Avenue; that's where he met Mom. Most of the rest of my family lived within five blocks, and at any time there could be at least fifteen people for dinner, sometimes, on holidays, fifty or sixty.

Papa (my grandfather) was really the patriarch of our family; he was born in the seaside town of Cinccola in the Foggia region of northern Italy. He lived in the finished basement apartment of his house on 42nd Street, which connected to his backyard garden. He grew everything in that garden, saved rain water in large barrels, and fertilized it with horse manure that he would gather from the horse-drawn carts that frequented our neighborhood. He also grew grapes and made killer homemade red wine stored in big wood oak casks. As kids, many times for fun Grandpa would let me and my cousins squash the grapes with our feet. A famous family story is one day while my cousin Bea and I were playing cowboys and Indians in the basement, I dipped into the wine barrel too many times and during our play acting, she claims, I hit her over the head with my two pearl-handle Lone Ranger silver six shooters. I only remember drinking the wine.

Every year on Papa's birthday, the entire family would get together in the basement. All the aunts, uncles, and cousins brought food. Aunt Millie did most of the cooking. She was the best. At the end of the feasts that lasted for eight hours, Papa would sit at the head of the long extended table. His family surrounded him, and one by one, people would line up, children and adults, all waiting to kiss him and receive anywhere from one to five dollars, depending on your age. You got your money only after you answered his question, "Have you been good?" It was a great time, and to this day my cousins still own and live in Papa's house. During one visit to Papa Pedone I brought along my new girlfriend and future wife, and Gramps wasn't shy. He politely asked her, as he asks everyone he meets for the first time, "Do you work?" while at the same time grabbing her arm and feeling her muscle, saying to me "good stock," then to both of us, "Getting married is like two weeds in the field. You both must bend with the wind." Charli and I bend in the wind every day.

Grandpa Frank Yandolino the First was different than Papa Pedone, more like a patriarch dictator. They both had and taught different values, philosophies, and stories. Grandpa would have something to say like, "Why do you have those side boards?" He meant my long sideburns, à la Elvis. He really liked my individualism and character, and this was his way of giving praise and acknowledgment without breaking his own character and position, also evidenced by his humble references to his father, who brandished a very long handlebar mustache, the original "Handle Bar Pete." At one of those family dinner encounters, explaining why I was a hippy and looked like a guru in white Indian robes, sandals, prayer beads, a beard, and a ponytail, my answer was, "Why not? What is wrong with it? Jesus and I look the same." That didn't sit well with anyone. After that shock, no one ever asked me anything again about the things I do and why I do them.

Grandpa was born in Sicily, in the town of Massena, on the other end of the island from Palermo. He was known as Iandolino, his real name. When he came over to Ellis Island in the early 1900s, he had to sign his name on a form next to the X mark. The mark and his Iandolino looked to the customs agent like a Y. The "I" became a "Y" and his name became Yandolino. My grandfather said that's not my name, but the answer was, "It is now."

The meaning and the origin and history of my name has a direct relationship to who my great-great-grandfather was, what he did and where he came from, and it relates to some degree to what I do to this day. It is derived from the Latin/Greek words that described what your family is known for. Iandolino. I-an (*I, me, am*)-dol-ino (*keeper of*).

I am keeper of the *dole*—keeper of the wine, food, money, important papers, and treasures that comprise the dole. First names were given to identify you, so Franco III means the third-generation son, named Franco, born of the keepers of the dole.

In a recent excavation of the ruins of the palace of King David— the second King of the Kingdom of Israel, from 1040 BC to 970

BC—archaeologists uncovered large casks (doles) of alabaster and pottery, vessels imported from Egypt, used to store collected taxes paid to the King. In those days the taxes were paid in the form of produce and various other edible items like seeds, spices, and wine.

Today I maintain a similar tradition by keeping everything I collect, in case I grab a ball that I might want or need later. Charli and I fight about this dole-keeping constantly; she wants to turn the large room in our apartment where I keep everything into a den. Why, I don't know. We already have seven other rooms, so let me keep my stuff (it's my stuff!) in my dole! People jokingly say, "Call Frank. He must have (whatever they are referring to) in his room." And I often do. I am truly the keeper of the dole.

CHAPTER 18

Russia and Hardknocks

My office at Bert's 1775 Broadway was a magnet for what was happening in the music business. I had at least five different projects going at once. One was my representing Joel Spiegelman, a Jewish-American composer and conductor who taught at Sarah Lawrence College. Joel had been married to at least five Russian women and spoke better Russian than most Russians. We became partners in National Exchange Productions (NEP), funded by the philanthropic Mrs. Pratt, descendent of the Pratt family who settled in America in 1622. Joel, Charli, and I visited Mrs. Pratt in her Long Island estate. She was a very distinguished-looking older woman who liked Charli immediately.

In Charli's Words

The minute we met, Mrs. Pratt and I liked each other. She was my kind of woman. She took me by the hand and showed me around the house and the sunroom where she painted. We sat listening to her tell stories of her family heritage. Mrs. Pratt served English-style high tea on her great-grandmother's handpainted flowered and gold-trimmed tea set.

Frank explained the mission. It first began when he and Joel were hired by High Fidelity *magazine to write an article and interview someone with whom Joel had an ongoing relationship, the extremely controversial head of the Soviet Composers Union, in charge of all the arts in Russia—a position that doesn't exist in America—Tikhon Khrennikov. They explained that the original idea had grown into a plan to develop a performing arts program to initiate dialogue and implement a new cultural exchange program between Russia and the United States.*

Frank showed her letters and correspondence that he was having with top-level government officials in both countries. Mrs. Pratt was excited, especially since she was very interested in the advancement of the arts. Several days later Mrs. Pratt invested in the project.

Now that we had the funds, I began direct correspondence with Khrennikov via telex or letter. As Joel and I were getting closer to leaving for Moscow we had to first be officially invited by the Soviet government, and then get approval from the US government. It was a serious and delicate time; the cold war was truly a war.

Out of the blue one day I received a phone call from an assistant to the director of the United States Information Agency (USIA), who asked several questions regarding my past and purpose of my requesting a visa to travel to the Soviet Union. I got the feeling he seemed to already know the answers before I gave them.

He then said, "You must be aware that relations with the Soviets are very strained at this time and our government is having private meetings to begin formal talks regarding a cultural exchange. We would appreciate that under these delicate circumstances we not confuse the issues. We strongly suggest you cancel your trip."

Well, I was having none of that. I politely answered, "I don't think we will do that."

He was not happy. Just as the Army does not like or understand the word "no," neither does the government. He followed my remark by saying, "I see. Thank you for your time. We will get back to you." Several days later we were summoned to Washington, DC, for the first of several meetings sitting in the director of the Information Agency's office. He asked with a suspicious intent, "How do you know Tikhon Khrennikov and why are you corresponding with him?"

Joel explained his ongoing relationship, saying that although they've never met, they both are composers, have discussed working together, and have sent letters to each other for many years. The director then looked at me, "And what about you, Mr. Yandolino? I see you have been having direct and personal conversations and correspondence with Mr. Khrennikov as well, and now he has invited you to Moscow. The reason for my question is that for the past several years, while our representatives have been trying to negotiate new talks with the Soviets, Mr. Khrennikov has avoided our attempts to discuss plans for a renewed cultural exchange program. Since you both have extensive knowledge and experience in the arts and seem to have a direct line to your counterparts and have decided to travel to Moscow, we have reconsidered and are now asking for your cooperation in discussions to help bring about ideas and opportunities for a cultural exchange."

He then got real serious, making a statement that had more meaning than just the words. "Oh, finally, since you are continuing correspondence, I request that you don't lick your envelopes."

I didn't get it right away, but after some thought, I realized this was his way of saying that after reading our letters to Khrennikov, he would lick them himself and then send them.

In 1948, the premier of the Soviet Union, Josef Stalin, had personally appointed a prominent composer and pianist, Tikhon Nikolayevich Khrennikov, as the head of the Composers' Union and all the arts in Russia. Khrennikov held that position until the collapse of the Soviet

Union in 1991 and died at the age of ninety-four in 2007. He was best known in the West as an official antagonist of Shostakovich and Prokofiev, having denounced them in his infamous speech at a Communist Party Conference in 1948. At the time, however, he was playing both sides of the political fence, quietly providing help to those musicians and composers who fell out of government favor. He wrote a good reference letter for composer Moshe Vaynberg, for instance, when he was arrested during the anti-Semitic purges of 1952–1953, and initiated the selection of Shostakovich and Prokofiev for the Stalin Prize in 1950.

The *High Fidelity* magazine article was really supposed to be a story regarding the controversy between Stalin, Khrennikov, and the widespread belief among Jews throughout the world that Khrennikov was responsible for suppressing Shostakovich, the most beloved famous Russian composer. Although Shostakovich was not Jewish himself, he had become more and more interested in Jewish themes as his career and life progressed. Stalin did not like Shostakovich's political views or his compositions that leaned toward the West, and he was accused of being on the side of the Fascists.

It was a very exciting time in the political landscape, and as the talks for a new cultural exchange began, we were granted rare freedom to move about Moscow on our own volition. Naturally, we took advantage of this and did several other things on the side that no one knew we were doing. In line with what we were supposed to be doing, we made an arrangement for Gideon Timplet, the head of the Cincinnati Philharmonic Orchestra, to come to Moscow with us and meet the officials and begin plans to perform in Russia and to bring Khrennikov and his Moscow Philharmonic to America.

I'll never forget the sight and eerie feeling of landing in Moscow for the first time during that tense period. It was a real awakening. I flew Aeroflot, the Russian airline, and sitting in the first-class cabin you could count the rivets holding the plane together. The rugs were not secured to the floor and the seats were cheaply put together. I couldn't help but wonder how the hell these guys managed to fly to outer space. As soon as I arrived at the gate, I knew I was in Communist Russia. It looked and smelled like industrial machines, dark and damp, stale and cold. Walking to customs, I felt enclosed by the low ceilings, dimly lit by light bulbs that looked like they were giving out only half of their light over the sterile steel gray and brown interior. Heavily armed police and Russian army soldiers dotted the scene, with machine guns in hand and German Shepherd dogs at their side, just like in the movies. Then it dawned on me this isn't the movies; this is the enemy.

We stayed at the National Hotel in Moscow, across the boulevard from Red Square and St. Peter's Cathedral, with its design and architecture that looked like multicolored Carvel swirled ice cream, with iced donut peaks at the top. The Cathedral is where Stalin is buried in his simple coffin for everyone to see. One early morning I was walking around Red Square. On this particular day, the square and St. Peter's had thousands of people waiting in a line that circled the building. Today was the anniversary of the death of Stalin. I decided to join in, waiting to view his body, shooting secret videos. My camera captured people who had come from all over Russia. From the north, they looked like Eskimos with slanted eyes and dark skin. Others were light skinned and blond, some young, some old. I joined the line not so I could pay my respects, but just out of curiosity. After waiting several hours to see Stalin's roped-off, open casket surrounded by armed guards, I saw a dead man who looked like most dead people, sleeping stern and strong. I remember thinking this little mad man was Stalin, the tyrant everyone feared. I felt sort of happy that he was dead. After all, I still was of the belief that the Russians were the enemy.

The National Hotel was a classic Russian hotel with a unique twist of contemporary, blended with complicated antique decorations. It was

213

very charming, dark, and sexy. There were no elevators. You had to walk up a wide, maroon-carpeted, beautifully thick mahogany spiral staircase to my suite on the third floor. On each floor landing was a desk with an old Russian matron seated behind it, a major league Russian woman whose job was to monitor who was going into the rooms and look out for questionable women of the night, sort of like a guard. I'm sure she was paid off and let them in anyway. Everything had a system in Russia; everybody had an angle to beat the government.

One evening, I was sitting at a small bentwood-type table and chair in the hotel lobby bar. Joel had gone to his room. Now on my second Stoli, I looked up to see a young, handsomely dressed girl approaching me. I think she was a hooker, although she looked young and sweet, even too innocent to be a professional. Maybe I was just being naïve. In those days people were poor and desperate; everyone was a prostitute in one way or another. She spoke broken English with a strong Russian accent, right out of a foreign espionage black-and-white 16 mm movie.

"May I join you?"

"Sure, please sit down. Can I offer you something to drink?"

As she made herself comfortable, she said, "My name is Isalda." My mind exploded. Another Isalda, I thought to myself.

"Well Isalda, my name is Tristan."

She was surprised and amused by my answer. I continued with my standard position. "I must warn you . . . if you want to have sex you gotta rape me."

She looked at me, not saying a word, but I could read her mind. *Who is this guy?* I took another shot of Stoli. "And then I would have to have you arrested for rape. It's the only way I can explain it to my wife."

Now she took a swig of Stoli, and I continued. I had her on the run. I knew she could tell I was not your ordinary easy mark tourist.

I never had to call the cops. I look at having sex much like how I approach fishing. You have to jump on my hook; that's how I know I got a fish and not seaweed. You see, I really don't care if I catch anything even though I fish all the time.

Always looking for some kind of ball to play with, I found one in Moscow when I met a very slick opportunist. This guy could get you anything you wanted, legal or not. He knew someone who was planning shows and exhibits to launch a worldwide tour that would eventually head to America. His idea was to present—for the first time legally—a photo exhibition of totally nude Russian models. The photo exhibit would be accompanied by some of the models as hostesses for press and photo ops. Naturally I agreed to help. They eventually came to New York. It was quite a show; this was a first. No one had ever been allowed to present or see nude Russian women before.

Joel and my connections to and in Moscow were growing. We now represented famous Russian opera singers, composers, and Bolshoi ballerinas.

Times were changing fast in the Soviet Union. You could see and feel it. The Cold War was taking its toll; food and products of all kinds were scarce. Little shops barely had enough food to supply the lines of hungry. The price of their beloved vodka was sky high—so unaffordable that people were drinking 100-percent grain alcohol filtered through slices of bread. Sidewalks and hospitals were packed with sick and dying alcoholics. People began colluding in secret. The black market and underground was growing and so was the "me" generation. Everyone cheated the government and the government cheated the people.

There I was, seeing how they needed everything. I could feel rock 'n' roll and Woodstock Nation coming down the pike. The desire for freedom exists in everyone, and it can only be caged for so long. Just like in America, from the Revolution to Woodstock, it all happened underground first. Most American rock 'n' roll was banned in Russia; you couldn't listen to it or buy it. But I've learned where there is a will there is a way. Rock clubs and Russian rockers developed the one-night rock club. The club and location would be promoted underground and would only be there for one night. The clubs and the groups that played there were becoming very popular and an issue for the government.

I had this conversation with Khrennikov. He often confided in me and referred to me as his American friend. I was trying to get him and his colleagues to allow me to bring American acts to Russia for shows and sales of records. We were discussing inviting Khrennikov to America to perform with major philharmonic symphonies, along with The Bolshoi, prima ballerina Maya Plisetskaya, and anyone else I could represent. During our private conversations I presented my argument and theory by telling him something he already sort of knew, but with a twist he may not have thought about.

"You know, Tikhon, there are rock clubs I have visited all over Russia now."

"I know this . . . we must, like a teakettle, let off a little steam or it will blow up."

"Well, realize this, Tikhon: once you let rock 'n' roll, jeans, and T-shirts stream out, it's like letting worms out of a can. You can't get them back in."

"We will see how this revolution will end."

I answered him, "It will end like all others—the people will win." He answered me with a smile, "Good."

Moscow's subway system is something I imagine the rest of the world is not very familiar with. Most of the time you enter it in a seemingly normal way, down gray concrete steps into a gray dark tunnel and then take an escalator straight down a gray quarter of a mile. But when you enter the platform, you are shocked by the beauty. Each station has its own image and theme. You see crystal chandeliers, three-story-high columns made out of marble. You see frescos, oil paintings, sculptures, vases filled with flowers. Other stops felt futuristic with brass, chrome, and glass. It was unbelievable being down that far in such an ornate maze of tunnels and connections. It was very strange to see how above ground the people lived very modestly, some like peasants, while down below the subways looked like expensively decorated mansions. That is where the underground world operated, in the subways and tunnels, where you could buy or trade anything: US dollars for rubles, drugs, contraband, and women.

The government tried to track every form of currency entering and leaving the country; whatever you brought in had to be counted at customs and documented in your passport. If you brought in $1,000, that amount was documented, and when you left you had to show receipts for exchanging your money for rubles and for everything you bought. Any leftover balance had to be held in cash. If you spent more than you had brought in you could be subject to high fines and penalties or risk your purchases being confiscated.

The Russians have become very resourceful; under years of struggle they discovered ways around things we would never think of. The more the government took or controlled, the more resourceful the people became. Once, I was eating alone at the restaurant on the corner of the National Hotel. The menus were in Russian, the waiters were Russian, everything was very Russian. I asked the waiter what's on the menu. He said something, shrugged his shoulders, and smiled. I couldn't understand him.

It reminded me of my friend Joe, the shoemaker's son from Brentwood, Long Island. We were working after school at Hill's Supermarket as stock boys. I was working in the produce department; and there was Joe, who always had a broom in hand, pretending to be working—a method I later adopted in the army. Replying to an old lady who requested he reach up to get her something she wanted on the top shelf, he answered her, faking a strong Spanish-like accent.

"Me don't understand. Me sweeping the floor." No matter what she said or how hard she tried, he answered her the same over and over.

"Me don't understand. Me sweeping. Me sweepy the floor, me sweepy the floor." The old lady turned to me. Not wanting to be outdone by Joe, I replied: "Sorry, I work in produce."

She walked away. I still regret not helping her and have never done that again.

So this waiter was not fooling me. I had learned from the master of "don't ask me I don't understand," Joe Gambino.

The waiter was very persistent, though, and wouldn't budge from sort of forcing me to agree on chicken Kiev. So I did. I mean I had no choice. It didn't take long to get it either. After dinner, I requested the check, and several minutes later the waiter returns with a piece of paper with Russian scribbling, the total amount due written in large numbers. He wouldn't give me the bill, not even to hold. Every time I motioned for it he backed up two steps. I was beginning to smell a rat now. I will never give up till I win, like a scorpion, so I paid him and asked for a receipt. Twenty minutes went by, no waiter, no change, no receipt. Now demanding to see the waiter, a new waiter came over asking, "What would you like to order?"

"Order? I don't want anything except my receipt, from the waiter who I already paid." Now somehow this guy spoke perfect English.

"Oh, that guy, he is not here."

"Where is he?"

"He went home." I quit. They wore me out. Later, I found out from Joel what the scam is. The waiter and the cook have an arrangement. Every food order a waiter writes down is connected to a piece of meat, fish, chicken, whatever, and the cook must account for it at the end of his shift. If they have twenty written orders there has to be cash to coincide with the twenty orders. So in their scam, the waiter reuses the same signed order form. They then have an arrangement with the cashier, so they all share in the stolen profits from the meals sold and not accounted for. The cooks may do this with several waiters at a time. This event taught me an important lesson: before you make decisions, before you grab the ball, it is always wise to understand your opponent's position, even though I don't always do that.

Another major scam was called black money—money the government didn't control; hidden, illegal funds. If you dealt with black funds you were given better rates than the banks. In Moscow, becoming a crook was the only way people could make any money. It was all controlled by the Russian mafia, who spread their territory from Moscow to Brighton Beach, Coney Island, in Brooklyn. All Russians wanted US dollars; with dollars you could buy anything. There were dollar stores where you could only buy things with dollars; rubles weren't accepted. These stores mostly sold items only available to foreigners and not available to the Russian people—rare or illegal things like amethyst and gold, or hand-painted Russian folk art. With my dollars I bought it all and took it all back to America with the help of Khrennikov.

Joel, as I said, had many friends in the arts, especially Russian composers, conductors, and musicians. One such friend was Maya Plisetskaya's husband, Rodion Shchedrin, a fellow composer. They invited us to dinner. Maya was cooking a traditional Russian meal especially for us at their Moscow apartment. It was a modest five rooms, well appointed, filled with art, antiques, knickknacks, and photos of their past performances. Velvet and carved mahogany furniture that looked a little worn was neatly arranged with colorfully embroidered pillows, doilies, and throw blankets to keep you warm when there was little or no heat. Another thing I couldn't help but notice in every home I visited was that people would turn the dials of their telephone and stick a pencil in one of the finger holes to keep the round dialer from returning to its stopped position, believing that by doing so no one could listen to their phone conversations. Russians were extremely paranoid, convinced that all phones and even light fixtures were tapped.

After a wonderful dinner, Maya told us parts of her life story as we looked at old pictures of their youth and a simpler Russia. As we were leaving after many kisses and hugs, she gave me a present: two tin cans of rare Russian clams and a glass jar of Beluga Caviar. I still have them, twenty-five years later, in my refrigerator in New York.

Several days later, we attended Maya's performance of *Swan Lake* at the Bolshoi Ballet. I smuggled in my tiny Sony camcorder, so small no one ever saw it before or knew what it was, so I was able to record the entire performance. I also recorded private meetings and conversations in the Kremlin, regarding the exchange of artists' performances that included Khrennikov, Billy Joel, Maya Plisetskaya, ballet, opera, philharmonic orchestras, and musicians of all kinds.

The original idea we pitched was to go to Russia to interview Khrennikov. At least that was our disguise. In reality, we went to help resurrect the cultural exchange for our own personal interests. I was interested in tapping into and getting rights to the untouched insular Russian entertainment products, shows, and stars and of course in opening up their markets to American products as well, in order to import and export as much as possible. Joel had deeper and more personal goals. Behind the scenes, unknown to the both governments, Joel and I were arranging marriage agreements between US citizens and Soviet women, who agreed to marry and go to America to get their families out of Russia. I had at least a half a dozen balls in my hand and pockets.

On my second trip to Moscow, walking through customs was a snap. I brought in banned music CDs that Khrennikov had requested. As I went through customs, an agent simply took out the CDs, never saying a word, as though he knew they were there. Weeks later, as I was departing from the Moscow airport, going through customs, the CDs were returned to my bag, again without a word, although now opened and accompanied by a slew of gifts. I was never questioned or checked. It was Khrennikov's gift to me, sort of our own fair trade agreement.

On another special occasion at the Bolshoi, Khrennikov was honored and presented an award for his contribution as one of Russia's leading composers and writers. On that evening his ballet was presented. After the performance and the press party, Khrennikov introduced me to one of the ballerinas, Isalda. Yes, can you believe it? Another Isalda. She was at least six feet tall, and she looked and danced the part of the Spider Woman very well. I was in awe of it all. Khrennikov said a few words to her before she turned to me. "Come, I will take you home."

We got into her small Russian sports car and started to drive out of the city. The first thing she said was, "I could really use a radio for this car." Why would she say that? I paid no attention to the comment and answered with, "Where are we going?"

Before I go on, writing this episode about my experiences in Russia reminds me of the time, many years later, while I was a promoter and producer of live music and boxing events staged for TV broadcast from the Taj Mahal Casino in Atlantic City, New Jersey, owned by multimillionaire developer Donald Trump, who was into everything he could get into, especially if it got him media exposure.

Donald Trump

I first met Donald Trump, a meticulous man who wore makeup along with his trademark bouffant teased hairdo to hide the fact that he was almost bald, at a sports luncheon in New York City where he was a guest speaker. At the meet-and-greet session, I mentioned my partner Louis Neglia, and explained Louis was a world-champion kickboxer and instructor and that we were producing kickboxing events in large clubs in Brooklyn and would like to do the same in Atlantic City. He liked the idea and invited us to meet at his office at the Trump Tower. During our meeting he agreed to let us promote matches at his Taj Mahal Casino.

Everyone went to the club hoping to see Trump. I doubt many went hoping to see Trump pole dance.

I still have the same philosophy and attitude I had then regarding paying for women. I really didn't like the whole premise and didn't understand how these gorgeous nude women were rubbing and dancing all over men who were sticking money in their bras and panties. In New York City a friend of mine just recently opened a multimillion-dollar strip club. While I was standing at a table the guy next to me arranged to have this pretty little girl strip, dance, and rub up against him, and he must have given her five or six $20 bills. The minute he stopped inserting money, she stopped dead in her tracks, got dressed in a blink of an eye, thanked and lightly kissed him on the cheek, and moved over to me, smiling with a look that said "You're next." In a strong Russian accent she flirtingly asked, "Can I dance for you?"

I answered, "I just saw you dance naked right over there."

"But for you I will do a special dance."

She continued to undress again. She was no more than twenty-one, if that, a stunning little thing with a great body. I had to stop myself not to be blinded by the light. I had to set the record straight.

"Look, let me explain something you should know. I'm from Brooklyn. Where I come from, if you show me your tits I'm supposed to fuck you. And there is no money involved. Actually, the way I look at it, if there was, you should pay me." I'm sure that's how Mike Tyson saw it . . .

This time, if you could believe it, she got dressed even faster and scooted off to the next customer as she cursed me out in Russian. Even though I had no idea what she said, I got the vibe and answered back, "Don't give me anything I'm not supposed to have."

To tell the truth, the closest I ever came to paying for sex was when I was very young. My cousin Joe D paid for it. It was my first time at a cathouse, at a bachelor party for his brother-in-law, my cousin (I won't mention names), and five other cousins. I was scared to death, but at least I didn't have to ask for sex. It was the same back in Moscow; I refused to ask or pay for it.

Now, Isalda the ballerina continued her quest as we drove out to the middle of nowhere. "Where are we going?" I asked again. She answered with a slight giggle.

"We will go to my place, have a glass of champagne and a little something to eat. The radio I want is only $250. Can we buy it?"

I again avoided answering. We arrived at a building complex, parked her car, and went up the elevator to an unmarked floor. Once inside her apartment, she excused herself, returning in a robe, champagne in hand.

"I really want a radio."

"I'm not buying a radio."

I thought to myself, *This is totally against my principles. I will never pay for sex. Besides, how would I explain it to Charli? Maybe if I was seduced and raped by a Bolshoi Ballerina, but not for the price of a radio.*

Isalda was not being kind to Tristan. In one swoop, she guided me to a steel side door, pushed me out to a landing and staircase, and bolted the door. I had no choice but to go down and out.

Now standing in the fog on an almost paved street, I realized I was in the middle of nowhere on a deserted road walking back to Moscow, wherever that was. There was nothing. I walked past a closed factory-looking plant, and to my amazement a car came out of the fog and screeched to a halt. As the window rolled down a cloud of weed came rushing out. The kid in the car saved my life, got me high, and drove me back to the hotel to meet Joel, who was waiting for me. We were going to Khrennikov's home to finish the interview.

During our talks, I did actually ask about Shostakovich. He got a little excited, summoned his wife, and asked her something in a loud Russian tone. She answered, "I'm a Jew."

Khrennikov added, "You see, I married a Jew. My kids are Jews. I was a colleague of Shostakovich. On the side we wrote music together. I didn't suppress him. I was protecting him as best I could under the circumstances." He paused for a beat, reflecting. "What could I do? I worked for Stalin."

Upon my return to New York, after release of the Khrennikov article, I tried several times to defend that position, especially to the Jewish Defense League (JDL), who were now calling and threatening me with just short of death for my position on the issue. They didn't want to hear the truth. Condemning Khrennikov made them feel better and gave them something to spread more propaganda and guilt.

I enjoyed my trips to Russia during that period. It was an exciting adventure. I liked the history, people, and the food, however, I couldn't care less if I ever go back. Instead, Charli and I often go to Brighten Beach, Brooklyn, now called Little Russia, where we eat in Russian restaurants and buy classic Russian food in the supermarkets.

Whenever I'm there I'm reminded of the propositions for sex I received from those Russian women. As I say, I never have and never will pay a dime for sex. I will, however, accept payment from them. Charli, of course, doesn't want to hear anything of the kind, but as she thoughtfully doesn't begrudge me for taking advantage of the special moments of my life, she has made me promise that if anything with another woman were to happen, she must be a queen or a princess and I've always kept this understanding in mind.

CHAPTER 19

Back at Bert's

I was now back in New York full time. Michael decided he wanted to move on and out of the office we shared at Bert's on 57th for many reasons, but that's another story. Charli and I as usual were spending a lot of time together, especially since we had just bought our new thirty-eight-foot sports fishing boat. I was working on several projects at the same time and interacting more and more with Bert Padell.

He was at the peak of his career. New clients and companies were given office space everywhere, even right outside the men's room. Everyone wanted an office at Bert's. It was a prestige thing, to have your own spot in the center of the entertainment industry. We hung out all day and sometimes into the night, often inviting friends and clients to come interact with each other. You never knew who would pop in. It was the height of the music business in New York.

Now working on my own for the first time, I could make my own plans and decisions, and accept the opportunities I wanted to work on. My reputation was growing with every new encounter, event, and person who came my way. I was now able to pursue projects that I could totally control and, in a sense, if you'll pardon my French, grab my own balls. And I met some of the most interesting and extraordinary people you could meet along the way.

"I'll Try Anything. If I Don't Die I'll Do It Again"

Peter Friedman was one of those new clients. Bert gave him a desk straight across the hall from my secretary's desk outside of my office. Peter was very young. He represented the beginning of a new breed, the new managers, movers and shakers, some of whom were gay and wouldn't hide in the closet anymore. He was developing his new band, Live, and several other up-and-coming acts. I really liked Peter, who would ask me a hundred questions a day. I learned a lot from him as well. He was a lot like Joe Lombardo, constantly working the phone, the room, the record companies, and anyone who passed by his desk. Everyone liked him, and it didn't hurt that he was very friendly with Clive Davis. Their personal preferences and lifestyle had much in common and Peter was part of Clive's private inner circle. Peter was doing well, on his way up until his untimely death at the hands of AIDS.

Murder á la Carte

Another company sitting in makeshift offices in the outside hallways was also a new client of Bert's. On their way up as well they were headed by a very creative Tom Chiodo, producer of road tours of popular Broadway shows. Tom had a concept he called Murder á la Carte. Seeing an opportunity, I grabbed the ball and became the managing director of the company.

Murder á la Carte became one of the first murder mystery event producers, staging real lookalike murder mysteries for audiences in hotels, restaurants, trains, planes, and other locations. On one occasion we presented a murder mystery at the famous restaurant Club Régimes at the Waldorf Astoria Hotel in New York City. The idea of this event was to surprise the invited guests who were positioned throughout the restaurant. Sitting among them were our actors, who were part of the scripted show. The guests never knew who was who.

At my table was my family, Charli, Mom, and Dad, sitting next to Joe Franklin, other guests, and several actors of all ages and sizes, dressed to fit their part. After the first course was served and everyone was settled in intermingling at their tables—all in all about sixty people in the room—no one had a clue what was going to happen. In walks a good-looking woman and a suspicious looking guy dressed smartly. The next thing, a couple at the next table start arguing, and our waiter approaches and spills a drink on a woman, who jumps up screaming. Her date starts an argument with the waiter and then the maitre d'. The tension and action builds, people are stirring everywhere, total confusion, then suddenly, a gunshot rings out, the guy who was arguing, sitting next to my mother, is now dead with his face in the soup (a personal touch I added to this scene, á la Joe Cocker in the soup at the Kurhaus in The Haag in Holland).

Two detectives now on the scene focus in on the investigation. They're asking guests who shot this guy and why? The couple that walked in is nowhere to be found. Mom freaked; she never experienced anything like this, nor had most people. It was done very well and completely convincing. On the other hand, my father was cool as a cucumber, never showed any emotion, sort of like he'd seen it before. Just kept on eating and refused to answer questions directly. That's my dad. Mom still talks about that night; she had a ball. Throughout my life I have always included my family at my events. They're one of the main reasons I do it.

The Beach Boys

Steve Altman was someone who would come in and out of my life for years. He touted himself as a producer of events and knew everyone. Steve was similar to Norman, who at Arlan's constantly bit off more than he could ever eat, not knowing when to stop or how to say no. But Steve had a great personality and everyone liked him. It was with him that I formed a company to develop and produce special events for Caesars

World Casino in Atlantic City, including a circus, karate competitions, TV commercials, and the July 4 Beach Boys outdoor concert and TV special.

The day before that Independence Day concert, I picked the Beach Boys up on the tarmac at the airport and sat in one of the limos with Mike Love, his girlfriend, and Brian Wilson. Brian was out of it, staring into space and rambling on. In order to make sure the show went on as planned I had to lock Brian in his room with a doctor in an adjoining room and a nurse in the opposite one to make sure he didn't get away and get into trouble. Just like Joe Cocker years before, he of course got out anyway.

We built the stage on the beach along the pier across from Caesars Casino. Herb Wolf, president of the casino at the time, was a nervous wreck. He came to my room the day of the concert at six in the morning after having been to the site, very concerned. I have done many shows all over the world and it's always been the same; just prior to the start, all promoters and clients ask the same question: "I don't see anyone here. Are you sure they're coming?"

"Oh, they're coming. Don't worry. They will be here."

Later that morning, a crowd of over three hundred thousand people was swarming on rooftops, the boardwalk, on the beach, and on a hundred boats offshore. There were so many people there that we had to hoist the mayor of Atlantic City with a cherry picker to the rooftop so he could see the show. People came to show support for the Beach Boys, who had been banned for the first time from performing an outdoor concert in Washington, DC. When we learned about the ban, ordered because their lyrics were not politically correct for the administration, we immediately hired them to play the Atlantic City show, knowing we would get plenty of free publicity. The show was filmed for a TV special and commercials for Caesars. The event got worldwide press and more importantly my mom, my dad, Charli, and my kids were right there.

In Charli's Words

Frank had just started a new project—producing outdoor concerts and other events in Atlantic City. This one turned out to be a concert that drew a few hundred thousand people.

All of the production for this concert and festival had to be done on site, so Frank and I and the kids were actually living at Caesars Palace for about six weeks before the show. A typical day for me would be to take the kids for a walk on the boardwalk, then to the beach. We would walk through the casino, eat in the best restaurants, and of course have access to room service twenty-four hours a day. The kids and I loved to eat a huge little-of-everything breakfast and snacks all day and of course shop. I never paid for anything—since Frank was the producer the casino paid for everything. After being there for a while it was a true learning experience I'll never forget. It was like living on another planet, another world. People who go to casino resorts and those who work there live in a bubble, a totally controlled environment. All they hear are the sounds of slot machines and horns announcing winners. Some never go outside; the casinos even have walkways and tunnels connecting each other. In Atlantic City the beach was empty most of the time—maybe a hundred people scattered throughout the the miles of beach. Luckily, I was not a gambler.

The members of the Beach Boys were and are a great group of guys, and so terrifically talented. Being behind the scene is totally different than being in the audience. Through all of the shows that we have done all over the world my kids and I have been backstage, and I've missed a lot of music from the audience's point of view, but I've learned a lot about the artists and their true personalities through what goes on backstage and what they do to prepare for shows. They are all different; some stay secluded, others surround themselves with so many people you can't move.

The show was very complicated to coordinate and produce. They had to bring in sand to extend the beach and build a gigantic stage for the band and the Corvettes and palm trees. I helped Frank as much as I could but he had the entire production in hand and as always he made it look easy. Suddenly I looked up and there were the people, the entire beach, boardwalk, and rooftops of Atlantic City covered with thousands and thousands of people. Many came by boats anchored offshore. The music was amazing. I remember sitting on the bleachers (VIP) with my son, Frankie, a year old and my daughter, Jaime, three years old, and with Frank's Mom and Dad. Frank always made sure they were there; they were so proud of him. One of the things that was constant with Frank is no matter how busy he was he always made sure his family was safe and always found time to spend with us. It was a huge, exciting event, as always, and I am lucky to have been a part of it.

Michael Jackson

Steve and I even tried our hand with the Michael Jackson family and their reunion tour, the Victory Tour. We developed and presented our proposal to Marlon Jackson. It seems in order to keep some sort of peace and sharing of the pie, it was agreed by all in the family that each Jackson would be responsible for some part of the total tour and all its rights. Marlon was in charge of movies and films, among other things. Our involvement was made possible because as a kid, Steve grew up in California living next door to the Jackson family. Because he was Jewish and maybe ate a lot of them, they lovingly called him Bagel.

The Jacksons appeared to be very close in the early years as kids growing up, even though Joe Jackson was reportedly a tyrant. The Victory tour proved that, like most families, sibling rivalry develops to various degrees and tends to stick around in one form or another. In my family it is minor—a little here and there but never to the point of not talking to your sister or brother. Neither my parents nor Charli nor I will tolerate that; we were taught and teach our kids love and respect for each other no matter what. There is just no other way. Unfortunately it took Michael's death to bring the Jacksons back together, at least for now.

We partnered with NFL Films. I had come up with the idea of interspersing the concert footage with behind-the-scenes events, sort of telling a story by combining the live action scenes and funny events á la The Beatles in *A Hard Day's Night*. The first day of shooting was the last day of shooting. I flashed my pass to the security guards in the Hilton Hotel lobby and got on the elevator. The most beautiful girl in the world got on as well, and we both pushed the same floor. She was sort of petite, a light-skinned black girl with perfect long black hair, eyebrows, and colored eyelids, red lipstick with liner, and most importantly real gold-tip fingernails. I never saw anything like her. We both got off the elevator on a floor completely secured for the Jacksons. I entered the room where our partners and coproducers from NFL films were setting up. It quickly became total chaos. One of our producers noticed another camera crew setting up as well across the room, and when Michael Jackson was asked, "Who are they?" Michael's shy, put-on reserved comment was, "Oh it's just my own personal crew, for my personal movie."

After hearing that, our crew and producers walked out. That was the end of our movie. The beautiful girl was La Toya Jackson.

A short time after the failed Michael Jackson film, the FBI contacted me. My partner Steve Altman had suddenly disappeared, and was being investigated by the FBI. An agent came to see me at our office. I convinced her Steve never did anything to me or I to him except produce our shows. After the meeting she determined I posed no problem for the FBI. I never heard from Steve again, but maybe it had something to do with his brother-in-law, the famous Chuck Barris of *The Gong Show*, who as it turns out was allegedly a secret agent for the CIA. As I always say, what you see is not always what you get, and sometimes what you get is not always what you want. Some balls are funny that way.

Fantasy Fest

I was producing another concert on the beach, this time in Key West, Florida, billed as Fantasy Fest with Peter Allen and friends. At the time Peter was a very popular pop singer briefly married to Liza Minnelli. Peter was known to be gay, but like Ricky Martin he didn't flaunt it. The day of the show, Peter's manager, Dee Anthony was stressed, sweating and high as hell. "I need $10,000 more or no show," was all he kept saying. To make matters worse, Dan Coglin, the producer who hired me, was a big problem. I had just bailed him out of jail a few minutes before for being drunk and fighting and resisting arrest. All the while Peter was involved in his own fight with his boyfriend. This dramatic sideshow was starting to resemble the stage, which I had designed to look like a wrecked cruise ship colliding with the shore and landing on the beach.

In Charli's Words

Frank was producing an event with Peter Allen in Key West, Florida, and we were lucky enough to spend a few weeks there with our children, who were really young at the ages of two and five. Key West during October is very famous for the annual Fantasy Fest, when literally thousands of people come to participate in the parade. It's around the same time as Halloween and it attracts a lot of amazing characters, both gay and straight. Everyone comes dressed in amazing, elaborate costumes and headdresses, playing instruments, singing and dancing. It's very similar to the Mardi Gras Festival in New Orleans, mixed with the Halloween and Gay Pride Parades of Greenwich Village.

Peter Allen was the star performer of the Fantasy Fest Parade. He rode though town on the lavishly decorated lead float. Peter and his band and backup singers were great to hang out with. They had a great vibe, our children loved him, and we met the most fun people. The parade was a great success for us, our family came to visit, and Dan and his family were there too. This was a first time experience for Dan, though: all his money was on the line and he struggled to handle the pressure.

Paul Butterfield

The first time I saw Paul Butterfield was during Woodstock 1969, when he was already famous. The Paul Butterfield Blues Band with Mike Bloomfield and Harvey Brooks from The Electric Flag was one of the best groups around, ever since they began playing during the mid-sixties at the Fillmore West. Right after Woodstock, I met Paul at Michael Lang's house, "tapooz," in Woodstock. We talked and smoked a cigarette outside on the porch.

Paul had a knack and a need for getting pity from anyone he could, and he was also a great complainer. He would whine, rant, and rave to constantly borrow money from everyone. He of course never personally paid them back. I couldn't go anywhere without being told Paul owed someone money: shows, clubs, studios, especially on the road, sometimes two or three people, bartenders, security, doormen, waitresses, club owners, and of course the road crew. They would approach me saying that Paul told them I would reimburse them for the money they gave him. Paul was a master of the game. The hustle was part of his blues and was of course meant to get money to buy booze and drugs.

I would calculate these debts to be paid well in advance of accepting or sending him out to do shows; it was always part of my budget when calculating how much he or any of the bands I managed would get paid. I didn't always pay back everyone. It depended on their story and what Paul used the money for; if it had anything to do with drugs I wouldn't pay them.

As a manager, the main thing is the artist must trust you. In order to do your job and make decisions without them constantly interfering, you must not break that trust. Once you lose that trust, it's over. Their paranoia and insecurity take over, and then you can't trust them, either.

Butterfield was living at the Gramercy Park Hotel, as was bandleader and keyboard player Paul Shaffer. We would often meet at the hotel restaurant. In order to save money, Butterfield wouldn't ever buy bottles of booze, opting to drink in his room. On one occasion we were having dinner, which of course meant Paul would order something very expensive, take two bites, not finish his meal, and have several drinks. That night I asked him why he doesn't finish the last few sips of his scotch and coke, always leaving about an inch in the glass filled with ice. His answer surprised me.

"There's no booze left at the bottom. It rises to the top of the drink so that's why about halfway down I order another." Sometimes there would be two or three glasses on the table because the waiters weren't sure if he was still drinking them. They didn't know he already drank all the good stuff.

Butterfield came close to dying on several occasions. One night in particular, I called his room but for several hours got no answer. I began to worry as it got late because he usually checked in with me. As I had done several times before, I called the hotel manager, asking him to use his key and check on Paul. By this time the manager knew my voice. He would usually either say that Paul was not in his room, that he was sleeping, or—the worst reply—that I better come over. This time he told me he had banged on the door, rang the bell, and called the room but got no answer. Extremely upset, he gave me that most undesirable reply: "You better come over right now." When I arrived, the manager was visibly shaken. He let me in, and there was Paul, still dressed, lying on the bed. I wasn't sure if he was alive or dead. He was blue, his mouth wide open with foam coming out. This was the second time I had to revive him, mouth to mouth, before the paramedics came in, hooked him up, and took him away to the hospital. I took a taxi to Bellevue Hospital.

After he was stable, I left the hospital and got into a taxi heading uptown. As I'm looking out the window I notice, out of the corner of my eye, the driver's head fall back on the headrest. He was fast asleep. It all happened in seconds and the next thing I know the taxi smashes into another taxi or car or something, so now I'm laying on the floor of the cab, holding my hand to my head, sort of delirious as the paramedics take me in an ambulance back once again to Bellevue.

There I was, four in the morning, lying on a gurney with a brace on my neck in the middle of Bellevue. People are being wheeled in with holes all over their bodies, everything from gunshots to stabbings and bat beatings. It was like watching animals at the zoo. I don't know what was worse, the people being worked on or the people who brought them there. I couldn't believe my eyes; a guy to my left was arrested lying down, not moving, as the doctors tried to save his life while different colored fluids came out of every opening in his body. He died of an over-dose. He was wearing a suit and apart from the unnatural colors looked like a stockbroker or an insurance agent. Meanwhile, a woman on the other side of me was holding her head in her hand trying to stop the bleeding after being hit in the head with a frying pan by her boyfriend, who was being arrested by the police. After about four hours no one was even paying any attention to me. I was insignificant compared to what else was happening. I got up, took the neck brace off, and walked out of the hospital, got in another cab, and this time made it home unscathed.

I guess I was still a little delirious, though, since after having trouble opening the door with my key I had no choice but to ring the bell, which woke Charli and the kids, who came to open the door. After seeing my cuts and bruises, they were shaken and worried, asking me a hundred times: What happened, Dad? Are you okay? I assured them I was, but the kids continued to cry anyway.

Several weeks later Paul had finished recording his latest album. I designed the cover and concept and named it *The Legendary Paul*

Butterfield Rides Again. To support the album release I put together various musicians and different variations of bands, including Paul Shaffer, Anton Fig, Harvey Brooks, Blondi Chaplin, Rick Danko of The Band, Jaco Pastorius, Danny Draher, Crusher Bennett, and others.

But Paul's downward spiral continued. Nothing was working. It was never enough for Paul, no matter what I did for him. I personally saved his life several times at the Gramercy Park Hotel and committed him to rehab. Just ask Paul Shaffer.

Butterfield unfortunately was a seasoned junkie. In rehab, he would "cheek the medicine," which is a term used when a patient moves the pills over to the inside of his cheek instead of swallowing them.

After releasing *The Legendary Paul Butterfield Rides Again,* a new band was formed. Unfortunately some members had the same problems as Paul. Rick Danko and Jaco Pastorius were also junkies. Once, after running out of excuses to borrow money, Jaco told me his wife was dying somewhere out of state and that he needed a few hundred bucks. That night I tracked her phone number down and called. She had no idea what I was talking about and hadn't heard from Jaco in weeks. I gave him the money anyway. After all, it was Jaco. He was strung out, hanging out in bars and studios hoping to get work, and I guess deep down I hoped he would do the right thing and send his family some of the money. I never did find out if he did. Jaco died a short time later.

I put together a US tour for the Paul Butterfield band with featured guest Rick Danko of The Band. I was busy working on several other projects and could not accompany them. I needed a replacement, and I knew I could trust my brother Robert to act on my behalf as road manager, protect my interests, and most importantly keep Paul and Rick in check. But, knowing how difficult it was to manage a tour and all the expenses, asking him was a dilemma. And indeed, it became a nightmare. Robert called me several times a day requesting instruction on how to put out one fire after another. Despite his inexperience he rose to the occasion, gained the respect of the band, and got through the tour, doing a great job. He learned the hard way, however, by throwing himself into it head on, much like what I did when I became the manager of Stuff. Being a manager is a twenty-four-hours-a-day job. Artists have no respect for your time. They want what they want when they want it and no matter how much you do, some still complain and wonder why you deserve to get paid. It's the nature of the beast. Robert and I laugh about it now, but he never volunteered again.

Later on I arranged for Paul to perform at the "Crack Down" benefit concert at Madison Square Garden. When I got backstage Paul was there with several other musicians on the bill. He was already high, while others were hiding in a corner, getting higher. How appropriate that a benefit meant to raise money and spread awareness of the widespread epidemic and to ask kids to stop the use of crack was being performed by some who were high on one drug or other themselves.

Back in the dressing room, Paul and I were sitting around when Carlos Santana came over and sat next to Paul. They exchanged salutations, hugged, and promised to do something together. Carlos seemed very sincere but deep down he knew the real Paul. People always said they would definitely like to do something with him but in this case no one from Santana's office called me back. It was the same later on with Big Daddy Kane, while making his record and promotional dates. Kane got a lot of "I would love to do something with you. Count on me," but most didn't show up. They knew Kane like people knew Paul.

Just before Paul was to go on, Bill Graham came over to him, irate. "How can you do a crackdown concert high?"

Paul just looked at him sadly, suggesting, "I'm not high." And in Paul's way of thinking, he was right. He wasn't high, he was always like this; in his eyes he was normal. I could not do enough for his insatiable disease. I made sure he had anything he could want, except drugs. And everyone knew if I found any I would destroy the drugs immediately. But it didn't matter. Paul always seemed to be able to figure it so he would win. He always said, "I can't help it. It's not my personality. It's in my genes, a chemical imbalance. Ask any doctor." Unfortunately he was one of us who couldn't do anything about that gene.

In 1987 Paul moved to LA, the elephants' burial ground of creativity. A place you go to die. Artie called me from California saying Paul wanted a few-hundred-dollar advance against an upcoming show, asking if it was okay. I said yes. Two days later I got the phone call: "It just came over the news. Paul Butterfield Dead, of a drug overdose." Paul was dead. He just couldn't help himself or allow anyone else to. I guess he got what he wanted.

Too bad I tried everything. No matter what I gave him, he would say, "If I only had blah blah blah . . ." It was never enough for him. Before Paul died, I asked his doctor for advice. "What should I do? How should I help him beat this catch-22?" If I did nothing, Paul would get more depressed and get drunk and get high. If I gave him what he wanted he would take his money, drink and get high. The doctor said I was in a no-win situation. No matter how much I did for Paul, and I tried everything—I delivered new records, a new band, a car, an apartment, worldwide tours, any kind of luxury you could imagine, even a new girlfriend—he would continue to get high. By the time he died he had already OD'd several times. I guess that's why they are called junkies—they will always find a way and an excuse to get high.

In Charli's Words

Paul would come to our apartment often. Although I would make dinner, he rarely ate, but would pretend to eat by moving the food around his plate while he drank his scotch and coke. One night we went to see him perform at a club in the city. He was great. Paul was a terrific performer, with so much heart and soul and more blues inside him and that harmonica than anyone I ever met. One thing I remember about him is that he taught Bob Dylan to play the harmonica. That was a great thing. When we traveled to England to the Cambridge Folk Festival he was so amazing; everyone said the sound of his harmonica would bring German Shepherds out of the woods. We spent a lot of time together. He was a very kind and soulful man with a lot of compassion and this was why his music was so well received, especially by real musicians who knew he was gifted musically. He never had a lesson and he could play without ever practicing. It was easy for him.

Unfortunately, he was so addicted to drugs and alcohol that that was what he lived for. The people that met him along the way didn't realize that most of the time he was really not there. He would come to my house after getting out of rehab and give me gifts that he made himself in the rehab. It was an honor to have known him and when I dust the shelves in my living room where his harmonicas are, a tear falls from my heart because he should not be gone. He was a wonderful person. Frank saved his life at least a dozen times. Paul's doctors always said, "Don't bother. He will be back in the emergency room again and again." We tried everything—inviting him to our house for dinner, going to his shows—but unfortunately we were able to keep him alive only for a few extra years. When he was out of our sight, when he went to California and got what he craved, it killed him.

I was so angry with him for a while after his death. Everything was going well, Frank had just gotten a record deal for him, and then we received the phone call that Paul was dead. Frank left the next day to take care of the funeral in California. I recall Frank saying most of the people there were drug addicts, too, just coming from one rehab or another. Those who spoke at the eulogy all spoke about their addiction and how much they will miss Paul. Frank came back from that very depressed and so was I. It took me a long time to say goodbye to Paul. My heart was broken, mainly because his death was self-inflicted and senseless. Paul is greatly missed; luckily we have his music to remember him by. Unfortunately some people just throw themselves into life without paying attention to the danger, just living for the moment. As Frank says, "I still look both ways when I cross a one-way street."

CHAPTER 20

India and "God Man"

Charli and I were having dinner at Mughlai, a local Indian restaurant of the Upper West Side, eating Indian style with one hand scooping up the food with a piece of naan bread. Most Americans at the restaurant ate with knives and forks. I guess our style of eating and our cool look got the attention of several men sitting nearby. One of them approached us and introduced himself as VJ Gupta, the owner of the restaurant. He asked me what I did. Telling him I was a producer of sorts, he suggested we meet his friends, Prakash Mehra and Mahendra Shah. We joined them and two other guys at their table. Prakash was introduced as India's leading and most famous film producer/director.

We hit it off immediately talking about an idea Prakash had for his next movie, *The God Connection*. We ate, drank, and swapped ideas and story lines till 4 a.m. Prakash was so excited he invited me to go to India in order to get a feel for the country and become the producer of the film, and to help get a screenplay written that would work for a film made in India and, for the first time, partially shot in New York with American and Indian stars and music. Psyched, I grabbed the opportunity. I was going to India. Since then I've gone back seven times. I love everything about India.

I was the partner of the biggest award-winning director in India, in Pakistan, and throughout the Far East. Prakash Mehra was king. They bowed to him and kissed his feet. He was a great storyteller and his ability to tell them became a business, like me. And so my ideas became stories. We both made a living out of what we loved to do, telling inspirational stories.

His movies gave people hope, took them off the street, kept them out of trouble, taught and showed them things they could only dream of. Everyone in India went to the movies, some indoor, others on a screen in an open field. They were grateful to see the stories come to life that depicted old fables passed down for generations mixed with new tales, done "Bollywood" style—their version of Hollywood and Broadway musicals mixed together.

You only have to go to India once; from the moment you get off the plane, you will never forget that smell. Just close your eyes and immediately you know you are in India. Hot, stagnant air no matter what time of day, the smells and ingredients all come together like Indian cooking filled with hints of old dirt, burning embers, fire, smoke fumes, and Indian spices. People are cooking everywhere on every corner and beach. And during the monsoon season of course you know where you are because it rains every day. Torrential downpours for months, and then it smells even older. I love it.

On the way to Delhi from Juhu Beach, on a sightseeing trip, the route you must take first goes through the outskirts of town before you realize it's all town, town never ends, it's all connected like one big town spread over an entire continent—India. It was a very hot sunny day as usual, and while videotaping the journey, looking through the camera, I realized that along every inch of road, under every building and structure, was a little hut, a house of some sort, some made of brick, wood, cardboard, some with tin roofs, others made of sheets of plastic and tarp. All variations and combinations of them, one after another, stuck together among the debris, garbage, animals, mud, and kids playing and most visibly laughing, always laughing and smiling, barely dressed.

I was shooting video of everything. Looking through the viewfinder I realized something I couldn't believe—that on every one of those little tiny structures was a TV antenna. I asked the driver, "Are those TV antennas on the roofs?"

"Oh yes, sir. They all have TV and VCR as well." I was shocked.

"They have electricity?"

"Yes sir, they pay rent as well to the local mafia bosses, just a few rupees a month."

"What are you saying?"

"Oh yes, sir. They pay from money they get from begging, odd jobs, and hiding illegal contraband for the bosses."

In this life there is one of everything.

We continued driving on the road, River Side Drive, oddly the same street of our apartment in New York, but what a remarkable difference in the scenery. My driver insisted we stop on the side of the road to eat at the most famous paani poori street stand in India. A simple hollow doughnut ball, this guy has been selling paani for many years. He punches a hole in the hollow thin dough pastry with his thumb and fills it with broth. I ate at least ten, hoping I wouldn't die. I didn't; they were very good and I can still taste the distinct flavor. All day and night at least ten people wait in line, eating on the spot as fast as they can, or as fast as he can make them. He must sell a million a week, and they only cost a few rupees for six.

Back in the car, it was a hundred degrees. I was sitting in the back seat with Prakash's driver up front, with no air conditioner, windows wide open. It's a long ride, with traffic and stop lights all along the way. Wherever you look all you see is poverty, overcrowded masses, somehow in a hurry going in all directions to do I don't know what. At one stoplight, a woman approached my open window, lifted her sari, flies circling her head, and exposed her breast, sticking her hand out for some rupees. The driver started screaming at her, telling me to stop encouraging and tipping them. There were guys with missing limbs and I felt terrible for them until the driver said some of them actually have their body parts removed so they can gain pity while begging.

And then there are the little boys and girls all begging and pleading or trying to sell you something while chasing the car. And yet again I was enlightened to the reality of Indian life. It seems the local mafia handlers supply these kids with the trinkets they sell. You are led to believe they are handmade and painted by the kids and that they keep the money they get, but not so—the items are given to them on consignment for whatever price the mafia fixes, the kids sell them for what they can mark up, they keep the markup and must pay for whatever they sold, or return the unsold items to their handlers. It's a form of low-level street distribution, and this system is used in many ways you would never dream of. I got the shock of my life, for example, when all of a sudden a young girl came to my open window and dumped a newborn baby on my lap. "Shit, what the hell is this now?" Then the girl starts moaning and begging, the baby is crying, the driver goes ape shit, the girl is now almost in the car, the car starts to move forward. What should I do? I'm panicking. I have no choice, I don't want this baby so I give her a handful of rupees, and she grabs the baby and runs off.

Knowing I was about to be reprimanded, I said, "I'm sorry. What could I do? That poor little girl . . . the baby?"

The driver snapped back, "That poor little girl rented that baby for the day and must pay the mafia that owns it."

"What? She rented it? Shit."

My visits to India were, to say the least, special and exciting. They made me see things I couldn't imagine. I felt energized visiting places five thousand years old and motivated by India's history and the demeanor of its people. Even though they had nothing, they all seemed content and happy. They taught me to be thankful and humble.

Prakash was the best host, a true old-world gentleman. He put me up at the Sun and Sand Hotel, in a two-floor penthouse suite, with thick winding mahogany stairs and banisters leading to balconies and bedrooms. It was the most lavish room I had ever seen, full of rare furniture and art. Every night was the same: Prakash and his gang of merry men—actors, producers, politicians, musicians, rich businessmen—would come for the night, like a ritual. Sometimes as many as ten or twelve guys would all send for their concubines to bring over the freshly made food they individually required. These women would come prepare the cooked food, serve and sometimes sexually service their man in one of my bedrooms, then leave. After gorging ourselves on food and drink, they got drunk, I mean real drunk, and some would crash unconscious all over the floor and rooms.

The following mornings, I would gather the containers of leftover food and begin my own ritual of placing equal amounts of every variety in little plastic bags and then throwing them out the window to the growing masses of people who, after several days of feeding, grew to as many as fifty or more who gathered out on the beach, under my window, waiting every day until I appeared like the Pope at the Vatican window. It eventually got to the point where entertainers were showing up, snake charmers, dancers, singers, monkeys, and camels, all there to entertain the crowd. The hotel begged me to stop and I eventually did but only after I got them to agree to distribute the food they were throwing away, even though they did so reluctantly, suggesting it would cause a trend that would grow and grow all over India and that the people would now expect the free handouts and never work for their food. It made me think: Isn't that what we do in America? I still occasionally threw some more bags out anyway.

Much like the Middle East, India was truly a man's society, where everything revolved around the men. It was the same when Charli and

I stayed in a log cabin in the Adirondack Mountains near Saranac, New York. The men there went without women off to hunting camps to stay for days in little wooden cabins, drinking beer and moonshine all day. To kill bears, deer, pigs, even frogs and turkeys, and drink till they passed out. Unlike in India, though, the mountain men—as they refer to themselves—lived off the land and ate whatever was in season. During deer season they ate deer and when the frogs were out they ate frogs, actually only frog legs. They would hunt them at night on the lakes and ponds, bringing their young kids along on their first hunting trips, and the next day you would see hundreds of dead cut up frog bodies with no legs all over the banks and roads. During bear season they ate bear, turkey season they ate turkey, and when it was dandelion season they even ate dandelions, in every way you could imagine. The same with mushrooms. The new generation mountain men were mostly Vietnam vets who also had large pot-growing fields hidden in the woods. I always found it ironic that these men were sent to Vietnam, supposedly to improve the world, and then they came back with no new skills and resorted to the marijuana business. Even today, the Adirondacks are a big hub for the marijuana trade.

India is a country full of festivals, with a festival for everything, what seems like every month.

Prakash took me everywhere and introduced me to all the famous Bollywood stars. One evening he invited the most famous Indian actor of all time, Amitabh Bachchan, to meet me at his home on Juhu Beach. Amitabh was a god, a king among men, the most famous man in India. Prakash was about to make what would turn out to be his last film with Amitabh. I was now one of the producers, helping Prakash make his film. It was something to witness how movies are made in India. Back then the crew walked around without shoes and built sets by hand moments before shooting the scene. It was pure chaos. Prakash was in complete control, directing everyone while wearing his signature gold-trimmed sunglasses, holding his silver cigarette case and handkerchief in one hand and a glass of Johnny Black in the other.

During the music production, Bopi Luri, the main producer, was as masterful as Prakash. The studio was filled with fifty musicians, lead vocalists, and singers all sitting around in makeshift booths and partitions, some sitting on the floor and of course most without shoes. All of them were plugged in to the mixing board, probably at least a hundred microphones and playback amps as Bopi recorded the entire song live. Truly amazing.

As we were attending the opening of one of his movies, Prakash revealed an interesting side note as I commented on the size of the crowd of people waiting to get in. He said the reason why he demands his money guaranteed up front is, you see the line? Well in many cases the last guy in line is carrying a gun, and when he gets to the ticket booth he steals the cash. In this way the theater owners cheat the movie companies and producers and the government tax, claiming they were robbed even though we all know they are in on it. Mahendra Shah suggested that he could put together an international traveling musical road show featuring Amitabh, other famous actors and actresses, dancers, singers, and musicians to tour. Months later the events were selling out. The next year we did the same type of show with Rekha, the most acclaimed actress/singer/dancer in India. We organized the show, playing a sixteen-city live tour in the United States, Canada, and Great Britain. Performances included sixty additional Indian musicians, dancers, and singers, culminating with two sold-out shows at Madison Square Garden in New York City with thousands of Indians and two others—me and Charli.

Before that happened, however, we had a major problem. After Rekha's shows in Canada, US customs and immigration denied all seventy-five visas for the traveling troupe and their equipment. One of the reasons they presented was that the Indian musicians and dancers performing in the United States were taking away union jobs from the union musicians and dancers at the venues they were performing in, and also avoiding fees and taxes. We were in big trouble. The first show at the Garden was just days away and due to time-limited visas we had to get out of Canada as well. Where to go? What to do? Charli to the rescue.

In Charli's Words

Frank came home so down, saying the entire Rekha show might have to be called off, and that we were going to lose the thousands of dollars we had invested in T-shirts, posters, and program books that were already printed. He explained the problem with the visas and the union, believing there was totally no hope. Well, I said, "Of course there is hope. I can call our congressman or senator. They can help us. Don't worry." Frank answered, "You are so naïve. You don't know how this world works. There is nothing we can do." Well that irritated me; he had taught me better. I'm not naïve. I am always positive, full of hope and faith, so this time I grabbed the ball and ran. I simply picked up the phone book and I looked up the telephone number.

In those days we had telephone books, not the Internet, so I telephoned Senator Alphonse D'Amato, and guess what? He personally answered the telephone, and in one very long sentence I explained the visa and union problem, going on and on, totally excited and out of breath, how the band and the dancers and the singers are stopped in Canada, and how we had invested all our money in this show at Madison Square Garden, and how we are expecting fifty thousand people and I really need your help, you must help me, please. Well Senator D'Amato said, "Of course I will help you. I will call Vermont, where all the visas are taken care of and everything will be all right. Please calm down. I will fix this." I calmed down and he fixed it and when he did I said to Frank, "It's fixed. The show will go on; now apologize for calling me naïve." He did and he never said that again. And I was the only blonde at the show.

On my next trip to India I agreed to write the script for *The God Connection*. I changed the title to "The God Man." The storyline I wrote was about two American businessmen who come up with a scam to go to India, find a young God Man, bring him back to the United States, and exploit him by using him to raise money and donations like Reverend Ike and Billy Graham. They find a God Man alright, bring him back to the US like Mighty Joe Young, but they don't realize he is truly a real God Man with mystical powers. The sting comes at the end after millions of dollars are raised and our God Man tricks the scam artists, takes the money, and distributes it to the poor. In order to do some research, Prakash arranged a trip to various ashrams throughout India. It was amazing. At one ashram I visited with Guramaya, the sister and spiritual leader of Si Babba, one of the most famous young Guru God Men. I witnessed incredible sights on that trip, God Men who walked barefoot across hot burning embers and held them in their palms without getting burned, pierced skewers through their bodies without drawing blood, stood on one leg or sat in meditation without moving or eating for days.

Every day I learned something new. India is truly an adventure.

In Charli's Words

On a side note, I love Indian food, although in reality there are not too many foods that I don't love. I will try most anything. When Frank would go to India and call me I would ask him what he was eating and he would say, "I have no idea." That would be a little too much for me; I have to know what I'm eating and where it came from. I would attend every Indian dinner with our Indian friends in New York at five-star restaurants. These dinners would very often be a "boys' night out," except Frank would always invite me. Our Indian friends would mostly like to go out only with the boys, though, so sometimes Frank would be out till two or three in the morning with Prakash, Mahendra, Rag Joshi, and VJ Gupta.

Prakash was a king. He would go to the restaurant owners' apartments, requesting they get out of bed to go to their restaurant and personally cook everything on the menu. They were all honored to do it, since it gave them bragging rights to tell other owners that Prakash came to see them and what a great time they had doing it. Every time this happened Prakash would order a takeout dinner for me because he knew I loved Indian food and he liked me a lot. He would tell Frank to make sure he takes something to Charli. Frank would come home from those all-nighters with bags full of food like naan, broiled jumbo shrimp, tandoori chicken, black and yellow daal, raita, mango and green chutney, vegetable and potato samosa, lamb tandoori and saag, and assorted vegetables curry. He would pass the bags full of food under my nose as I was sleeping but the aroma would make me sit up from a deep sleep. Without even opening my eyes I would eat all the food and go right back to sleep. It was a ritual and one of my favorite things. I loved Prakash and his friends and the amazing food and great conversation. They were wonderful friends and I will always feel happy that I knew them and they liked me.

The King of Nostalgia

Joe Franklin is an icon. He invented the talk show and is known as the first talk show host. He started in 1951 and is credited for having the longest-running radio/TV talk show in history. Joe Franklin's *Memory Lane* was the first show to talk about gossip and the behind-the-scenes stories and events of the stars of the entertainment world, complemented with trivia and a healthy dose of nostalgia, including photos and movies. His TV show would have major stars of yesterday and today, like

John Lennon and Yoko Ono, sitting next to relatively unknown guests like local singers, comedians, and would-be actresses.

Joe claimed he gave everybody a chance to make it big and as a matter of fact he did launch many major stars' and celebrities' careers—the likes of Barbara Streisand, Woody Allen, and Julia Roberts, to name a few. Joe has said Marilyn Monroe, Jane Mansfield, and Veronica Lake all threw themselves at him.

How and when I first met Joe in the mid-sixties is a funny story that not many people know. Joe himself still doesn't know the whole true story. Somewhere around 1986 I was sitting in my office, when in walked Joe Franklin. I hadn't seen him for over twenty years; as a matter of fact, the last time I had seen him he crashed my engagement party, a posh affair at the Huntington Townhouse on Long Island. I was sitting at my table, looking at all my friends and family getting gigantic amounts of food from the buffet tables, when one of my friends came over to me and said, "Isn't that Joe Franklin, the television guy?"

I replied, "What's he doing here? Who invited him?"

I decided to ask him myself. He was still standing and eating right off the buffet table.

"Hi, I'm Frank. This is my party." At this point I was surrounded with friends and family.

"Hey, great party, kid. What do you do?"

I was caught off guard by his quick response. I came to ask him questions, not for him to interview me. "I'm a graphic designer." He was quick, a real pro. He knew what I was about to ask and never gave me a chance to ask him what he was doing at my party.

"Great, kid. You have a portfolio? Call me, I'll put you on my TV show, you can show your stuff, launch your career. Here is my number, kid. Call me next week. Don't forget."

I was so excited. We all took pictures with Joe, and the next day I told everyone I was going to be on TV. So that week I called him and left a message, then a few days later called again. I called and left messages several times, until finally he picked up the phone.

"Hello, is this Joe Franklin?" I asked.

"Hey boss."

"Hi, Mr. Franklin. Remember me? You were at my engagement party two weeks ago. You asked me to call to set up an interview to appear on your show."

"Oh yeah boss, I'm on the other line. Call back tomorrow same time, okay boss? Don't forget."

Well, two more weeks went by, and needless to say Joe came up with two hundred excuses. I never did get on his show nor did I even see him again until twenty years later, when standing in my office was the King of Nostalgia himself.

"Are you Frank?" he asked me.

"Yes, I'm Frank." I like to say that. I could tell the Joe Franklin ball was now mine. "What can I do for you?" I never let him know about our past encounter. A short time later I contracted a book deal for Joe with Bernard Geist. For those wondering, yes, I did slide down Bernard's fireman's pole and got a nude mechanical stripper pen after landing in his office. I was now Joe's manager. Over the years he had amassed a huge collection of various memorabilia, hundreds of thousands of things like photos of stars and celebrities, postcards, newspapers, magazines, hundreds of 16 mm films and movie trailers, TV shows, posters, marquee cards, classic old records, and sound recordings, radio shows, and on and on. He kept it all around him in his office on 42nd Street and in various warehouses. We decided to inventory it all with the idea to sell and license the collection by forming Joe Franklin Productions.

Joe had some connections with a group that was interested in merging our company with a private shell—a company that is already public and waiting to merge with another company they believe can generate stock sales and income revenue. We began to negotiate with the various parties. It was recommended we hire a Wall Street attorney to draw up the necessary papers and do the filings. That lawyer was Harold Horowitz, a seasoned attorney who had orchestrated and successfully taken several companies public. We went to see Harold to request he consider representing us. Harold was at least three hundred pounds. You could not help but notice he was a very religious man with a black longish beard, wearing a yarmulke that, when it wasn't falling off his head, sat above his long curly peyos. He wore dark, horned-rimmed, thick-lensed glasses that accented his crossed eyes as he sat behind a big oak desk with piles of papers scattered everywhere. He looked up as if to say what do you want, so we introduced ourselves. When he spoke to me, I wasn't really sure he was talking to me because of his eyes, until he said, sort of half jokingly, "What are you doing here with all these Jews?" I immediately responded with, "Excuse me, you don't know who I am." Now he was on the defensive. "No, I don't. Who are you?"

"I'm the Shabbos boy of 42nd Street in Borough Park, Brooklyn."

"What?" he replied.

I went into my Shabbos boy story, and after I finished he shocked me by saying, "I know who you are. You're the kid who held up my grandfather for more money."

With that he stood up, saying, "Okay, I'll be your lawyer."

Our company, Joe Franklin Productions, did a reverse merger initial public offering (IPO) and went public on the day of the Stock Market Crash of 1987, or "Black Monday." It was the largest one-day market crash in history. The Dow lost 22.6 percent of its value, $500 billion dollars, on October 19, 1987.

1986 and 1987 were banner years for the stock market, with low interest rates, hostile takeovers, leveraged buyouts and merger mania. IPOs were also becoming a commonplace driver of market excitement. An IPO is when a company issues stock to the public for the first time. The euphoria of these years made investors believe that the stock market would "always go up." Many people lost millions of dollars instantly with IPOs. There are stories of some unstable individuals who lost large amounts of money and then went to their broker's office with a gun and started shooting. A few brokers were killed. What a ball I'd grabbed. Forging on, I hoped this wouldn't happen to me.

I was now president and CEO of the public company that was formed and based on Joe's vast nostalgia collection. In addition to the production and distribution of rare classic and nostalgic entertainment products, we offered a monthly magazine and various rare music, television, and home video programs. Joe really liked the girls. He would send them to see me all the time—wannabe actresses, strippers, dancers, health fitness experts, singers. Lady Allison Asante came to me wanting to release her record and Broadway musical, *Lady Bird*. Lady Allison was something special, elegant and charming. She'd married some Count Something or Other and when he died she inherited a vast amount of art, money, and property, so she was very wealthy, living on Park Avenue, and I was fighting off her very provocative advances.

Charli would say half-jokingly I should marry her, and then I finally would be happy having all the money I ever wanted, and of course to give her some. It wasn't easy to overcome the temptation. Lady Allison was a beautiful woman. I often would escort her to formal affairs and it was she who introduced me to the Knights of Malta and Father Zorza. I will get into that story later.

First comes the main reason for the story of Joe Franklin Productions. Joe was beginning to become subversive, dropping hints how more should be done with the company even though he didn't do much to help. I realized he was developing a plan to sell the company and get rid of me. All he kept saying was, "We should bring in a real shark to run the company. We need a shark." He would tell this to everyone. But everyone, including our stockholders, was happy with our progress, having built a business from nothing. It didn't matter to Joe what or how much we did; he was always unhappy and divisive, so it was Joe that no one trusted. He set up meetings to discuss a merger takeover with a public company headed up by an Israeli—as he called him—shark. I was sure he had hand grenades in his pockets. I decided this was the time to make my move, that during our merger negotiations it was time to sell and get paid. After several days of intense meetings, I began stalling and becoming difficult, then while sitting around the conference table after everyone agreed on the terms I grabbed the ball, throwing out my own grenade by declaring, "I changed my mind. I don't want to sell my shares. I want to buy everyone else out." I thought there were going to be several heart attacks after the gasps of "What did you say?"

"I said I want to buy you all out." Joe was taken by surprise, since he thought he already had a side deal with the Israelis that I would accept. Shaken by my counteroffer, he asked me if I would talk to him privately. Everyone left the room. Joe seemed very perturbed.

"What are you doing?" he asked. "What is it you want, Frank?"

"I want more money for my third of the company," I cooly answered.

Joe shot back, "They won't give us any more than we agreed; where is it going to come from?"

My answer was simple and direct: "You." He was shocked and realized I was dead serious. He agreed to pay me off. I figured that paid me back for the food he ate while crashing my engagement party. I didn't tell him that, of course, and he still doesn't know, so I say: sorry, Joe.

"If you, look, smell, and act like an ass, look in the mirror; you're an ass."

Vatican Deal Maker

"I'm the cause and effect."

One evening I escorted Lady Allison Asante to a Knights of Malta extravaganza dinner. She introduced me to Father Lorenzo Zorza, a handsome young priest. He told me he represented the Vatican in Rome and that the Pope himself had sent him on a mission. I invited him to my office, and he showed up with his assistant Chauncey, a very tall, sexy, attractive short-skirted redhead. What was that all about? I should have gotten a clue.

Zorza, as he called himself, claimed to be a real authentic practicing priest and dealmaker for the Vatican. In fact, he told me one of his projects was keeping the Archbishop out of Rome, sort of on a traveling banishment.

It was sometime in September 1986 when Zorza introduced me to Emmanuel Milingo, this former Archbishop of Lusaka, Zambia. He gave me a signed copy of his new book, *The World in Between: Christian Healings and the Struggle for Spiritual Healing*.

During our conversations, I was to learn that in 1973, Milingo began preaching his ideas regarding the spirit world to a growing number of followers. He was convinced, after personally experiencing and participating in several events, that by placing his hands on those who believed he had the gift of healing, he was able to cure them from being possessed by the evil spirits; in short, he was practicing exorcism of the spirit. In 1982 Milingo was summoned to Rome. The church and the Pope had had enough, since the church was totally against the use of exorcism and denied the existence of evil spirits. While in Rome Milingo was accused of witchcraft, and after pleading his case with the Pope in 1983, he was forced to resign in 1984 and was put into exile, banned from practicing and forbidden to make any contact with his dioceses in Rome and Zambia.

In order to guarantee this, Father Zorza was appointed by the Vatican to take Milingo away from his disciples and followers. Zorza took him to America, which led to my meeting with the two of them several times. Milingo explained his beliefs in detail and requested I attend a hands-on healing he was planning at St. Joseph's Church in the West 40s. As I entered the church packed with people, there was

Zorza, dressed in full priest collar, robes, and crosses, presiding with two other priests at the altar. Until that point I wasn't really sure Zorza was a real priest since he talked and acted more like a playboy. After the priests finished their ceremony they requested everyone place their hands in the air to demonstrate accepting Milingo, who now took center stage and mumbled a few words as everyone but me waved their hands to the heavens. Milingo summoned those in need to come to the altar to receive his hands of healing.

Reluctantly, I joined the line, and one by one people of all ages and colors approached Milingo. As he placed his hand on their heads, some wept and shouted out loud, and many fell to the floor and shook violently. When my turn arrived I was scared to death. What would happen to me? Would I faint? Would I be cured? Cured of what? I walked up to him, and as I got close, an inch away from him, a terrible smell filled my nose and brain. I thought, *What the hell? This guy smells like shit.* Milingo must have felt my vibe, and instead of placing both of his hands on my head, he forcefully threw me off to the side, more like a hands-off healing. I was immediately taken away by his protectors. That was the last time I saw Milingo.

Several days later, Father Zorza was on his way to our apartment, but just like Abbie Hoffman coming for dinner, Zorza never showed up. Then, wouldn't you know, Charli and I saw it on the news and read it in the papers that the Hoodlum Priest had escaped from a police dragnet. It turns out one of the other things Zorza did was smuggle heroin, using real Church nuns as his mules. I never heard from or saw him again, either, and he was never caught.

Hi, Zorza, wherever you are. Call me. My number is the same.

What you see is not always what you get.

CHAPTER 21

Snow White in Happily Ever After

I n 1993, despite being bedridden in the hospital after suffering a slipped disk, I grabbed the ball and launched my next project, a Disney-type animated film called *Snow White: Happily Ever After*, a sequel to Disney's original *Snow White and the Seven Dwarfs*. Charli was there in the hospital every day. She set up an office on the bed next to mine making and answering phone calls, never letting on to anyone that I was in the hospital. I was a partner and president of Technovision Industries, a theatrical film and television distribution and ancillary sales company in association with First National Films, a publicly traded company who owned the film.

The film was created by famous onetime head Disney animator Lou Scheimer and starred the voices of Dom Delouise, Ed Asner, Phyllis Diller, Zsa Zsa Gabor, Tracy Ullman, and Irene Cara as Snow White (on a side note, back in the early seventies, Michael Lang signed to Just Sunshine Records a group of very talented singers and dancers called "The Voices of East Harlem," featuring Irene Cara).

The project was part of a major plan for company insider stockholders to increase Technovision's stock value by producing and launching the film and using it as a marketing tool—sort of a loss leader. And it worked. We distributed the film nationally to theaters and then home video. We planned a private dinner, invited all the stars of the movie and the press including an actress and actor dressed as Snow White and the Prince, my kids, and Mom and Dad, who took pictures with all of them. Our efforts raised the public stock price of Technovision from just under $2 to about $10 per share and produced several million dollars in profit from theatrical, ancillary, and merchandising sales.

This was all preceded by a landmark lawsuit by First National Films who beat Disney but lost the war. The battle began when Lou Scheimer left Disney to start Filmation to compete with his old boss. He then contested Disney's claim of ownership of the name Snow White, claiming the character was an old German fable and not copyrighted or owned by Disney.

The battle was on. Lou was right that "Snow White" herself couldn't be owned, as she was now in public domain. Walt Disney was very shrewd when Disney studios first made the film, however. In order to camouflage ownership and copyright, Walt created the seven dwarfs, which he did own the rights to, and included the seven dwarfs in the title, so by connecting Snow White to the seven dwarfs, Disney gave the illusion they owned it all, and no one contested it, until Lou. It went to court in a major lawsuit. Scheimer won the case, giving him the right to use Snow White's name and image, but not the seven dwarfs, so Lou came up with a solution. He would make the film about what happened to Snow White after she met the prince, sort of a sequel, this time with the seven dwarfetts. All girls. While the male dwarfs are away whistling while they work, their wives and girlfriends tend to the village with Snow White and the Prince. The film was great and looked exactly like what the Disney Studios had done fifty years ago, if not better, and Disney knew it.

The problem I now faced was the marketing, what to call the film and how to use the name Snow White. Ultimately, Disney allowed us to use the title Snow White in *Happily Ever After*, with restrictions. On all printed material, her name had to be half the size of *Happily Ever After*.

I realized, though, that in all my ads on radio, TV, and in the theaters the audience would hear the entire title, unbounded by percentages: "Snow White in *Happily Ever After*." Sounds great, right? Except Disney didn't think so. Although we can't prove it, they blocked us in most if not all distribution channels.

We managed to do something, though—a limited theatrical release, licensing the sale of home video cassettes with Blockbuster, and securing other licensing on merchandising, toys, dolls, and a soundtrack album.

Even though the film was not a box office smash, the publicity still caused the stock to go up several dollars per share, so investors were happy. It was not easy. Even though Lou Scheimer won the lawsuit, if you're not careful you might say: winning the battle can cause you to lose the war.

Ponte's Restaurant

Years later I would come to visit Ponte's restaurant again. My cousin Bea's husband, Donald Mazza, had a cousin, Pauli, who was the son of a very well-connected New York family in the construction restoration business. As a matter of fact, they were the ones who constructed and secured the giant King Kong on top of the Empire State Building in the sequel to the movie. There was nothing subtle about Pauli, who also played drums in a rock band. We would meet at Ponte's restaurant. You never knew who you might be sitting next to or pissing with in the bathroom.

Among other things, as I mentioned earlier, the Pontes were deeply entrenched in the garbage business in the tri-state area. The first time I went to the restaurant was with my father to try to put together a garbage disposal deal for Guccione. That's when my I met my soon-to-be friend Ted Fay, who introduced me to John D., who I call the Shoemaker, the Godfather of garbage and recycling. The two of them were going to introduce me to the powers that can make these things happen. I was introduced to Anthony Dilorenzo, who had just come out of prison and was celebrating with friends at the restaurant. Ironically my father also knew The Hick, as he was called. Charli and I had met him at a New Year's Eve party Dad threw for his partners, friends, and associates several years earlier.

Conversely, on a similar occasion, Pauli and I were invited not to a coming-home party but rather a going-away party for one of the mob big shots who was going to prison the following week. Something I have witnessed for years is that for some reason these guys can't get enough of being noticed and being treated special by the maître d' and owners of restaurants, whom they tip handsomely. It is an important badge of honor to be known in restaurants, to look good in front of your guests and all the other restaurant patrons watching your grand entrance. Another observation is that these guys travel in packs with other close associates and their gumadas, their mistresses, while their wives stay at home with the kids.

At these dinners they are liable to say anything. Inside secrets, stories, these gumadas hear everything. It's quite remarkable how much is revealed and bragged about as the big shots boast about going away. It is traditional to order pasta puttanesca, a dish known for and made famous because it was a fast dish the gumada could prepare on the spur of the moment as the wise guy visited her for an unannounced quickie. The recipe is simply olive oil, garlic, tomato sauce, black olives, pepper, and anchovy cooked in one pot until it gets hot, then served over tubalini spaghetti, with Italian bread and a glass of wine. The entire visit would take ten minutes; in and out.

Sometimes, once you have grabbed the ball, it takes longer to develop or to achieve its goal. Even if it lies dormant for years, hold on to it. Oftentimes it can be joined or merged with other past and future balls. Some things may just be ahead of their time. Also, you have to do something with it; having a ball is a waste unless you use it. Sometimes, though, you can't. It's tricky. A ball may simply be out of your scope.

For instance, one day I was sitting in my office with my friend, the New York family–connected Shoemaker. He would come to visit me sometimes, presenting ideas and opportunities he had, or just to talk. I really liked the Shoemaker. On this day, Vickie, Bert's receptionist, called my office phone to say there was someone here to see me. It was common for someone visiting someone else or who happened to be in the neighborhood to just drop by. That's how it was at Bert's; you never had two days the same, ever. I went out to the front desk. It was Teddy, who had lived in Artie's apartment building on 56th Street fifteen years earlier. I invited him into my office and introduced him to the Shoemaker. Teddy proceeded to lay out his idea to the two of us. He was involved with a company, a foreign one. His mission was to get the company set up in New York to introduce their technology and machinery, and take over the building-cleaning and maintenance industries by introducing a machine that could do the work of ten men, and, as he boasted, do it better and faster, therefore making zillions. But with one simple statement my distinguished older guest, who was connected to the men this machine would replace, said, very calmly and very seriously, "Who's going to let you in to do it?" I never saw Teddy again, nor did his plan work. He had a ball without a plan . . . or connection.

One day while waiting for Pauli I was sitting at the bar at Ponte's having a Myers and coke, watching the baseball game. At the other end of the bar was this old man, a scruffy-looking guy. We got into a conversation about the game. He had one viewpoint, I had another, and just as our conversation was getting heated, Pauli arrived. All of a sudden Pauli starts franticly rubbing his chin, eyes wide open, suggesting I stop the argument. I had no idea what he was doing; he kept on rubbing and rubbing his chin, so I looked back at him as if to say what the hell are you doing, until he leaned over and whispered in my ear, "That's the Chin Vincent."

Vincent "The Chin," Gigante, the Godfather, head of the Genovese family. I stopped talking and ordered another drink, looking at the TV, then raised my glass and smiled to the Godfather as if to say you are right. He never smiled back. I then realized this was the same guy who, while sitting at the bar a few days before, was approached by a man presenting a big paper bag to him. The old man looked into the bag and reprimanded the deliverer. "You are paying me with small bills. What are you, crazy?" The deliverer answered back, "I'm sorry; that's what I collected." With that the old man called over Angelo Ponte, saying, "Hey Angelo, lend me $5,000 from the back room." The back room was where the bosses would play high stakes card games. Angelo, without questioning the old man, went back and came out with a stack of hundred dollar bills, gave it to the old man, and after a short pause the old man handed Angelo the paper bag saying, "Here, I paid you back."

As I said, it was always an adventure at Ponte's. One day I got an urgent call from Pauli, saying it was important, that Joe Ponte had died and in order to show respect I had to attend the funeral. I was to meet him at the restaurant and we would go to the funeral home together. As I walked in, there was Mary, the coat check woman, who would officially greet and screen everyone. "Hi, Mary," I said. "What a tragedy."

She looked at me confused, saying, "Yeah, it's terrible."

"When did it happen?" I asked. She was further confused, but not wanting to offend, she replied, "Yes, it was terrible," and hugged me at that moment. I was surprised to see Angelo Ponte come in the door. I ran to him and hugged him.

"Angelo, I'm so sorry." He hugged me back, and I said, "I can't believe Joe is gone."

"Yeah, what are you going to do?" he said. "That's life."

Hugging him again, I said, "I'm waiting for Pauli. We are going to the funeral home." Angelo sadly said, "I'll see you there."

When Pauli and I arrived at the funeral home we got out of the car, and Pauli commented, "Why don't they let us alone, let him rest in peace," referring to all the FBI and others staked out behind trees and cars, photographing everyone attending the funeral, even me. I was nobody; it didn't matter that I was documented. Once inside, the place looked like a botanical garden. The flower arrangements were gigantic, covering every wall and aisle up to the coffin. Well-wishers kept coming in groups, all decked out, some young, others old with canes, all with pinky rings, hugging and kissing cheeks and extending hands. Pauli and I got in the line to view the body, and as we got up to a very elaborate coffin, we kneeled down. That's when I saw Joe lying there, rosary beads in hand, a giant Jesus cross on his chest, surrounded by photos of his family. I turned to Pauli and whispered.

"That's not Joe Ponte."

Pauli answered back, "No, it's Joe Piney."

"Joe Piney? Who the hell is that? I don't even know him." Nor had I ever heard of him.

None of that mattered to Pauli. Joe Piney was a made guy, and in Pauli's mind he had to go to the funeral to show respect and, mainly, to be seen doing it. I quickly made the sign of the cross, mumbled a few nondescript words, and asked Pauli, "What am I doing here? Let's get the hell out of here," and headed for the door. Pauli stopped and hugged and kissed everyone along the way. We got back in the car after being photographed again and sped off.

This experience was a ball that I never felt comfortable with. I wasn't interested in anything business-wise ever happening; it was purely just entertaining, and it always felt like a movie set.

Woodstock 2, 1994

Almost twenty-five years after Woodstock '69, in 1994, my longtime friend and partner at the time, Peter Saile, and I approached Michael Lang with the idea to organize Woodstock 2 on the twenty-fifth anniversary of the original festival. In our attempt to bring all the ol' players back together who hadn't spoken to each other in twenty-five years, we set up meetings with Warner Brothers Records, John Roberts, Joel Rosen, and Michael Lang. One name was missing: Artie Kornfeld. It was made clear they did not want to include him, and he was not invited to any of the meetings. Although Artie was devastated, he will never admit to it. I couldn't believe it myself; one of the original creators of the most famous music festival of all time is still, to this day, left out. Some people will never be able to share. They need the spotlight, always keeping their thumb on others and surrounding themselves with serfs and followers, not other generals. They especially exclude you if you are equal or of greater worth than them. I have learned this the hard way and work diligently to avoid that conflict daily with people who live by this Machiavellian theory.

Based on those preliminary meetings, we drafted contracts and agreements and put the money we raised in an escrow account. Then in the middle of negotiations, things went left: they all got together without me and Peter, deciding that they could get a bigger and better deal by partnering with Pepsi. Needless to say, this deal did not include Peter and me.

There was, however, one problem with that maneuver: the town of Bethel wasn't agreeing to let it happen. They would not let Michael back. Since 1969, the town elders never forgot the mess of the first festival, and resented never being included in the festivities or the opportunity to make any income. So the town of Woodstock and the Yasgur family decided to make their own plans for the Woodstock Twenty-Fifth Anniversary on the original Holy Ground of Yasgur's farm.

I have come to learn that if you stay true and honest, things have a knack of turning around.

Bert Padell was at this time representing Sid Bernstein, the original Beatles organizer responsible for first bringing them to America. Sid was brought in to organize and produce a three-day Woodstock event on the original site. Bert set up a meeting with Sid and me and I was hired by Sid to help produce his event, funded by the Rulens, a wealthy family from upstate New York in the real estate business. And so the war began between both Woodstocks. One had the original name; the other had the original hallowed ground. Since Artie was not involved with either side, I convinced Sid that it would be a good idea and valuable marketing tool if I invited Artie to participate and lend his name to add credibility to our event by having one of the other original creators now participating on the original site. I made arrangements to pay Artie a fee and have him come to New York from Florida. At that time he had a phobia with flying, so we arranged for him to come up by train.

Even though I had been left out of Michael's plans I felt obligated to meet with him to explain I was working on the original site. We discussed a plan I had come up with to join together the two Woodstock festivals. Since both events were happening at the same time and going to be filmed and broadcasted, we agreed that at the perfect moment we would do a live TV feed switching between the two festivals, bringing them together without anyone knowing. The entire thing would be a closely guarded secret, the perfect clandestine coup. Both festival goers and TV viewers would get what they wanted, the old and the new together. I thought Michael agreed in principle. It was a surprise to me when he changed his mind.

The battle between the two festivals "escalated." Sid could not use the Woodstock name since it was owned by Michael's group, Woodstock Ventures. Letters, TV stories, and newspaper articles filled with threats and allegations, one side accusing the other of not being the true Woodstock anniversary. Festival reporters showed up in droves. Sid and the Rulens decided to name our event after the town of Bethel, where Yasgur's farm is actually located: "Bethel '94 the Reunion at Yasgur's Farm."

Instead of Bethel, Michael was forced to have his version of the Woodstock Twenty-Fifth Anniversary festival in Saugerties, New York, ten miles east of Woodstock. Everyone wondered, *How can it be a twenty-fifth Woodstock anniversary miles away from Yasgur's farm and without any of the original 1969 performers?* It just didn't feel right. The show we were putting on, meanwhile, included many of the original '69 acts: Richie Havens, Judy Collins, John Sebastian, Mountain, Sha Na Na, Country, Canned Heat, and Joe Cocker, just to name a few.

Construction on both sites and stages began. After several weeks, we were in full swing, and then out of nowhere the Rulens got cold feet. They pulled the plug on our festival on August 1, 1994, ten days before the event. My tail was more than between my legs. Charli talked to Michael. I don't know what she said; all I know is Artie, Charli, my kids, Frankie, and Jaime, and I were invited by Michael to participate in his event.

One great thing I must thank Michael for is that Charli and I, along with our kids, got to stand on the stage of a Woodstock festival together. Who would have thought that would happen twenty-five years ago?

It was weird, though. Artie had no job to do, nothing but bum cigarettes, steal backstage and all-access passes and food vouchers so we could eat at the commissaries. He walked around with an old wet news article showing him as one of the original producers, and showed it to everyone. It was hard to see him reduced to that. This was the great Artie Kornfeld.

The Label Records

In 1995, I formed LeisureTime Productions and The Label Records out of necessity, since the bottom of the rock market fell out along with every other kind of music, except hip hop. I signed my very first hip hop artist, The Soul Snatchers, to "The Label," as everyone referred to it, and their recording of "Blam, Blam," distributed by Morris Levi's son Adam on his hip hop label "Warlock." In a flash I was immersed in the world of rap and the hip hop lifestyle.

The record started with a bang, or should I say a stabbing. MC Hakim of The Soul Snatchers was arrested for violating parole because of a domestic dispute. After I visited him at the Queens House of Detention and paid for his bail, he was released. I finished the deal with Adam Levi, the record was released, but then Hakim stabbed someone to death and went on the lam. I lost my bond money. That's how my first hip hop experience started; unfortunately it didn't stop there. My reputation was growing within the hip hop community, and that's when I met Travis "Spunk" Macklin and Eric "Rud" Rudnicki, the famous Rud of Casanova Rudd and Supper Lover Cee, MCs of the classic "Do the James." My other hip hop artists included T-Roc, Tommy Gunn/Miss Jones, Sham and the Professor, Pop Mega, and Sound Mind, a Nine Inch Nails–type rock band from Cincinnati.

All of a sudden my office was the hub at Bert's, crawling with my crew. Almost every day we were smoking three or four blunts at a time made with my twenty-five-dollar Cuban Monte Christos. There was so much smoke that it would travel out the vents and smell up the whole building. We smoked and burned everything to hide the smell, and I naïvely believed or maybe I just didn't care that no one was sure it was us. Those that did know usually came in to join us.

I was now a hip hop maven, showing up at recording studios and clubs in Queens, Harlem, Brooklyn, and Manhattan until four in the morning. I guess I was experiencing a version of that wise guy walking into a restaurant with wanting-to-be-seen-as-very-important syndrome. Charli and the kids and all of my friends thought I was crazy. I wasn't crazy; I was stupid. I mean stupid, but not as dumb as Pop Megga. Pop was in line to be the next Biggie Smalls. Everyone was talking about him, waiting for our record to drop. We finished the record *Ghetto News* and I made a deal with Sony. They were excited and so was I. They agreed to shoot a video. Now comes the good part.

On the day of the shoot the story that is now famous folklore in the hip hop world began. Pop and the crew gathered in Queens to make their way to the city. As they entered the subway, some paid the fare, but not Pop, since he didn't have the money and none of the crew would lend him the $1.25. So all 350 pounds of him decided to jump the turnstile, and as he struggled to get through, he was caught and arrested. When the cops checked his record it turned up that he had an outstanding out-of-state warrant and was on probation in New York, so they immediately took him to jail. That was the end of the video and the beginning of the end of the record deal, but not the end of the story. I visited Pop at Rikers Island before he was extradited to Maryland and put in prison for six months. All he kept doing was calling me collect and requesting money for himself and his kids. Pop over the years must have cost me over $50,000 dollars.

In 1997, after Pop, I thought I had had enough of the good life, until Big Daddy Kane showed up at the office. Kane said he was interested in coming out of retirement and wanted me to put out his comeback record. This guy was a true legend, one of the founders of hip hop. I always believed my theory when it came to a song: "Once a hit, always a hit." Everyone knew Kane, so I thought to myself I didn't have to reinvent the wheel. I signed him to The Label, produced and put out his new record, *Veteranz Day*. The Label had worldwide distribution through PolyGram/Mercury and Blackheart Records, which was owned by my longtime friend and manager of Joan Jett, Kenny Laguna.

After we shot a music video for the single, Kane changed his mind; he wanted a different song to be the single. We shot another video, but everything we did he would say, "I changed my mind." He cost us hundreds of thousands of dollars. As you can see, even though I grabbed the ball I wasn't any good at making money with hip hop. I must say through the ups and downs I really liked all of them and I know they liked and respected me. How do I know? It's been over thirty years now and they still call me. I truly liked playing with that ball and on occasion I still do. Even if some of the balls don't bounce, in most cases they lead to others that do.

I'm a hammer waiting for a nail.

In Charli's Words

For a while, Frank was constantly surrounded by rappers, and some-times our apartment was filled with ten guys or more. Jaime and Frankie would stay in their rooms; I don't think they ever understood what Daddy was doing with all of these guys. I would walk in the house and I was never sure either what they were up to, but really, they were the nicest guys and very respectful to me. Upon looking at this group of guys, though, you just have to do a double take. Our building is primarily religious Jews who have never experienced anything close to a group of guys like these. Our neighbors must have looked through the peep hole on their apartment door and been cautiously interested, probably wondering what exactly was going on in my apartment. A few times the cops even came to check on us; they too wondered why our guests kept showing up at all hours.

I did like them, Pop, Rud, and Spunk. They were very affection-ate and respectful, commenting on our great family life whenever they came over, and I treated them like they were family. I always had food and drinks for them, and for the holidays presents for their kids; they were fun and they really loved Frank and still do. They know that he tried very hard to help all of them. There was a real bond, a friendship, and there was nothing they wouldn't do for him, and nothing Frank would not do for them. If Frank needed their help all he would have to do is make one phone call and twenty guys would show up. For years, I would get collect phone calls from the Concord Correctional Facility asking if I would accept the call, and I always said yes. It would be Pop calling to say hello and that he just wrote a dozen or more songs. Frank said he was the most talented songwriter he ever knew.

One day Pop telephoned and said he was up for parole. We were delighted and asked when.

He said, "Well I decided not to take the parole. Knowing me, I will do something else and be right back in so I might as well finish my time, get out and be free." What happened to Pop was very discouraging because we always thought, being such a natural talent, he would be a great success, not only for us but also for him and his family. But it never happened because he kept going in and out of jail. Just the other day some guy called asking for Frank. I asked, "Who is it?" He said, "Mick," and I said, "Mick Jagger?" He started to laugh. No, not Jagger. He needed to talk to Frank right away and said he was around the block. I could sense something was up, and he reluctantly gave me his name, saying Pop asked him to call. It sounded familiar, and I told him to call back because Frank was out of town.

Tommy Mottola

While Peter Saile and I were doing well raising money for various projects with The Label Records, Bert Padell was representing Tommy Mottola, who was a big shot manager and producer in the record industry. He had a management company called Champion Entertainment. Among other artists, Tommy was responsible for Dr. Buzzard's Savannah Band, Mariah Carey, Hall and Oates, and John Cougar Mellencamp. Tommy's buddy Walter Yetnikoff asked him to become president of Sony Records and Tommy accepted. In order to avoid any conflicts of interest between him, the artist, and the label, he would have to sell all his interests in Champion Entertainment.

As soon as Bert told us, I grabbed the ball. Peter and I immediately jumped on it. What an opportunity. To slide right into a major management company would be a major coup for us. Bert set up a meeting at

Tommy's office, which was followed by several more meetings, and ultimately a decision by all parties that Peter and I would raise the money, $5 million, to buy Champion Entertainment from Tommy. I thought I died and went to heaven. We brought in accountants, bookkeepers, lawyers, secretaries, and assistants all to analyze Champion's value and ROI. Our investors were requesting backup to all the numbers, including profits, loss, loans, operating expenses, etc. Then came our own accountant's initial review and summary of what had to be done.

That's when problems surfaced. We found out the books were not consolidated; each group had its own set of books and records. Some things were cross collateralized between artist and production companies, and some things were simply misfiled. We also discovered that documents between the management company and the artists had lapsed, expired, or in some cases didn't even exist. It was a nightmare.

It took us a couple of months to put it all together into a package acceptable to our investors. Tommy was already working at Sony. We visited him in his big plush office. His whole demeanor had changed. He was now the serious president of Sony records, and along with that position came paranoia and hints of Machiavelli. His office was dark, the shades were pulled down, and rumor had it he had a gun in his top drawer. He told us that as a matter of fact he did. Now that he was at Sony, we would have to speak to John Sykes, a media maven who had been brought in by Tommy to run Champion with his associate partner Al Smith. That's when I felt something was wrong. I didn't realize I had just lost the ball, which was confirmed at our next meeting. It was a lesson I thought I had learned at Burlington Mills about killing the Indians and selling them Bibles. Now this all backfired in my face Tommy and the others at Champion decided to take all the information and work that we gathered and do it themselves without us, sort of a leverage buyout. That is a lesson I will never let happen again. Yeah, right!

Woodstock 3

The third Woodstock Festival in 1999 was definitely not the charm. Michael's Woodstock Ventures again was unable to secure the original site. Woodstock 3 was held at the Griffiss Air Force Base in Rome, New York, with concrete airstrips and roads for the kids to sit on in ninety-degree heat. There was very little shelter and there were still land-to-air missile silos all over the site. What a dichotomy from the original Woodstock—1969, stop the war, peace, and love.

This time Michael agreed to let me get involved. Again, Artie was not invited, nor did he attend. The rift between Artie and Michael goes back to the beginning. They never could agree on anything, starting with what to call the festival, what acts should be invited to perform, is it an anti-war festival or a peace festival, how much to spend on who and what, what happened to the money, how to promote it, who was boss, who was king, and on and on. Although they are seemingly cordial to each other they have not done anything together for forty-five years. Who knows if they ever will?

I arranged for my brother Robert's company to have food and concession vending rights for the festival. Right from the beginning the vibe was off between the acts that were booked and again the message and purpose of the event. There wasn't one, except to make as much money as they could. Just like all the other Woodstocks, even that didn't work out. This version of Woodstock was very commercial and had the wrong mix of performers that drew a wide range of audience. The new, disjointed vibe caused the burning of Woodstock 3 on the last day, when rioters started fires and burned down the house, so to speak. Despite all of that, Michael again developed spectacular-looking stages that were huge, beautiful, and magnificent.

For the fourth time, including Riviera 76, a giant monsoon rainstorm came; fences were torn down by the festival goers who again didn't pay to get in; gate revenue was lost; no movie was released, just music, raves, rapes, and riots. What had happened to the Woodstock Nation?

The original Woodstock Nation was the birth of a new generation that began way before the festival on that hilly farm in White Lake in 1969. The Woodstock Nation was a mental and physical way of life. Woodstock the festival was a place to gather and listen to music from groups symbolizing a generation of young people who believed in the same things. Even though the mixture of folk and rock music was different in style, the message was the same. People gathered to show unity against the corrupt government, the war, and the establishment, and to be free to exercise their rights. Woodstock '99, on the other hand, was a microcosm of the change running through society at that time: the mixture of rap, rock, pop, and electronic dance brought an eclectic mix of styles and certainly mixed messages that caused the clash between festival goers.

Michael's and Artie's Woodstock didn't end after that first festival in '69. They couldn't let it be over. The never-ending dramas continued for decades. For me, Woodstock was only a period in time that came after and before others, like Picasso's Blue Period. For Artie and Michael, it was different. They never left the Woodstock world. They say the word every day.

The three of us say we are all best friends and do care for each other, but the Woodstock saga continues. The common thread we all love is Charli. She talks to Michael and Artie more than I do. She is the one with the "diplomatic" nature, always displaying true friendship, the one who really cares and is the voice of reason. She's the one whose thoughts and actions you never have to second-guess, and she goes through life without prejudice and free of ulterior motives.

CHAPTER 22

Marilyn Monroe and Lena

Lena Pepitone was eighty-six years old when she passed away on June 11, 2011. She was Marilyn Monroe's seamstress and part-time cook during the last five years of Marilyn's life, 1957–62.

I met Lena over twenty years ago at the company party to celebrate the launching of Joe Franklin Productions. After meeting her, I saw the ball and I am still running with it. That meeting and many subsequent conversations with Lena brought me to write a screenplay. "Marilyn and Lena" is a true story about two women and their lives together. Over the years, I have uncovered many things about Marilyn that most people don't know. Lena has revealed new and provocative personal information she didn't put in her book—a book, by the way, even though she is credited as the author, that she never read, nor did she really have any idea what was written in it by her co-writer. The details of her stories revealed to me during the years we spent together were much more detailed and scandalous. Among other things, Lena told of Marilyn's suicide attempts and relationships with presidents, movie stars, and other influential men. Those stories and others have led me to questioning how Marilyn may have truly died.

Charli became a very close friend to Lena, a lot closer than I, and many times she would intervene between me and Lena by keeping her on point, especially when Lena would become impatient and complain that things were not going fast enough with the screenplay. Lena would meet and discuss with others her ideas regarding her story. She was always looking for the grass to be greener on the other side. She didn't know it could be Astroturf over there.

Charli is, of course, a very likable person. She was able to listen to Lena and understand her. Lena would tell Charli things she never told anyone else, especially about her relationship with her estranged family. I'm sure Charli's ability to focus and show that she cares helped her relationship with Lena.

The world has always been fascinated with Marilyn Monroe. More than forty years after her tragic death, Marilyn continues to intrigue us. She's transcended generations and has been crystallized into our minds and our culture. Marilyn's life story has always been told with a mixture of success, struggle, and controversy. Her life as a film actress in Hollywood's golden era, her relationships with some of the world's most influential men and her unexpected death are among the elements of Marilyn's life that have been documented and portrayed in many ways over the past fifty years.

Lena was an attractive young Italian woman who loved to sing and play act, always dreaming of Hollywood's glamour and a rich, famous life far better than the one she had in war-torn Italy, where she was unhappy and disappointed. Lena's sister arranged a meeting with an American GI stationed in her town, and Lena grabbed the opportunity to get to America and married that soldier, Joey Pepitone. After leaving Italy they found an Italian community on the east side of New York City. The life of wife and mother with two small boys, however, was not what she had in mind when she moved across the Atlantic. She was not satisfied, still dreaming and wanting to be a star, an actress, a singer, anything that would bring her fame and, most importantly, fortune. Joey never wanted her to work. In those days, a woman would stay home with the children, cook, and clean—especially an

Italian woman. That did not sit well with Lena. So she decided to get a job and not tell Joey. She secretly went off to an employment agency and was sent on to her first interview at an apartment on 57th Street, the apartment of a very famous person. Arriving at the appointment, walking off the elevator, she rang the bell to apartment 3F. The door opens, and she is greeted by May Reese, a tall, stern, gray-haired woman who coldly invites her in, where the interrogation of Lena begins.

"Tell me, have you been a maid before?"

Lena was insulted by that question. One thing about her is she would tell you what was on her mind no matter how it came out of her mouth.

"A maid? I don't think so. How 'bout you?" As Lena tells it, suddenly she got distracted as a door swings opens and out bursts a woman into the room, á la Loretta Young. Lena is shocked to see Marilyn Monroe fresh out of bed, totally nude.

Seeing Lena, Marilyn responds, "Oh, hi. Excuse me. I'm Marilyn, are you here to help me?" Lena nods her head as May helps Marilyn into a robe.

"You seem so nice. What's your name?"

"Lena. Lena Pepitone."

"Are you Italian? I love Italians. And their food! Can you cook? I can really use a good cook around here. Can you make lasagna? I just love it."

"Oh boy, that's my specialty! I could show you how to make it. It's easy."

And Lena was hired on the spot, beginning a strange relationship. Lena cooked for Marilyn and was present at unique events and several risky situations where she attempted to find her true love. Over the years to come Lena would give Marilyn what she never had—her own family. What Lena got in return was the chance to be the closest she would get to becoming a great actress.

*The following scenario and dialogue was told to me personally by Lena and Henry Weinstein. *

Back in Hollywood, Marilyn was on the set, shooting *Something's Got to Give*. Directors, cameramen, the producer Henry Weinstein are all there, except no Marilyn. She walked off the set and days later she called in sick. Now Weinstein called her phone.

"I'm sorry, Henry," she answered. "I must go to New York. I promise I will be back in a few days. It's for the president's birthday, you know!" Weinstein fired her.

Before her untimely death, Marilyn Monroe spent most of her days living on 57th Street in New York City. During those days, Lena arrived at Marilyn's apartment, where Marilyn was standing in a corner, talking on the phone with her head in her hand and her back to Lena, who, unknowingly to Marilyn, overheard the entire conversation.

"Well, if it's okay then I could come there."

Marilyn paused for a minute then hung up the phone. She realized Lena was in the room. Lena was embarrassed.

"Excuse me, Marilee." (Because of Lena's strong Italian accent she called Marilyn Marilee.) "I didn't mean to listen."

Marilyn was uneasy. "No, Baby Lamb. Don't be silly. I'm sorry. I must go out and get something at the Carlyle Hotel."

Marilyn was never really good at lying, so she decides to confess. "Oh shit, to see Jack."

"Jack. Who's Jack?" Lena asked.

"Jack Kennedy. JFK, silly."

"You call the President of the United States Jack?!"

"Yes, Jack. He said it was okay ever since we became, you know, friends. He told me to be careful what I say and never to tell anyone what we do so that means you too, promise?"

"Never. I promise." I don't think Lena said anything else, but it wouldn't surprise me if she was thinking *I don't know what your plan is, but I'm pretty sure your secret's out already*, Marilee.

A touching part of their relationship is how Lena taught Marilyn how to cook. They prepared dinner for Arthur Miller, Joe DiMaggio, Frank Sinatra, Yves Montand, Montgomery Clift, and several others who came to visit.

An important element of what I uncovered in my collaborating with Lena had to do with wiretaps and secret recordings. As Lena tells it, while talking from Marilyn's New York phone to Marilyn at her house in LA, Lena asked, "What is all that clicking and humming sound?"

"It's not me," Marilyn answered. "I hear it all the time, must be the wires, the taps." Lena, surprised by that remark, replied, "What tap? You got taps?"

"Yes, on the phone and in my room. Well, whoever you are," Marilyn continued, "I'm listening too."

"If they can, so can I," she tells Lena another time. "I hired this private detective, Fred Otash something, to record and find out who's listening to me. He said he is hired by everybody famous and that they all do it to each other."

Lena was very suspicious. She warned Marilyn, "Maybe people listen to you talk too much, Marilee."

"Let them listen and let them talk. I don't care anymore, anyway. You plan a big dinner for twenty-five people, lots of food. Everyone is going to see the new Marilyn Monroe! I'm letting it all out, once and for all! I'm going to tell them all about everyone."

"Marilee, what's this about? You mix me up. Why do you want to stir this up?"

"I'm gonna show everyone, even me. I'm not crazy; I'm not a drunk anymore. I'm going to call a big press party and tell everybody everything, what they have all done to me and how I don't need them anymore."

"You be careful what you say on the telephone."

A short time later, Marilyn was invited to a barbecue at Peter Lawford's home. He told her Jack Kennedy would be there. She refused to go and told him about the same plans she had told Lena. Lawford paid her a visit later that day. She was found dead.

After returning from India and working with Prakash Mehra on his latest movie that I had written with him, I attended a producer's seminar and dinner at the Waldorf Astoria Hotel in New York. Sitting at my table were ten other producers, directors, and industry executives. I was explaining my experiences working in India, and when asked what else I was working on I mentioned my latest screenplay in the works about Marilyn and Lena. As usual, I was bombarded with questions. Everyone always wants to know the same thing: How do I think she died, did she screw the Kennedys, and on and on, until one of the older guys sitting at the end of the table, a heavyset gentleman, asked, "Do you know who I am?" and with a smile he said, "I'm Henry Weinstein, the producer you're talking about in your script."

That was it. The ball was in the air. We immediately sat next to each other and swapped stories the rest of the night. We agreed that Henry would come to my boat and spend the weekend, where we would discuss my concepts and his recollections. We did just that; it was amazing. Henry and me, Cuban cigars, rum, and my favorite topic, Marilyn Monroe. Neither Henry nor I am quite sure how she died.

After all is said and done and more than twenty-five years of working on this story, I now see the most important aspect of it, one of the underlying stories in the relationship between Marilyn and Lena. Lena, along with Marilyn's other so-called close friends, were nothing but enablers. They fed Marilyn what she wanted in order to get what they wanted. Just like Michael Jackson, Elvis, Anna Nicole, Whitney, and others, Marilyn died because of the enablers. I also realize people aren't interested in personal or good things about Marilyn; they want to hear the dirt. I have talked with producers somewhat interested in my nice story about Marilyn and Lena, but most of them are more interested in hearing whether they were lesbian lovers, who she slept with, or who killed her. They don't care what Marilyn was really about, what she did as a person, or whether or not she ever cooked a meal or ate a hamburger. I wrote a screenplay, "Marilyn and Lena," based on this relationship, about two women searching and wanting what they didn't and couldn't have. Not a porn movie.

In Charli's Words

Frank was very passionate about his screenplay. He believed a different side of Marilyn should be told, the side none of us really saw, the side of her as a lonely woman, not a sex goddess but just the girl next door. He would often say, "No one really knows her. They only know the same old stories, book after book, movie after movie, the same old thing. We don't even know her. Did she ever eat a hamburger?" When he met Lena, he set out to write that story, a story about two women, one who happens to be Marilyn Monroe and the other an unskilled immigrant from Italy. Frank would wake up in the middle of the night, as he often does when writing, and write until morning, putting down his thoughts, completely immersed in his work.

Lena became my friend. Yes, she was a client of Frank's, but most of the time when he finishes a project he leaves it behind and moves on to the next. He is not a good smoocher nor does he continue relationships when the project ends. He says he is working on that flaw but he is still not good at it. Luckily our phone number was the same for thirty-six years, so many times some of those people eventually call him again with new ideas, requesting his help. They all say the same thing. "Boy, am I glad you still have the same number." There are a few exceptions, a select few people, maybe six or seven he has remained friends with for over forty years. Frank, who doesn't trust anyone, is a great judge of character and is usually right. I, on the other hand, generally stay in touch with people we meet. And Lena was special, someone I felt was more like a family member. Sadly, in the end I was wrong.

When I first met Lena we hit it off right away. She did not trust or respect most people she met in her life, but over the years I gained her trust and respect; she would tell me that many times.

Lena lived at 309 East 76th Street. Marilyn visited her there several times. The apartment was not far from my office, so she would drop by often and I would take her to lunch. Lena was much older than I—old enough, in fact, to be my grandmother—but she called me daily and we became very close friends. When I originally met her many years ago she was physically and mentally much stronger, full of confidence, a strong character, but now as she's gotten older she's become bitter and very disappointed with her life. She has lived in the same three-room walk-up railroad apartment for her entire life since coming to America. Her life in Italy was good, she was brought up well, she had fine tastes, and when she married a GI, Joe Pepitone, she left her loving family, ambitious to be a famous singer or a Hollywood star. Otherwise I don't think she would have married Joe or left her family. Many people that I have met have been disappointed with America, left only with their visions that did not materialize.

Lena came here not speaking English and suddenly was one of the millions of immigrants without any money, now with two young boys and a husband. Unfortunately for everyone, that was the last thing on her mind. She was disappointed and depressed, and then she met Marilyn. Lena was torn with emotion. In one sense she envied Marilyn, but in another way she enjoyed how being her seamstress, maid, and cook made it easy to fantasize being her. Even though Marilyn thought of her as a friend, inwardly Lena was always ambitious and jealous of her money and fame.

Marilyn was a weak, needy person; Lena strong and aggressive. They both needed each other. After Marilyn died, Lena wrote a book about their lives together, only wanting the fame, the money, the high life, not caring or paying attention to the true facts or what the cowriter of her book says, and whether there's some scandalous discrepancy between what was written and what was expected to be written, and whose expectations they were actually writing about—essentially, they were stories filled with false controversy all for pure shock value. Because of that, the book has received very negative and damaging reviews and has painted Lena as a money-grabbing opportunist.

Lena's children always resented the time she spent with Marilyn. They felt and still feel that Lena abandoned them, sold them out for her own personal needs. All children want their mother to be at home, but that was the last place Lena wanted to be. All the way up to the end of her life she was hoping for a new apartment and a lot of money. Money was her real love. I found her to be a person who totally looked down at everyone, thinking she was better than them. She refused to go to the West Side of New York, for example, because she thought it was beneath her. She lived on social security but would only shop in the most expensive food stores on the East Side and would look at everything as if it was not good enough. People were not good enough, and the deals and opportunities were never big enough.

Still, I liked Lena. She did have some good qualities and I guess I wanted her to like me. I spent many afternoons with her. Whenever I would stop by after work she would make me dinner. She was afraid of being alone, so I would sit with her, leaving Frank at home having dinner alone. After Frank finished working on the screenplay he had an idea to write a cookbook based on the dinners Lena prepared for Marilyn and her famous guests. I helped Lena write her stories, taking notes and writing down all of her recipes; the book turned out great.

With the money she was paid for her first book she invested in an Italian restaurant that she owned and operated. It was a lot of work for her and her family, and as it turned out, grabbing this ball still wasn't glamorous enough or lucrative enough in her eyes. Continuing to be a cook was not part of her dream, so she spent more time in the dining room entertaining the customers than in the kitchen. She would wear her mink coat that she also bought with the money from her book. A few years later because of poor management the restaurant closed. Lena only had one "vision" of what her ball was like, and as a result she suffered. She wanted to be the star, and she knew stars like Marilyn did not cook.

One day we got a call that Lena had had a heart attack, and I spent a lot of time in the hospital with her. I would bring her food and feed her. I was the daughter or friend that she never had.

With Lena, everything revolved around how much money you had. She would ask you straight out, "How much money do you have?" and if there was a room full of people she would sniff out the people she believed had the money. That was her downfall. She was very transparent; her loyalty was not there and it was obvious. I am the type of person that truly likes you; rich or poor, I am there for you. Lena was not that person.

Her sons felt neglected right from the beginning of their young lives. She was more interested in her fame and fortune, and if Marilyn called, no matter when, she would leave them. During one of her son's birthdays, a telephone call came from Marilyn and right in the middle of the party she left and went to California. I was to find out later Marilyn would pay her extra cash for those extra requests but she never told her husband, Joey. The boys never got over that. They actually wanted Frank to make a movie about how sad they felt and how sad they still feel. A mother can scar a child and Lena did just that. She was one of a kind. Never satisfied or really happy, always looking for something better, never enjoying what she had.

Lena's apartment was like a shrine to Marilyn. Sometimes I felt her presence and I would wonder what Marilyn might have thought of how Lena would do anything for money. Everyone made money on Marilyn, but I am sure Marilyn would not have believed how Lena took any and every opportunity to make money on their friendship. You are what you eat and you reap what you sow. Unfortunately, that was true for both Marilyn and Lena.

The screenplay feels like I hit a ball that's going to be a home run. The ball is in the air, going and going, but not yet out of the park because the outfield wall keeps on moving back. As it turns out this ball is still in the air. Just today, in fact, September 10, 2012, I got a call from a Marilyn lookalike actress who heard about me and my script. She claims a producer friend of hers may be interested in making my movie or producing my original idea to put it on Broadway. Hopefully this ball will get over that wall sooner than later.

As far as I'm concerned everybody is full of shit except me and Charli.

CHAPTER 23

Signal to Space Concerts

*J*n a flash, the Internet can spread photos, videos, ideas, messages, and stories worldwide. The proverbial ball was in the air again in 2006. Michael Luckman, founder and director of Cosmic Majority, an organization dedicated to the cosmos and alien research, called wanting to know if I could help him figure out what he could do with an idea he had regarding a music concert revolving around aliens and outer space. Even he wasn't quite sure what he or that meant.

I have discovered that most people don't; the ones I meet usually just have a thought or an idea and do not or cannot think it out, and that's when they call me. Mike questioned whether I thought it was a good idea. They all try to get a quick fix without paying their dues. That's when I say, "This is your dream. You woke up this morning with this idea, not me, and in order for me to work on your dream this is my fee."

After several discussions and an arrangement between us, a concept and idea was born. My goal was not just to do a concert predicated on the belief of aliens. I thought it may be difficult to sell to investors and especially sponsors without a better hook, concept, and plan—one they could use to promote their brand and get a return on their investment. So we developed the germ of an idea. We would broadcast the concert music and visuals into outer space and spread the word of peace and harmony. Now we were on to something that I could bite my teeth in.

When I realized we could actually beam images to the moon and beyond, it hit me. I made a comment: "Wouldn't it be funny if we could project Michael Jackson actually moonwalking on the moon?" The idea began to grow. We called the event the Signal to Space Concerts. Mike had connections to Michael Jackson and, equally important, to Michael's mentor, healer, clock stopper, and spoon bender at that time, Uri Geller.

I called Uri Geller, got him on his cell phone while he was in London, and told him the concept. Uri flipped out, saying that he loved the idea and thought it would be great for Michael. He said he would talk to him and get back to me. Several days later, we spoke again. He said Michael liked the idea and wanted Uri to put it together and get back to him with more information. That is when Uri asked me to send him a first-class round-trip airline ticket to New York and $5,000. Two days later it hit the press, first a full page with photos in the *New York Post*, then internationally, in all media including the Internet.

"Whacko Jackson to Moon Walk on the Moon," read one of the many headlines.

I immediately called Peter Saile, my funding partner in past events, and ran down the idea. He thought it would be a fantastic moneymaker and so we were off to the races, forming a company and setting off for Germany. Flying into Tempelhof Airport in Berlin is like no other experience. Imagine the plane approaching the airport by flying in just over the treetops and houses, and then landing in the middle of the city. The idea to surround the airport by houses and buildings was conceived by Adolf Hitler in order to protect him, his troops, and the airport from Allied bombs. He knew the Allies wouldn't bomb the airport if innocent people living in those houses protected it. So instead of bombing it, the Americans flew into it and delivered the famous Berlin Airlift. The planes flew in under fire and delivered food and medical supplies to a starving, cut-off city. What a history. And now we were proposing to stage our event right there at Tempelhof.

I felt like an alien on our way to Switzerland from Berlin during our fourth attempt at getting the big money. We booked a flight on a new airline, Berliner Airlines something or other. During the flight, the stewardess came around taking drink orders. This was when airlines for the first time decided to cut back on what used to be free services.

"Sir, would you like something to drink?"

"Yes, please, may I have a cup of coffee, dark with skim milk and one sweetener? Thank you."

Several minutes went by, and as she walked by again I asked her, "Excuse me, may I have some water, please?" She answered me in a strong German accent in a tone natural to Germans; they weren't and still aren't fond of Americans.

"No." She realized her curt response, forgetting she was the servant, and came back with a forced smile. "You already had your free beverage."

"What? I just want to take my pills. I would like some water. I can't believe this. I have traveled to the jungles of India; they gave me water . . ."

By now, everyone on the plane was listening to my conversation. She wouldn't budge. "Sorry. Would you like to purchase something?"

"No, let me ask you a question. Since we are only entitled to one beverage, what if I ordered a half cup of coffee and a half cup of water—would that be acceptable?"

I was joking, of course, but she walked away saying, "I will check." She came back moments later with an answer only the Germans could give. "We had a meeting regarding your request, and it was decided you could do that as long as next time you fly, you let us know in advance."

She was dead serious, and the whole plane burst out laughing. To add to the ridiculousness, several minutes later we were all given free Coke samples as part of a promotion. Go figure.

Peter and I continued trying to raise millions of dollars for the Signal to Space Concerts. Our idea was growing, and so was my confidence that we could beam, via pulsed lasers and satellites, music and images of the live performers and concert goers to the moon and beyond. There was also room to push the possibility that it might reach intelligent life and the hope of receiving a signal back from space. I added the spin that the concerts would also be a showcase for science and technology, hoping to lure additional sponsors. The initial three SIGNAL TO SPACE CONCERT™ events were to take place in Germany, Japan, and the United States.

These concerts would represent the largest live outdoor music events in the world, and would feature performances by leading rock and pop superstars. But this would be much more than just an outdoor concert; it was a full-blown music cultural festival with scientific experiments, featuring exhibitions and displays that would focus on the future of our planet and developments in new technology, alternative energy, health, and the environment. We acquired actual flying saucers that could hover over the crowd with interactive robots and brain wave machines that could take signals of your brain and turn them into projected graphic images, and much more.

We hired Jerry Standish as our due diligence expert. He always said no. I always say yes. He was hired to attend all our meetings, take notes, and report back to the board of directors on what he learned. He was great at it, except he always found too many problems with the potential projects. We couldn't go forward. One day I called him into my office.

"Jerry, you are very diligent, you see all the problems, but if you keep finding problems with everything and saying no to new business opportunities we won't have a business. So instead of no, please find a solution. Like the little Dutch boy finding a hole in the dike."

Stick your finger in the hole and say yes or I will be forced to fire you.

But he couldn't do it. Saying no was easier for him. The Chicken Little theory applied, so I shot him. The show kept growing and growing and everybody wanted to get involved. Among the scientists and celebrities on the future SIGNAL TO SPACE™ Advisory Team were Dr. Edgar Mitchell, the former Apollo 14 astronaut trained to be America's first man on Mars; Brian O'Leary; radio personality Art Bell; Dr. Tom Van Flandern, former chief astronomer for the US Naval Observatory in Washington, DC; and Stanton Friedman, a Canada-based nuclear physicist.

Many celebrities have reported close encounters with UFOs. John Lennon and his then-girlfriend, May Pang, claimed they were completely naked when a UFO as big as a house maneuvered near the roof of their building. John allegedly ran out and yelled loudly to the flying saucer, "Stop! Take me with you!" World boxing champion Muhammad Ali was jogging in New York's Central Park early one morning while training for his title fight against George Foreman when he supposedly spotted a large UFO. A golden disc may have saved the life of actor William Shatner of *Star Trek* fame, who became lost in the California desert on a motorcycle when he was told telepathically which way to ride back to civilization. Singer David Bowie had a telescope peering through the roof of his limousine so he could search for aliens. Mick Jagger found that the alarm kept going off on his UFO detector every time he left his estate in England. The list of celebrities who believe in extraterrestrials and have had strange encounters is growing all the time.

In the early nineties, along with three other partners, we formed a company, Interconnections, whose only business was to present programs using new interactive voice technology. We joined and partnered with Unisys Technology, an early leader in the field. They helped us develop our own system. Our idea—allow a customer to have simulated interactive live conversations with celebrities and stars over the telephone, cell, or computer using pre-recorded audio and voice recognition—was way ahead of its time. I believed this was the future, and indeed it was. Unfortunately for us, at that point back then it was too far in the future. Now some fifteen years later, without me, that communication technology has made it into our daily life on computers, cell phones, and cars.

Speaking of cars and timing, while Peter and I were having meetings in Germany with investors and sponsors for our space concerts, we met with the president of BMW Motors. I presented our idea, emphasizing the fact that we were all about technology and how that could benefit the BMW brand. He responded by saying he liked the idea very much, but he pointed out that BMW is marketed to a slightly older customer and a high-end buyer than the younger audiences we were targeting. He suggested, however, that the Mini Cooper might be a better fit based on our market. I immediately grabbed the ball.

"I believe we could hit each of our goals and market demographics."

I had his attention and began to reveal my idea, developing it as I spoke. The more he seemed interested the more I went on until I painted the perfect picture.

"We would go after the college and young adult market and turn the Mini Cooper into an extension of the dorm room." I set the hook and he took the bait.

"Interesting. What do you mean by that? Extending the dorm room?"

"We will equip the Mini Cooper with the ability to do what you do in your home or dorm room in your car. It will be completely interactively voice-activated, hands free, plug in your cell phone, listen to your music or the radio, broadcast or Internet, get directions, go shopping, request movie theaters and restaurants, go online, Wi-Fi, Bluetooth . . ."

He liked it very much and suggested I speak to their marketing director. We had several phone and mail conversations, and once we were able to go forward with our funding and Space Concert plans, they said yes. This was 2006.

We never did launch our concerts, though; it was too big an idea, and cost too much to launch, even though we raised hundreds of thousands of dollars in development funds. I should have targeted the concept and developed the bigger picture at hand, which was to equip cars with these features. This has now in 2012 come to market, again without me. This is a perfect example of grabbing the ball without the ability to bring it into the market at the right time. I was too focused on what I perceived was the big picture, but not able to see what was right in front of me. The same thing happened when designing my sheets and pillow cases. I produced and created full color photo-like images on fabric, which itself became an entire business of its own. In order to be successful, you have to recognize your invention. With my sheets and then the technology, I just didn't see sometimes you have be able to see the trees from the forest.

Having a good idea ahead of its time is as bad as having a bad idea.

The Spirit of India 2007

Still, I was not giving up on my Space Concerts. Even as the possibility began to fizzle away I decided to call Artie Kornfeld. After I explained the concept he said maybe we could combine it with his new project, saying he was asked to produce a Woodstock festival in India. He knew he wouldn't be able to get the rights to use the name without losing control to Michael. So he did not want to call it Woodstock anything, thereby avoiding having to deal with Michael and Woodstock Ventures entirely. Artie knew my past history in India, so he arranged to bring me along to assist him as a line producer, or coproducer, or adviser, or consultant; he was never quite sure what to call me. He just knew he needed my help. The investors in India agreed they would put up the money without Woodstock as part of the name. Artie came up with The Spirit Festival. It reminded me of Frank Costanza's Festivus Festival from *Seinfeld*. The generic name ended up being beneficial though, as I later expanded the concept to the rest of the world by first calling it the Spirit of India then the Spirit of Africa, China, Dubai, or anywhere they might want to do one.

During Artie's first trip, his investor and copartner Lalit's family and friends put up the initial investment. They were getting nowhere and going crazy. Artie, playing all ends from the middle as is his custom, made a similar deal at the same time he was working with Lalit, with another group headed by Jackie Shroff—the famous bad-boy Indian actor—that ended in a disaster of mudslinging articles, rumors, and stories in the media. Artie couldn't avoid disaster himself; he claims that while he was looking to score hashish from Jackie's friends, a group took him for a ride, hijacked him, and stole all his money. I doubt anyone will ever know the reality of that story.

At this point Lalit realized he needed help with Artie, so I was brought in to meet all parties, introduce my own vast network in India, and above all try to make it happen. As we would always say, it was truly another Kornfeld Production. The fun began one memorable night at a dinner party in Mumbai, sitting around a large round table with about eight people. Indians love to drink. I mean love to drink. Stupid drink. Prakash Mehra never went anywhere without his bottle of Johnny Black. In the trunk of his car was a wet bar with ice, and he always could be seen no matter where or when, private or public, with a glass of Johnny in one hand, his gold and silver cigarette case and lighter and a white embroidered handkerchief in the other. Prakash was much like Dali; they never carried money and somehow someone else always paid.

The waiter brought everyone a small bowl filled with a hot liquid and a floating square piece of white something, garnished with a piece of leaf on the side. Artie, always the first to indulge, no matter what he is indulging in, takes the hot white thing out of the bowl and proceeds to wash his face with it. We all looked in amazement as he scrubbed his face with what turned out to be, to his shock, a thin piece of sticky noodle dough, now stuck and glued to his face over his eyes and hands. It was a sight to see. He was then told it was a soup, not a hand and face wash. We and everyone in the restaurant including Artie laughed for hours.

Every day is an adventure with Artie and his piles of pills, outbursts, fights, meetings, and interviews. One morning we were off on a several-hour drive to the remote town of Puna to meet with a Guru at his Ashram. Lalit hired a car and driver, but while cruising down the highway in the middle of nowhere we ran out of gas. It seems that in order to save some money, Lalit did not fill the gas tank, waiting to get gas cheaper outside of Mumbai. His calculations were wrong. I have learned this is the Indian way, that you have to account for how Indians think and do things into your own equations if you want to do anything in India. Kornfeld, Lalit, and I had to push the car miles to the next gas station.

When we finally arrived at the Ashram to meet Guru Shri Shri Ravi Shankar Ji, who, by the way, has twenty million followers worldwide, there were hundreds of devotees spread out all over the building, hoping for a glimpse of the Guru. They were on the floor and on the steps, and we literally had to step over and on them to get to the third floor. At our first meeting, Shri Shri, as they call him, stood up from his high-back chair at the head of the large room. He was a small man with long strag-gly black hair and a long unkempt beard. He reminded me of Charles Manson. He approached me and asked, "And what is your name?

"Frank."

He answered back without hesitation, "And are you?" I answered right back, "Always."

He smiled at my quick and direct remark. I hugged him, he hugged me. I don't think you are supposed to hug Gurus.

As in most cases I did the feasibility research, market analysis, budg-ets, and pre-production only to find out the investors didn't have enough money to complete the project. All too often, investors only have the startup funds and are hoping to get other funds along the way, but that almost never works. That's why I get paid up-front and even then not always the full amount. Charli always says, "You have to pay Frank to come to a party."

After several trips, mishaps, and broken promises the investors got cold feet. The spirit was dead. Just when you think you're onto something and you realize you're on the dead ball, I say: sometimes you're on a roll, when you should be on a bagel.

Sanjaya, the False American Idol

Barry G. (I won't mention his real name) is someone who has come in and out of my life, like the locusts who hibernate underground for years then surface for a season and spread havoc. Barry does exactly that; every few years for the last two decades he resurfaces. I never could figure it out. I would come to learn he was manic-depressive, and would only contact me when he was manic. Having been in the entertainment business all my life, compared to others I have met and or worked with, he seemed normal. I had no frame of reference, so I thought that's just how he is. I found him and some of his music and lyrics interesting. He even had a style like Randy Newman meets Neil Young.

One day in 2008, after I can't remember how many years, he called me again, asking if I would help him put together his band and make a record. We agreed to meet at the City Diner on Broadway, where he proceeded to tell me that he was putting together a production company to produce a record for his son; I never knew he had one.

"Who is your son?"

He looked at me cool as a cucumber. "Sanjaya," the young kid from *American Idol* with all the crazy hair. I immediately flashed on his image—that little South Indian-combo-Australian Aborigine-looking kid with a Mohawk. The ball was in the air.

"Sanjaya, your son? What the hell is that? You're kidding me."

"No. He's my son."

"Your son? How did that happen?"

"Do you remember years ago I came to your office with a girl I said I was gonna marry one day? Her name was Jill."

I didn't know what time he was talking about; I did, however, vaguely recall a girl who he was with who didn't seem too keen on Barry's marriage comment.

"What does this have to do with Sanjaya?"

"Well, I married her and he is her son, Sanjaya, who I adopted."

I was in shock. Nothing he said made any sense, but he continued.

"We would like you to manage Sanjaya and put together his record and his career. We have a song ready to go. He needs to do the vocals over, but it's called 'Drive My KARMA.'"

Barry knew the drill. Especially with him, based on his history, I wouldn't do anything without getting paid first. We went back to his apartment. He played me the song; it was corny and dated. Politely I said to let me think about it. Then he said the magic words: "I will fund it all." A few days later Sanjaya's mom, Jill, called me, reminded me how we'd met more than ten years before, and said she would like me to manage her son's career. Barry was gonna fund it, and I would put together the package and make appropriate deals for Sanjaya and his sister, Shyamali. Several days later they all flew to New York. We met and agreed I would become their manager.

A few days later I was able to arrange a full-page article in the *New York Post*, photos and all. The headlines read: "Sanjaya and his sister are moving to New York." Everyone was talking about it. From the first day we met, my inclination at every opportunity was to grab the ball and run. Except it was almost always me alone who grabbed and ran; Sanjaya hardly ever existed. I had to be both Frank and Sanjaya. Sometimes, even if the timing is right, the ball just won't bounce. In some ways Sanjaya was the laziest piece of crap you would ever want to meet. I had to wind him up every day, and that's if I could find him.

In order to make that easier I had him move in with us. We treated him like family, like a son. My kids, Jaime and Frankie, weren't too fond of him, his character, or his dogs. However, they both did a great job on the Sanjaya campaign with Jaime's public relations ideas and connections and Frankie's web design and Internet skills.

Sanjaya entered my life much in the same way things have happened in the past. I never really was a fan of *American Idol*; my interests were only aroused at the end of competition to see if there was truly going to be a talent, one who was a future star, inspirational, innovative, entertaining, who could really contribute in some way. This doesn't matter to Clive Davis, though; he makes things happen anyway and somehow everything he touches turns to gold. He is a genius. Everyone knows that he controls all avenues of the show and its ancillary properties.

Clicking through the channels one evening, before I actually met him, I caught Sanjaya in the middle of a song, unaware of anything that had happened before that moment between him, the judges, and his sister. My first impression was, that's a strange-looking kid. He seemed very emotional and vulnerable, and had a great smile, but was it real or some deep-rooted psychological front?

That was it, though; I never really followed the show. I did see Sanjaya on an occasional press clip here and there. Later, after I met him, the ball was mine. The whirlwind of TV appearances, articles, interviews in newspapers and magazines, TV commercials, fashion shows, a memoir, a music record, and other events had begun.

Through it all, there he was, sleeping. He'd lie on our couch watching TV and social networking all night, then sleep all day and into the evening. He moved into Jaime's old bedroom with his new puppy, Padma, a crazy tiny little miniature Doberman Pincher who shit and pissed everywhere and chewed everything. Sanjaya rarely cleaned it up and if he did you had to do it again to make sure it was clean; that was part of his pattern. You had to do everything he did over or stand next to him to make sure he even did it. I liked him very much, but not the dog; nor did his mother, who, along with his sister, fortunately kidnapped Padma while Sanjaya and I were off somewhere. They went to Montana and gave the dog away to a shelter where they thought Sanjaya would never find it. To prove a point, defiant Sanjaya and his friend tracked down the little dog. After finding it, he brought it back, but eventually chose to abandon little Padma anyway.

Several months later he shows up at my door with a new puppy, Luciano, a French bulldog and terrier mix who also pissed and shit everywhere and chewed on everything—eyeglasses, slippers, shoes, wires, tables, chair legs. After a while he gave the puppy to his sister. Sanjaya as it turns out basically destroyed, caused to die, or abandoned every pet and plant he ever owned.

After we executed the initial management agreement, I immediately took over shaping his career. I didn't think he was showing his total ability as a singer, dancer, and entertainer. He was best as a total performer, a song and dance man. He and Shyamali should be like Kid Creole and the Coconuts, Dan Hicks and His Hot Licks, Ricky Martin, Louie Prima and Keely Smith, Donnie and Marie, Sonny and Cher. But that idea didn't work. Shyamali always said no to everything; her attitude was rooted in a deep resentment for her brother's fame that eventually resulted in nothing ever happening for her.

I began negotiating for him to star in a TV commercial for Nationwide Insurance. Sanjaya, his sister, and I were off to my favorite place, India, to shoot the spot. Arriving in Mumbai, we were treated as royalty, especially from my friends and connections, five star all the way. Sanjaya was blown away. His only other time in India had been to visit his father in a very small remote village in Bangladesh. His father was a musician and abandoned him and his family at a very young age. So arriving in Mumbai as royalty was a first. Everyone knew him, stopped him, hugged, kissed, and took pictures. It was amazing how all of India recognized him, even in the remote village where we shot the commercial.

Another example of grabbing the ball with Sanjaya was when Brian Shinn, a member of the Shriners organization, contacted me. They were exploring the idea of Sanjaya helping in some way by becoming a spokesperson and host performer at the annual Shriners convention in Fargo, North Dakota. We went there to help raise funds for the flood victims, and by the time I was finished, Sanjaya was the master of ceremonies for the three-ring circus and performed in front of thousands of screaming young kids. Actually, mothers, fathers, grandmothers, people of all shapes, sizes, and ages came out to see him. After the event, Sanjaya said that he had never been to a circus. Yet there he was, singing, surrounded by elephants and flying trapeze girls. That was one of the first of many firsts for Sanjaya. During that time, he also flew an airplane for the first time. He was gliding over North Dakota; we took pictures of the unbelievable floods. At Fashion Week in New York City, he modeled and walked the runway; he was a sensation and a natural model. We also wrote a book, published by Simon and Schuster, released a musical album, and performed live shows. He also starred on a television reality show *I'm a Celebrity, Get Me Out Of Here*, which was shot live from Costa Rica and aired on NBC for a month.

Then he disappeared back to his mother's and sister's arms and took his grandfather's name, Joseph Recchi, for some reason. His mom couldn't take it anymore; she felt out of control, knowing she couldn't control me, and thereby unable to control Sanjaya, but more importantly unable to control his money. With Sanjaya it became "rags to riches to rags" when he disappeared back to his mother. She sure did a great job; now he is broke again singing on the subway. You are what you eat.

Sanjaya is special and maybe he can reappear on top again, but the question is whether he will want to, and stop being the False American Idol. In this case I had grabbed the ball that wouldn't bounce.

In Charli's Words

The first time Frank and I met Sanjaya, he was with his sister, Shyamali, their mother, Jill, and Barry G. at a restaurant on Broadway on the Upper West Side here in New York City. Jill was Barry's ex-wife. I didn't say much. I just watched and listened. Sanjaya and his sister were adorable, well-mannered, and seemed very nice. I liked them, they liked us, but you could not help but notice as Barry spoke that Sanjaya became filled with anxiety and rolled up into a ball. He was definitely trying to cope with just being with Barry, let alone with what he was saying. He was completely traumatized. I didn't know why, but from the moment I saw her I did not like Jill. She was watching Sanjaya's every move and most of the time speaking for him; it seemed as if this is how he had lived his life, with his mother scamming people while the children did whatever she might say, no matter what it was. My initial impressions unfortunately became reality.

Jill had great plans for Barry. She knew how to manipulate him and was focused on his money, and he had a lot of it. Barry was totally in love with Jill and would do anything for her. She was very cute but cunning and could never be trusted. My basic instincts were to stand clear of her and she knew it.

It all came about quickly; it felt like all of a sudden we were managing Sanjaya. Soon Frank was off to India to shoot a TV commercial he had arranged for Sanjaya and Nationwide Insurance, and they would take Shyamali along. When they returned, Sanjaya, Jill, and Shyamali were going to move in with Barry. Shyamali would not stay at Barry's, though, and could not leave fast enough. The next day she was off to see her boyfriend in LA. I thought it was strange she had no desire to see or stay with her mother and seemed to resent all the attention Sanjaya was getting. Most daughters are so connected they can't wait to spend time and talk to their mom. Not this girl; she couldn't wait to get away from all of it.

Sanjaya was younger than his sister and very vulnerable. He grew up in a house of domineering women: sister, mother, aunts, and cousins, all women. He would do anything and everything they said he should do. He wanted to break his ties with them now, so he was going to stay with us, after refusing to live with his mother and Barry. He wanted to be free of their controls and begin to be himself. I thought that was unbelievable. I certainly could never just drop off my children somewhere with people I hardly knew. My kids would never stand for that either, but Sanjaya, like a robot, did anything Jill wanted. He must have been dropped off a lot as a child. He didn't have anything to say about it and now he was living with us in New York City. I think he was seventeen years old.

We became close. He was a really nice boy so I took him under my wing and tried to make him feel like one of the family. Well, my kids did not appreciate sharing me or Frank and more importantly could sense Sanjaya was a user, believing that with him what you saw was not what you got. It was obvious they did not like him. He was always looking in the mirror, posing, and always on the cell phone taking orders from his mother. I tried to explain to Frankie and Jaime that he was Frank's client and to give Sanjaya a break, but my kids did not give breaks, so they completely avoided him.

I suggested Sanjaya should consider going back to school, but no one liked that idea, especially his mother. She wanted him to have a career and make lots of money. In fact, she was the one who pushed her kids and became the annoying backstage mom during American Idol.

I took Sanjaya to 42nd Street to teach him the subway system. I thought he would have to get around New York and should have an understanding of where he was. We went to the train station and stood on the platform and then we got on the train. Everyone in the car recognized him and lined up to get his autograph, showering him with love and affection. He was a natural star. This was unbelievable; he was smiling and happy to meet all of the people on the train. Old, young, men, women, black, white, Spanish, and Asian, he was recognized by everyone and he had a charisma that was magnetic to everyone who came in contact with him. I have never seen anything like it. Wherever we went he was recognized and stopped and asked to sign autographs. He always did it with a kind and willing attitude. He was a natural and everyone was attracted to his smile.

Jill was kind of a free spirit, hippie type who found Sanjaya's biological father in Bangladesh, under a hut, and brought him and his entire family back to Seattle to live, and then they had two beautiful and talented children.

Sanjaya experienced all the influences to completely confuse a kid. Jill divorced his Indian father and latched on to Barry, who is an Orthodox Jewish, manic-depressive millionaire, perfect for Jill's plans. And then she went to work. She is a natural Svengali but something else must have happened; I don't know what, but something that really frightened her children. A manic depressive is something I have never been in contact with, but I could always sense that those children at a young age must have seen something traumatizing and been permanently scarred. I am sure it was not easy for Jill either, and eventually Jill divorced Barry.

Just about that time she was arrested for growing and selling a huge amount of marijuana with her new boyfriend in the woods behind their house in Seattle. Shyamali was also arrested. She was only a teenager and this was not easy for her because her mother had brought her in to this. During American Idol *the people working on the show found out about it on the Internet, and this was something that kept them from choosing them as winners. When the kids were auditioning for* American Idol, *Shyamali was not chosen but Sanjaya was, and I don't think she ever recovered from that rejection. Jill was a real backstage mother and very impressed with her kids. She thought they would be really big stars, and they could have been, but Jill caused havoc on the set of the show. She became overzealous that her kids were going to be such big stars and was so demanding the producer banned her from traveling and production. It was after that we met Sanjaya and Shyamali and we were hopeful to begin a terrific career.*

When Frank and Sanjaya were writing the book about his life and experience with American Idol, *the cowriter would call every morning. We would do everything we could to wake Sanjaya up after staying up all night hanging out at comedy clubs, then texting on his phone and playing video games till the early morning before going to sleep, and waking up again early in the afternoon ready to work when the rest of the world was about to end their day. It was a lot of work; Sanjaya was high maintenance. It was Frank and the writer who wrote most of the book. He was never ready to write. He did not want to do it, since if he did he would have to put some effort into it, just like his music. Sanjaya would do as little as possible, just enough to fake it or get by. In one memorable part of the book he revealed that he could in a flash turn on as he called it his* American Idol *Smile, and that it worked every time. Funny, when I see President Obama flash his smile it is identical to the false* American Idol *Smile that Sanjaya would flash all the time.*

After the book was finished, when he gave a copy to his mother, she told him it was mediocre and made him feel very bad. She never gave him praise for anything.

He went to Costa Rica with Frank who got him on the reality show I'm a Celebrity, Get Me Out of Here! *I thought he was great, he really should have won, but again something political happened and he did not make it to the end. I think Holly, another contestant on the show, really fell for him and the producers saw a great angle of Sanjaya and Holly. Sanjaya, however, couldn't do it; he did not respond sexually, so that was it for him on the show.*

Again, Jill decided Sanjaya did not need a manager, that she would be the manager. It was a plot to get control of his money again, like she had done before Frank took over. She knew he would not let her near it, so she worked her poison on Sanjaya and forced him to leave Frank. I know Sanjaya was disappointed. Frank and he had a real connection, like a father and son, but nothing ever happened for him again. That was really sad because we put a lot of time and effort into Sanjaya, and he was so talented. He had his moment and that was the end. I must say after all we have done for Sanjaya, not only Frank generating a lot of money for him by recording and distributing a record, shooting TV commercials, writing a book, starring on a reality TV show, doing endorsements, shows and events, but also giving him my home and taking care of him, feeding him, doing his laundry, and treating him like a son, I was very surprised and hurt by Sanjaya just walking away without saying thanks or goodbye. I heard he was singing karaoke in a pizza place somewhere in Seattle. It will take years for him to figure out what he should do with his life, but first he must get rid of his sister and mother. That won't be easy.

After Sanjaya disappeared and Lena Pepitone fired me for the third time, I'd had enough of working on everyone else's life and dreams. I decided to just do me all the time, like Hemingway, retire to my beloved boat and just fish and write this book, smoke cigars, and drink rum. That is all well and good, but it's not working. My phone keeps ringing and I realize I have to keep answering it. It is what I do. I am still and always will be looking for my next ball. "Does anyone want to play?"

CHAPTER 24

Woodstock on Broadway

*I*n the summer of 2010, the Woodstock saga, of course, continued. Lang called me with an idea he has had to produce "Woodstock on Broadway." Buried in the conversation was a subliminal "Don't tell Artie yet until I get it off the ground." Michael keeps telling Artie, "Don't worry; you will be involved," but no one believes it, not even Artie. They're already arguing about who came up with the idea for Woodstock on Broadway.

Michael invited me and Charli to stay with him at his home in Woodstock, along with selected guests who were involved in the original festival in some shape or form. The purpose of the visit was to contribute our thoughts on what Woodstock on Broadway should be. About a dozen of us sat around the living room, voicing our opinions one by one. No one had a clue what would or could work. I was the last to talk. A hush came over the room as I took my original glass vial filled with psychedelics from 1969 out of my pocket and placed it on the table.

"We should all take a hit before we continue, to get us in the right frame of mind." Everyone freaked out. I continued.

"Since a baby was actually born at Woodstock '69 and everyone and the media talked about it, I think a baby should be born at every performance, just like in '69. We could go live to a hospital delivery room, and project the image on stage in the theater. It would be great press."

Needless to say, since then Michael never asked me to participate in Woodstock on Broadway again. Shit, it's going on right now. Artie just called me to touch base. He brought up my book.

"I hear you're writing your book."

"I am."

This of course led to Artie's favorite topic: Woodstock.

"So," he announced, "I'm working on my own Woodstock on Broadway."

"Oh, with Michael?" I asked. Sarcastically.

"No, on my own. You'll be involved. Don't worry."

I am, I thought. I won't be surprised if Woodstock on Broadway happens . . . and Charli and I have to buy our own tickets to see it. Finally, Artie used the words that I knew he would: "Cheech, don't tell Michael."

The real Woodstock never happened. Its true spirit of peace and love, we are all one, was a myth that lasted for three days. So, it happened, sure; but it didn't last. Today there is no Woodstock Nation. Its true message disappeared in smoke and mirrors. Those first three days of Woodstock '69 were the first Berlin Wall, the first Tiananmen Square in China, the first Tahrir Square in Egypt. None of the original '69 festival planners had any idea what was about to happen. A million united people showed up, with no violence, and generated the momentum. There is no doubt that they grabbed a big ball of opportunity.

In my opinion, though, no one had a clear direction in mind where to run with the ball, and they all fell down before they got to the goal line. I have said many times to Michael and Artie to keep it going, but don't forget what was started.

The Woodstock Nation was supposed to be the birth of a new generation, a generation of Green Peace, Save the Whales, and No More War. It should have symbolized what was right and wrong with our world. The name Woodstock and its logo should have become the *Good Housekeeping* seal of approval for products and events worldwide. It was nothing like the Monterey Pop Music Festival in 1968, which was mainly a pop music festival. Instead, though, Woodstock only still exists today in name, several festivals later, and they're still missing the boat now about big business and mixed messages.

The film clip of Richie singing "Freedom" from the Woodstock stage should have been broadcast with every freedom protest across the world, from Serbia, China, Africa, Egypt, to Libya, to Wall Street and throughout Europe—wherever people need to be free to express and demonstrate their beliefs and make a stand against totalitarian governments and dictators. Even though we in the United States still have these rights they are slowly being stripped away by our own growing government, our increasing dependence on entitlements, and an overall moral breakdown as demonstrated in our TV shows, movies, music, and videos where anything goes. When I read what I have written here I wonder how I, one of the original Hippies, a pioneer of social and democratic reform and freedom, have changed.

Just the other night I was on the phone with Artie; as I hung up, Charli came home. "Get ready," she said, "we have to leave for dinner soon."

"Where are we going?"

She sort of scolded me. "Did you forget?"

"Forget what?"

"About our dinner, with Michael."

I had not forgotten. Charli never told me we were to meet Michael, Anne Lang, his ex-wife, and his new wife, Tamara, along with several others, to celebrate his birthday at the Peking Duck House in Chinatown.

When we get together, no matter how much time passes between meetings, it is like the three of us—Charli, Michael, and I—have seen each other every day. We laugh and reminisce about the great times and experiences we have shared for over forty years.

Charli brought us back as soon as we sat down.

In Charli's Words

Sitting at the table I couldn't help but say, "I guess we should have a duck for the table."

We laughed at the memory, traveling back in time to the Chateaus of France and England. At one point, Anne asked me about the mannequins in our apartment.

"We don't have them anymore."

One of Michael's twin daughters, now in her thirties, who had joined us at the table, jumped up from her seat. "What do you mean you don't have the mannequins anymore?"

Shala was distraught, although seeing such a strong reaction made me smile. I realize those mannequins made a profound, lasting impression, and many people ask about them.

Soon, though, the conversation came back to the present.

Michael stopped eating, put down his fork, looked at me, and said, "Artie told me you're writing a book."

"Yes, I am," I proudly answered.

"What's it about?"

"*You*, and everyone at this table." They all choked on their duck. I told him more than I should have. The authorship of ideas tends to be confused when you are dealing with Michael and Artie. I could literally hear his wheels churning.

"How do you like writing?" He fiddled with his fork, moving the food around his plate, never looking up. "Can you remember all the parts?"

He seemed to be hoping I couldn't. Waiting for my answer, he then looked at me with suspicion and began to reaffirm things, as if he could positively influence my memories. But I remember everything.

I love Artie Kornfeld. I will always remember his big heart and funny humor that fights through his devastation from losing his wife and daughter to drugs. I personally don't know how he lives with it. Every year, we talk about Linda and Jamie and losing my beautiful brother James. Every time I think of them, I cry.

In 2019 it will be the fiftieth anniversary of Woodstock. I will be seventy-five years old. Nothing changes.

I am very blessed and lucky to have lived at the same place and to have kept the same phone number for thirty-six years. This affords me the luxury of people from my past calling me, oftentimes years after we've last spoken, along with the many new people who call and say, "I got your phone number from so and so."

Just recently, I got such a call from an acquaintance who wanted my advice regarding an idea that had to do with the Mayan calendar that predicts the end of the world in December 2012. He introduced me to Joe Campo Jr., who is in the construction business running a company he took over from his father, Joe Senior. In the 1940s, Ray Kroc, then new owner of McDonald's Hamburgers, hired Campo Construction to build his first 1,500 franchises. Later on Joe Jr. expanded the business and helped his father build shopping malls and private homes.

Several years ago, he became one of the first builders of survival shelters. The concept they had was to raise capital and launch a new business to build survival sustainable living geodesic domes. I must say Joe's concepts and designs, along with several proprietary-patented products, impressed me, so I agreed to join him and to explore the possibilities.

I then had a thought. I believed there was a market to sell these domes, but I suggested that we expand our business to include what I knew was a bigger market, incorporating Joe's inventions and patents to build sustainable grow rooms that would allow private growers and farmers to grow vegetables hydroponically and organically in our self-contained grow rooms.

I am convinced because of the world's current economy that our grow domes are a perfect product. This product is needed in America as well in Africa, South America, India, China, and other countries throughout the world that need to have better resources for growing their own food.

It never ceases to amaze me how often grabbing one ball leads to another. In this instance, alongside our grow dome products, we developed what we came to call a healing wand tracking system. It was born out of the need for indoor marijuana growers; apparently the farmers lose a substantial amount of their plants because of mold, mildew, and spider mites. So, we offer a solution to that problem, which also works for fruits and vegetables. Our wand system travels above the plants, emitting an ultraviolet light and spraying a healing, non-hazardous natural oil solution that cures the sick plants. We copied this formula from the NASA space program. And this ball, too, led to yet another. After we developed the tracking wand I said to Joe, "Why don't we design a handheld mini wand that can be used in the home, in nurseries and flower shops?" So we did. We built a prototype and just filed for a patent. Just like that, the Plant Doctor Healing Wand was born.

I have decided I will keep going, keep looking for the next ball of opportunity, knowing, as I have said before, that I am extremely blessed. Eventually the phone rings with my next adventure. Today I signed an agreement to represent the Sanford H. Roth Collection, owned by Francesca Robinson Sanchez, the granddaughter of legendary actor Edward G. Robinson. Francesca's is one of those stories of someone who knows someone who knows me. It seems she got my name and was aware of my past experience with Joe Franklin Productions, the public company I formed to package and distribute Joe's vast collection of memorabilia. Francesca's collection comprised several thousand items from the world famous photographer Sanford H. Roth: original photographs, negatives, notes, stories, film of the most famous stars, celebrities and artists, travel photos and other one-of-a-kind items. Some of the photos include Albert Einstein, Judy Garland, Marlon Brando, Sophia Loren, Matisse, Picasso, and hundreds of others, including James Dean.

James Dean and Sanford, known as "Sandy," became very close friends. Dean adopted Sandy as his father after living with Sandy and his wife Beulah. Sandy was in Dean's Ford station wagon driving behind Dean in his new Porsche Spider on the way to the Salinas Road Races on September 30, 1955, when Dean died in a late-afternoon crash. It was Sandy who took the now famous post-accident photographs of Dean's mangled Porsche with him in it.

The Roth project and the Plant Doctor are both in the development phase. The ball is in my hand. The cookbook Charli mentioned is done, complete with photos, stories, and recipes based on the dinners Lena helped Marilyn Monroe prepare for her New York guests like Arthur Miller, Frank Sinatra, and Joe DiMaggio. As these balls are in play I have my eye on several others in the air.

Some things keep going and the ball keeps bouncing. I am now in discussions to package several other famous photographers and nostalgia collections, including the Sanford Roth collection, and do what I did with Joe Franklin's memorabilia in 1987 when we launched that public company. So I called Joe, who was thrilled to hear from me, and said he would be happy to make his collection available. Bert and I are having lunch with him next week.

I just got an email from Michael Rubenstein, one of the producers of Tony award winning show *Pippin*. He wanted to talk to me about a new off-Broadway show that he was working on about Marilyn called "Naked Marilyn." I grabbed the opportunity to get involved, as this topic was something that I have been covering for many years. When I wrote my original story twenty years ago about Marilyn, the concept was to launch the story on Broadway and later through a theatrical film. Meetings with agents and talent are underway.

CHAPTER 25

Charli, My Yellow Brick Road

One thing I can say for sure about Charli is that our relationship grows stronger every day. It feels as if we were meant for each other. I can't imagine being with someone else or that anyone else could put up with me like Charli does. Through all I've done, Charli has always encouraged me to be who I am and to do what I do, and I make sure to do the same for her. We share everything equally and spend a lot of time together; we kiss each other good night, every night, making sure never to go to bed angry at one another. Sometimes when she is not aware I look at her and smile, communicating without words and reflecting on a past moment. When we walk down the street together we often hold hands. Just like Papa Pedone said, we're like "two weeds bending in the wind."

My character is likened to the following metaphor most of the time. I share half of my English muffin, giving the person I'm sharing with half of the top half, and half of the bottom half. We both get exactly the same, not I get the top, you get the bottom. This is true if I care about you. Sharing with people I don't care for, on the other hand, I take the whole top half or whatever half is bigger, and of course if I don't like the person I may just offer them a bite or offer nothing at all, then declare the Brooklyn rule of "no a'kees."

Unlike myself, when people meet Charli, there is no split. They like her immediately; I have never met anyone who didn't. She adds a balance to my character, which can separate a room as soon as I walk in. I can't help it; my aura comes out. Maybe it has something to do with my long hair and beard, as Mrs. Benson of the Gurdjieff Institute warned me. In any case, people tend to react to my character right away; they judge the book by its cover. This is most evident when I enter a room full of people. Without Charli by my side the room seems to part like the Red Sea.

People feel it and see it in various ways, sometimes as a threat, sometimes enviously and resentful of my confidence and freedom. As a matter of fact, though, that's how I like it. I basically don't trust people. When the room parts it's easy for me to see who is who, the likes and the don't likes. Charli understands me, welcomes and respects my character. She is my social alter ego, bridging the gap for me. That's why I send her in first. When Charli is there with me, she brings both sides together.

I call her the parrot on my shoulder, always helping me by whispering in my ear and leading me in an alternative—usually better—direction I might never have considered without her. She puts everyone else before herself; her first focus is on me and our kids. She always says that our family is her career first, and her loyal trust and dedication to us keeps other distractions and men away from her. They just don't exist for Charli.

Charli's presence allows me to slow down and think before I react. It's a proven scientific fact that your feelings react faster than your thoughts. They are an alert system, a defense mechanism built in to protect us from danger. My reaction time is faster than instantaneous. This has both helped me and worked against me; it is the Brooklyn in me that tests and helps me evaluate the situation or judge people for who and what they are. In that immeasurably small moment I can read people 95 percent of the time. I am almost never wrong.

I have learned to find trouble before it happens, with my built-in antenna that signals my air raid siren to go off. I make calculated decisions in the blink of an eye, and then make my final decision during the blink. When I find myself in the middle of an imminent conflict my radar alerts me and my instinctual reactions to my feelings and self-preservation take over. I begin flying on automatic pilot and I react with quick, strong conviction. This can be a problem, and in some cases gets me into a battle. Once my trigger is cocked and my hot feelings take charge I don't have a nice switch. I enter the fight or war with everyone and everything as fair game, and you become the enemy; the ball I grab is grabbed to win at any cost.

That's where Charli comes to the rescue. She is the opposite; her natural instinct is to be nice when interacting with others. Even if they are aggressive, she defuses them. She is wonderful when considering other people, especially, of course, with her family. Our relationship remains strong because she knows that I want her by my side so I will always include her. Whoever I meet and wherever I go, she doesn't feel left out. I always say, "Let me introduce my wife, Charli." There are no boundaries between our personal and my business life. She gives me great courage.

I'm thankful that Dali taught me his secret when I asked how he and Gala get along so well. "Gala knows she comes first," he answered. "Always invite and include her, then she will pick and choose when and where to go, knowing she doesn't have to go to protect her position." Charli and I have both put in a lot of work to make our relationship as strong as it is. We reap the benefits of our hard work when people feel our vibe and togetherness, and people know not to mess with the unbreakable bond of "Frank and Charli." We trust and love each other, like Dali and Gala.

On one occasion, I faltered. Not too long ago, I stepped over the line. Tension and apprehension were building in Charli's mind, new anxieties that I wasn't paying enough attention to were combining with old feelings and thoughts of my escapades in Paris, India, and Russia that had been stifled but remained unresolved, and had been lying dormant for too long. Her uneasiness collided with my irritability from the boredom and pressure of a lull in my work and not having much income. My self-esteem and sense of worth were low and I felt like I wasn't contributing to my family's well-being. A simple disagreement over some trifle escalated to a major argument. I overreacted, ranting and raving and threatening her. She was shocked that I would or even could go there. I was equally surprised. It came out of nowhere. She really got scared and called the cops and then threw me out. I slept in my car, and the next day I begged to come back. I wrote her a letter explaining why she should reconsider. I explained how Dali, too, had had a rough road, how he had several other women and a gay lover boyfriend, Federico García Lorca. In that regard we are not totally similar, however in many ways we are. Sometimes things get turbulent and off track but no matter what it was Dali was able to make it work with Gala. Nothing could change his love for her, nor hers for him. He continued to include her in many of his paintings and you could always see her standing in the background or next to him no matter where he went. To my surprise, I recently learned that from his deathbed, Dali died listening to his favorite opera—*Tristan and Isalda*.

I promised Charli to never go there again, and thankfully her belief and faith in God and love for me helped us return to the Gala-Dali relationship, but with the major addition that I never betray my respect for her and threaten to damage the beautiful thing we've created together. She accepted, but it took a while to get back to normal. I had to be super cautious and still am. She believes in Gala's cashew bird theory. It helps her stay grounded, and to this day she lets me fly free, knowing that I will always come back. Still, I know I don't tell Charli I love her enough.

When I see old pictures of myself, I know I don't look the same but I also know nothing has changed inside. I still think and feel like I'm twenty-five, especially when I'm with Charli and my kids. We do every-thing together, especially cook. My kids learned how to cook from me, and I from my mother, and she from her mother, and on and on. As a matter of fact, when I met Charli she couldn't boil water. My aunts took her to their houses where she spent days learning how to cook our fam-ily's traditional meals. Jaime and Frankie always call me to say, "Hi, Dad. Are you okay?" I have the greatest kids.

CHAPTER 26

Conclusion and Reflections

Telling stories dates back to the beginning of man. The storyteller was and still is the most important link in civilization and his community. He documents the past and present, and then passes the torch to the next storyteller. From cave drawings to the Bible and Koran, then printed books, pictures, and movies, the storyteller has captured the moments and events of time. Stories are time capsules, preserving our history for others to learn, providing a guide to the past and a map to the future. And now social networking is a new form of storytelling, instantly reaching millions of people who can then share their own thoughts and comments instantly.

It was in the early sixties when I first began to write down my little stories and events, wondering back then and still today, why am I compelled to document my life experiences? What's the purpose? Who would care about me or what I have to say? Looking back and reflecting over forty years of my notes and stories, people and events, I decided to do it, to put it all together once and for all. Jarred Weisfeld, my agent, said, "Why not? You are somebody. People would be interested in your story." I, on the other hand, still believe you have to do something like blow up a building, have eight babies, or kill your agent to be famous enough for people to read your book. We will see.

I don't particularly care how many people actually buy this book in terms of making money. I am more interested that it inspires you, the reader, to live your life as what you are and who you can become, not what you or others think you should be, and most importantly that you "*Do it now!*" Grab the ball and run.

Writing this book is like emptying and freeing space on my mind's hard drive, leaving room to add more. Writing for me is like an addiction, a drug you use in order to secretly feed your ego, hoping someone will read your story, learn something, acknowledge your existence, and thus make you feel rewarded and important enough to keep going unless you're dead.

This book documents a true historical time capsule, a slice of life. I want it to be humorous, educational, and inspirational, with useful philosophies and tools. If it delivers these values for, say, $25, then you, the reader, are getting something for your money. You're happy you've read something of value, and I'm happy I'm getting paid for my work; everyone should be happy! If you're not, you can always, as I have said before, stick your fish in it.

I continue to share my life experiences with my partner, Charli, who in turn continues to let this bird fly. And I dedicate this to Frank W. Abagnale Jr., who thirty years ago walked into my office at Bert Padell's wanting to make a movie of his life. He began to unfold an unbelievable story, so unbelievable, in fact, that I couldn't imagine who would believe it. Who was this guy, anyway? How could he have done all these unbelievable things? Boy, was I wrong. It took him over thirty years to get his movie made. *Catch Me If You Can* had Hollywood's biggest stars and was nominated for two Oscars. History, however, as I've seen time and again, has a habit of repeating itself. A few months ago, I was sitting in my agent Jarred's office discussing the progress of this book. I revisited my experience with Frank Abagnale Jr. when Jarred jumped up and said,

"Wait here. I want you to meet someone." He returned with a woman and he introduced me to her. "Frank, I'd like you to meet a friend of mine, a Broadway producer. Tell her the story about Frank Abagnale."

I did and she was surprised at what I told her, but not as surprised as I was when she said I must come to the Broadway opening of the musical she had produced—*Catch Me If You Can*. You can meet Frank, she said. *A Broadway musical,* I thought. I was speechless. Years ago I couldn't imagine they would make a movie based on his outrageous story, and now a musical. I was convinced if he could do it, so could I.

My story is not just about my life, my business, or my art. It's about setting yourself free by grabbing the ball. It's about living the life of who you are, and working hard. It's also about how to deal with insecurities, which in my case largely dealt with my learning disability. All my life I've driven myself to overcome my dyslexia as best I could, or at least be able to work through it. Fears and self-doubts became my lightning rod; I looked them in the eye, grabbed the ball, and ran on by, past my fears of failing. I make sure I don't. You can do it, too.

I have come to believe we humans are the byproducts of manipulated energy, and that our ultimate goal is to cross over from the physical world to the spiritual, or perhaps the other way around. Either way, in order to be free and happy, you must lead a life of who you truly are, not what you have to be. I am amused by those who post photos and send messages to me on Facebook. Facebook is a place that narcissists use to post how they want to be seen. An investment banker I know, for example, constantly posts what new bands are in town, or which new albums or TV shows or movies he likes. But this "person" who is posting this material is not the investment banker I know.

Moving up the ladder of life, I have learned that you cannot be like or apply the Machiavellian theory, and surround yourself with people you keep under your thumb. Men get jealous, envious, and they resent it. Most Machiavellian men don't like to share their perceived throne, especially when others rise to become their equal or pass them by. They feel threatened.

Guccione, for example, resented my creativity and popularity. Eddie Gilbert was troubled that I was more well-known than him. Paul Parino couldn't share his perceived power. Michael Lang was unable to share. Artie Kornfeld had to be sole king and get all the recognition. Joe Franklin was never satisfied and greedy. Bert Padell sat at his throne alone until he got Parkinson's. Gunner Larson liked taking all the credit. My answer to all of this nonsense is: *You can be king or president as long as you pay me.*

I now know from personal experience and observations that artists of all kinds are resented and sometimes persecuted because of their freedom to grab the ball, make the first stroke and be successful without anyone else's help. It's that freedom that enables them to do and be who and what they truly are, living the life they want, not one that's dictated by others. But there is freedom to live the life you are, artist or not.

I am the opposite of whom I started out as; now I exude confidence and self-esteem and feel there is nothing I can't do. Through my evolution from shy kid to partner of the seas, I've learned that you must listen to your instincts and the voice inside your head. Go with your gut feeling. Trust yourself only, then you will have only yourself to hold accountable. Learn from your past experience and decisions—good or bad, right or wrong—without blaming anyone else. Don't second-guess, and realize this: Always do your best and you won't be disappointed. Determination is the key. Keep moving up, not down, don't give in to your fears or stop dreaming, never quit, take risks, teach yourself to excel, and always be driven to the point of exhaustion. Then get up and do it again.

Reflecting on events in my life, no matter where or when, I see that each of my encounters were all just part of the journey—necessary links in the chain of experiences that made me who I am; no encounter more important than the others. As I look back on my work now, I see things written over the years, the events and the people I've met along the way, one after another, all as parts of a painting, whose image and message became clearer as I put them down, one brush stroke at a time. Some strokes overlap others years later, and I often had no idea what was going to happen next or what the finished painting would become. But I never put my brush down.

I've taken advantage of opportunities, and I know that if I hadn't, life could have bounced right by me. Life is my ball, and many times it's allowed me to turn nothing into something. I have become very good at recognizing that the ball is in the air. You can, too. Find out who you are and what your yellow brick road is. To be who you are, you need more than financial success. You need freedom to do what you want, or as close to it as you can. Take control over the ball of life.

And when you take control, do it right. Just grabbing the ball without doing something with it is sacrilegious. You must always do something, even if you are juggling several balls at the same time. Otherwise the balls you've grabbed will disappear or grow old and life will bounce by.

I see now that my life's message is clear. The yellow brick road, the threads that weave through it all, holding each story together, all have the same thing in common: I grab the ball and run, knowing it's now my ball, reacting without hesitation and, as some have said, with a fine disregard for the rules. Every episode has been a risk. To risk or not to risk, that is not only the question but the true challenge in life, to go beyond what you perceive as your limits, regardless of doubt, fear, and uncertainty, and change those thoughts by simply looking at them as part of the process of evolution. "Anybody can do it, just do it now."

Grab the ball and run like hell.

That is my yellow brick road, the message, and moral of my story.

"I am what I am, and that's all that I am." (Popeye the Sailor Man)

I am the ball.

CHAPTER 27

Postscripts

Junior
Brooklyn 19 New York

There is something to be said about my belief: If you didn't grow up in Brooklyn, you didn't go through Basic Training.

The early years of my youth growing up in Brooklyn definitely shaped my persona and character. They influenced how I think and react. Those experiences taught me, above all, that if you snooze you lose.

The following stories reflect the events that developed and formed the early foundation of my life. Now, decades later, I can see in these stories the man, the artist, the ball grabber that I've become. I hope reading this book and its stories have been as enjoyable as it was for me experiencing them.

My First Job

I learned the art of trading and bartering at what I consider to be my first job. I was seven years old, standing at the top of a ten-step red-and-green painted concrete stoop, with four other young boys playing one strike two strike, scissor-paper-rock, and flipping baseball cards, all in order to win comic books from each other. I was learning plenty of applicable skills through buying, selling, trading, and winning as many comics, baseball cards, and marbles as I could. It's an obsession, and demands respect and power from the kids on your block.

The rules dictate that the winner of the previous round gets to pick what game to play next. Each round's winner gets the four comics put up as ante for each game. Little Michael Scarsella chose one strike two strike, and eliminated everyone else but me. Now it was just the two of us for the whole pile, all the comic books. The other kids had lost Spiderman, Batman, Dick Tracy, Archie, and Veronica (I never read that one)—about twenty comics in all. (As I'm writing this, my first girlfriend, Maryanne Piccorelli, just popped into my mind. I wonder what she is doing. Hey, Maryanne. Call me. Let's catch up.)

I'd picked odd, little Michael got even. He's looking at me with determination. "Ready," he says, and with a weak stare he starts the count. "One strike . . ." In perfect rhythm with the counting we pump our closed fists toward each other's face with a vengeance. ". . . two strike . . . three strike . . . shoot." I knew I had him. His weak stare was no match for my squinted-eye smirking smile. I throw out two fingers, he throws out one finger—it's odds. I've won. I knew it all along. I felt it. I could psyche him out. He hates me. He thought since I picked odds I would throw out one finger and so he would win with evens. Ha ha ha, "I win!" As I jump up, so does he, and the next thing I remember is falling over the stoop banister rail all the way down, one-and-a-half stories, hitting my head on the concrete landing of the basement floor. My aching head not only felt but had actually grown to twice its size and was spinning in circles like Linda Blaire's in *The Exorcist*.

On the X-ray table my mother asked me a hundred questions. "What happened? Oh my God, Junior, how did this happen?" Not able to see, eyes black, blue, and purple, swollen almost shut, sitting up holding my twenty-pound swollen head, convinced I was pushed, "Where . . . are . . . my comic books?!"

"There are no comics."

"But I won!"

That was when I got my first lesson: You don't always win when you win.

From that day on I made sure to stay in position, to never get pushed, and most importantly to not let anyone ever take my comic books again.

As we say, I became "Brooklyn like a motherfucker."

Little did I know that event and reputation would follow me throughout my life.

Danny's Bananas

On the corner of my block was Danny's Bananas. On Saturday I would report to Danny, a young handsome guy who always wore a white wife beater—the ones with straps and a low cut neck line that shows off your chest hair. Danny sold only bunches of bananas from his wooden stands, right off the street at the corner of 42nd Street and 13th Avenue. Huge stalks, the whole plants, they must have weighed fifty pounds, were delivered by trucks full to the top with green bananas. My job was to bring the new green bananas down to the basement through the sidewalk folding double steel doors, where the bananas were stored, and then bring up the ripe ones. I had to cut off and throw out the rotten and squashed ones. (Yeah—squashed bananas. Now you know why the girl on the blanket at the Nemerson pool with the squashed banana made me sick and still sticks with me.) I never forgot the smell of that cold, dark, damp banana basement.

It was one of the badges of honor to work for Danny. Only the chosen few did. Everybody bought his bananas. They came from all over the neighborhood and beyond. He knew everything about everyone and he talked to them all. Sometimes when certain individuals would come by he would go down to the basement, lock the steel doors and say, "Junior, watch the bananas. I'll be right back." This meant I got to run the stand, pick, cut, weigh, and sell bananas. On 13th Avenue Danny and I were truly top banana.

The Meter Boy

In 1956 I spent 75 percent of my time on the street in my limited neighborhood within Borough Park, which included 12th to 14th Avenues and stretched from 43rd Street down to the 38th Street park. Those were my blocks, including the schoolyards at PS 164 and Montauk Junior High School. I took regular trips to the Sunset Park pool, Coney Island, and Ebbets Field. Back then if you saved ten Borden's ice-cream pop Elsee the Cow wrappers and sent them in to Elsie with $1.25, two weeks later you got your Dodger ticket in the mail, then cut school that Tuesday afternoon, went to the ballgame, and sat way out in the bleachers. It was always full of kids. Living on 42nd Street I spent much of my time playing stickball, stoop ball, punch ball, off the wall on a bounce hit it yourself, Johnny on the pony, sculze, kick the can, hit the stick, salugi, mums eye mums eye 1-2-3, lucky strikes, and more. I never went anywhere without my thirty-five-cent shiny, midnight-blue with a diamond in the middle Duncan yo-yo in my pocket.

Today the iPhone has replaced the yo-yo.

One day while playing stickball on the street corner of 42nd, back when we used a mop or broom handle stolen from the neighbor's yard for a stick, I kept swinging and missing the pink Spalding ball. I was pissed, so I hit the new addition to the block, the newly installed parking meter. This time I didn't miss, and to my surprise the meter popped open. Dimes poured out; what was I to do besides take the money and run? That was the start of my first lucrative job: popping the meters with a screw driver and putting rubber bands around them so I could come back in two days and take out more dimes. You never opened them all and never took out all the dimes. That way the city wouldn't have to repair the broken ones and I could get some dimes from the ones with rubber bands. It took them a while to figure it out. I would stash the dimes in my six-year-old little brother Jamie's pockets, in his boots, everywhere. I had

326

dimes all over, bought anything I wanted. So many dimes it looked like my pockets had the mumps.

One sunny summer Saturday morning looking out of my bedroom window, curious to see if any of my friends were out yet, I saw police cars and cops everywhere. I heard one say to my hysterical mother, "We are looking for Frank Yandolino." Thinking they were looking for my father, she answered, "He's not home." The cop looked up and caught me peering out the corner of the window. The cop answered, "No, ma'am. We are looking for him. The meter boy." They all looked up at me and I ran to lock my door. By this time the entire neighborhood was looking on. As I was taken away in a police car I asked them to put on the siren. They obliged and off we went down the block. That was the end of Brooklyn for us. We moved to Brentwood, Long Island, from 1957 to 1962, my high school years, which are a whole other story unto itself. Sex, drugs, and rock 'n' roll was just beginning. Somehow I managed to play high school baseball, football, swim team, and dated a cheerleader without knowing how to spell, multiply, or divide. So growing up in Brooklyn must have taught me something.

It's been forty-five years and I finally finished writing today at sixty-eight years old on October 28, 2012. My birthday.

Bullshit. I'll never finish this book. It's now October 28, 2013, and I'm still writing.

"Happy Birthday, *Junior.*" Thanks, Charli.

Love Always, Frank

CHAPTER 28

Affirmations

*I*n order to promote positive thinking and confront my fears and self-doubts, I post the philosophical quotations and metaphors that I try to live by all over—on my boat, my apartment, my office, and several made it into this book. Here are some of my favorites:

If you see Chicken Little around me, shoot him!

Knowledge is wasted on the old.

I live the life I am.

I don't want other people's dreams to become *my* nightmare.

Absence makes the heart grow fonder; it all depends on how happy you want to be.

The grass may look greener on the other side, but you have to make sure it's not Astroturf.

If you find the shoe on the other foot, make sure it's yours.

I'm a vampire looking for a giraffe. I'm a flight waiting to take off.

I'm a balloon running from the pin. I'm a stranger in a familiar place.

Winning the battle can cause you to lose the war.

If I piss in the wind I don't want it to hit me in the face.

Every day is extra.

Paid for it, didn't I?

If nobody sees it, it's not interesting.

Sometimes you're on a roll, when you should be on a bagel.

I would rather be wrong than right.

Enough is too much.

I'm a hammer looking for a nail.

Just play me the hit.

If you, look, smell, and act like an ass, look in the mirror; you're an ass.

I'm from Brooklyn; if you show me your tits I'm supposed to fuck you.

Make sure the light at the end of the tunnel is not a train.

Don't give me anything I am not supposed to have.

Go with the flow, then turn left.

You gotta rape me.

In this life there is one of everything.

Let's talk turkey, not beef jerky.

It takes just as much time to do it wrong.

The iPhone replaced the yo-yo.

You don't always win what you want when you win.

I will sleep when I die.

If I had tits I'd be a billionaire.

I'm the cause and effect.

Lie, then learn.

I can hear a hit on a paper bag. What is a hit? It sounds like one.

If you didn't grow up in Brooklyn you didn't go through Basic Training.

I still look both ways when I cross a one-way street.

You can trace . . . if you make it better.

LA is the elephants' burial ground of creativity.

Food for thought may be too much to eat for some, so offer them a bite.

Art should never disappoint.

Since you are talking behind my back . . . why don't you bend down and kiss my ass. I'm the line between love and hate.

When I walk into a room it parts like the red sea. Those that love me and those that hate me.

My problem is I'm underfunded, always looking for a pope.

Only narcissists write memoirs.

Stick your finger in the hole and say yes.

You can lead a horse from water but they still drink.

I don't give a damn. I want what I want when I want it.

Innovation is the key to creativity.

I am what I am, what I am.

I'll try anything. If I don't die, I'll do it again.

What is your yellow brick road, that constant thing that makes you unique, that weaves in and out of your life?

What is the moral of your story?

I leave you now with this last question: *What is the moral of your story?* But before you decide, consider that "morals" are often interpreted differently from one person to another.

As an example, in the classic story of Cinderella, the enduring moral is to have faith, to be a good person, and trust that you will be rewarded in the end. One day your prince will come.

Still, I can't help but wonder, what if that glass slipper wasn't really Cinderella's shoe? What if the real moral of the story is: If the shoe fits, wear it?

Or, even better:

Grab the shoe and run.